Thinking after Heic

Thinking after Heidegger

David Wood

polity

First published in 2002 by Polity Press in association with Blackwell Publishers Ltd.

Editorial office:
Polity Press
65 Bridge Street
Cambridge CB2 1UR, UK

Marketing and production:
Blackwell Publishers Ltd
108 Cowley Road
Oxford OX4 1JF, UK

Published in the USA by
Blackwell Publishers Inc.
350 Main Street
Malden, MA 02148, USA

A catalogue record for this book is available from the British Library.

Library of Congress Cataloging-in-Publication Data

Wood, David (David C.)
  Thinking after Heidegger / David Wood.
    p. cm.
Includes bibliographical references and index.
  ISBN 0-7456-1622-4 (alk. paper)—ISBN 0-7456-1623-2 (pbk. : alk. paper)
  1. Heidegger, Martin, 1889–1976. 2. Philosophy. I. Title.
B3279.H49 W66 2002

2001007798

Typeset in 10.5 on 12 pt Sabon
by Kolam Information Services Pvt. Ltd, Pondicherry, India
Printed in Great Britain by TJ International, Padstow, Cornwall

Contents

Acknowledgements

This book has been a long time in the making, and it bears the stamp of many conversations and philosophical relationships, some which began at Oxford, others at Warwick, at the Collegium Phaenomenologicum in Italy, and at numerous conferences in the USA, in Europe and more recently with colleagues at Vanderbilt. Here most particularly I have to thank Darren Hutchinson, a real philosopher and companion in thought, for whose help and work, reading and arguing with me about this manuscript on innumerable walks around Radnor Lake, I will always be grateful.

I would further like to thank Andrew Benjamin, for many years of collaboration and friendship, which changed everything; Antje Kapust, for her inimitable grasp of the deep structures of exclusion; Keith Ansell-Pearson, for being stubbornly and enthusiastically different; Jonathan Rée, a friend and free-spirit for many years; John Llewelyn, for his sensibility, his respons-ability, and the uniqueness of his voice; Richard Kearney, with whom my story has criss-crossed for so long; Morag Patrick, who taught me to slow down; Jacques Derrida, for his inspiration and his tolerance of my anglish ways; Paul Ricoeur, for showing me the meaning of the philosophical life; Gianni Vattimo, for his generosity of spirit and for the example of his political engagement; and Hans Georg Gadamer, for firmly correcting one of my readings of Heidegger. Among friends in North America that are too many to list, I would like specially to mention David Krell, for daring to be himself; John Sallis, for his extraordinary example as a thinker; Charles Scott, for advice, support and tough questioning every step of the way; Dennis Schmidt, for his personal warmth and philosophical example; Jessica Benjamin, for opening up for me the space of constitutive intersubjectivity; Ed Casey, the best interlocutor

I know; Irene Klaver, for her liminal interrogation and her originality; and Robert Bernasconi, for having brought me face-to-face with Levinas and for demonstrating how some papers are worth more than books.

I have learned much too from colleagues at Vanderbilt, especially Gregg Horowitz, for his constructive perversity of thought; Michael Hodges, for keeping his head when all around are losing theirs; Idit Dobbs-Weinstein, for showing me how scholarship thinks; John Compton, for phenomenal and phenomenological friendship and his concern for things green; Jay Bernstein, for the challenge of his outrageous dismissals of positions he disagrees with, and Victoria McGeer, for refusing to recognize artificial boundaries within philosophy. Not forgetting Beth Conklin and Volney Gay, who remind me constantly, without trying, that philosophy has no monopoly on thinking.

Finally, a big thank-you to my one-time editor at Polity, Rebecca Harkin, whose patience, good humour, friendship and encouragement helped to keep this project alive through the years.

I would like to dedicate this book to the memory of C. Douglas McGee [1927–1993], philosopher and father-in-law, who never stopped searching for the good life, and to Gillian Rose [1947–1995], an indomitable spirit, who might not think I had contributed much to repairing 'the broken middle', but who raised my game by always expecting more of me than I thought was possible.

Introduction: Aspects of the Plot

Liminal interrogations

Philosophy is at war with the complacency of the concept. Philosophy serves as handmaiden to science only insofar as it preserves and renews science's liminal activity. The concept functions both to disclose and to conceal; its practical benefits obscure its selective operation. Where chaos threatens, philosophy may temporarily side with the concept, but when systematic conceptualization becomes the order of the day, eternal vigilance requires a liminal interrogation – probing, challenging, poking at the lines we have drawn on the map.

The task of philosophy is to disrupt any and every naturalization of the conjunction of the concept and the world, every unreflective naivety whether it leads us to fascism or foolishness. There is no one approved way of doing this; phenomenology, rethinking the history of metaphysics, reflection on the desire of philosophy, genealogical studies, critical theory, and deconstruction have all contributed to this enterprise. If remedies too often perpetuate the symptom, the hope of deconstruction was that it had new and sophisticated ways of counteracting this tendency to unconscious repetition. And, of course, the very temptation to turn interrogation or disruption into techniques is one that deconstruction both articulates and, inevitably, falls prey to. Although this book as a whole is not intended as an introduction to Heidegger's thought, Part I begins with an attempt to rewrite Heidegger's inaugural address 'What is Metaphysics?' in a contemporary idiom, an address in which, infamously, Heidegger makes much ado of Nothing. The second chapter develops this theme by talking about 'impossible experience', or the play between the impossibility of experience and the experience of the impossible, showing that Derrida,

Levinas and Blanchot each at a certain point endorses a liminal phenomenology rather than breaking with phenomenology completely. The third chapter, 'The Voyage of Reason', demonstrates that rather than being a 'discourse of mastery', as Lacan charges, philosophy is actually the space in which the very thematics of mastery can best be challenged. The best thinkers of the twentieth century did just that.

Dangerous intersections

If philosophy is to remain up to the task of vigilance against complacency, it must fight against its own corruption.[1] Dangerous intersections is a series of case studies of ways in which Heidegger deals with the threat of premature closure in Hegel's dialectic, and in Nietzsche's will-to-power. The very same issue is discussed in relation to Heidegger himself by comparison with Adorno and Derrida. We toy with the conceit that Adorno and Derrida can be treated as offering twentieth-century responses to Heidegger's readings of them, on behalf of Hegel and Nietzsche respectively. The danger of these intersections lies in the way in which, in these conversations, we have to offset the respect properly owed to the distinct problematics being addressed by each thinker and the historical situation in which they wrote, against the ahistorical pulse generated by the aporetic logic of thinking and representation in which they each find themselves caught up. 'Heidegger and the Challenge of Repetition' shows how, in *What is Called Thinking?*, Heidegger opens up a way of thinking that *repeats* Nietzsche's account of repetition and, by so doing, renews the project of protecting us from the spirit of revenge.

'Heidegger's Reading of Hegel's *Phenomenology of Spirit*' shows precisely how Heidegger attempts to translate what Hegel understood by dialectics into a thinking stripped of its teleology. 'Heidegger after Derrida', on the other hand, shows us just how far Derrida in many ways continues the same line of critique in relation to Heidegger himself, opening up a much more radical Heidegger than we had previously expected. In the last chapter in Part II, Adorno's differences with Heidegger's and Rose's readings of Derrida are compared for the insights they offer into both the relation between philosophy and the political and the 'necessity' of misrecognition.

Unlimited responsibility

Thinking 'after' Heidegger is not an innocent title – as if a 'title' could ever be innocent. A title is no mere name or description; it is closer to a claim, a proclamation, an announcement. It serves to identify, but it affirms an identity – it does not petition the right to do so. A title performs the affirmation of its own entitlement. As such, of course, it can fall flat on its face. It lacks innocence in another sense too by embodying a certain conceit – that 'thinking after' could be understood along the lines of 'running after' or 'looking after'. Or consider what we mean when we say a boy takes *after* his father. This conceit merges with a reading of 'after' that we find in art history books, especially with reference to Italian painting: 'After Raphael' means in the style of Raphael. To these senses we can add the sense of taking up where Heidegger left off, or in a way that responds to Heidegger's interventions, or one that tries to avoid Heidegger's terrible political errors. The word 'after' is not being problematized just because no self-respecting deconstructionist would let it out without a good dusting of polysemy. It is rather that this range of issues nicely captures the many threads and tracks that need to be taken up in working out where we go from here, both in response to Heidegger, and also in response to those who have in various ways measured their distance from him. His readers and critics have not always been helpful. Much of the noise created in response to revelations of his Nazi involvements set back the cause of serious discussion of the contribution a philosopher might make either to politics or to the political. But the readings and misreadings of Heidegger, especially by Levinas, Adorno and Derrida, have opened up Heidegger not just to objections from others but also to his ongoing conversation with himself, to his encounter...

In this way, reading Heidegger in the light of the thematics of responsibility is both an ethical reading (and a way of understanding reading in fundamentally ethical terms), and a way of thinking responsibility and 'ethics' in a manner that subjects the scope of the ethical to repeated displacement. Unlimited responsibility is not only a theme that pervades the space of intersection in which Heidegger and his best readers meet, but also the challenge that Heidegger offers us in reading him. Heidegger is one of 'the few and the rare' who set a standard by which even those who disagree with him may be judged.[2]

Part III begins with a critique of the ethics of deconstruction that attempts to rescue its positive significance from hyperbolic overstatement. It continues in '*Comment ne pas manger*: Deconstruction and Humanism' with a critique of the residual humanism in Derrida's attempt to think the animal, arguing that vegetarianism is not merely an option for deconstruction, but another name for deconstruction 'itself'. We conclude with an extended analysis of the staging of philosophical performativity in Heidegger's *Contributions to Philosophy*, in which Heidegger works to release philosophy from the systematic violence of the concept in the form of *Machenschaft* and representation. We show that, given Heidegger's premises to do with the inseparability of the manner in which we philosophize and the 'content' or import of philosophy, which many of the greatest thinkers have grasped, Heidegger's approach here cannot just be treated as one option among others. That it flirts with the risk of failure is no objection if to carry on with business as usual would have guaranteed failure.

Part I

Liminal Interrogations

I

Thinking at the Limit

In 1818, in *The Friend*, Coleridge asked his reader the following question:

> Have you ever raised your mind to the consideration of existence, in and by itself, as the mere act of existing? Have you ever said to yourself thoughtfully, It is! heedless in that moment whether it were a man before you, or a flower, or a grain of sand – without reference in short to this or that particular mode or form of existence? If you have attained to this, you will have felt the presence of a mystery which must have fixed your spirit in awe and wonder... Not to be is impossible, to be, incomprehensible. If you have mastered this intuition of absolute existence, you will have learnt likewise that it was this, and no other which in the earlier ages seized the noble minds, the elect among men, with a sort of sacred horror... [he is speaking, he says] of the idea of being in its essence.[1]
>
> (English slightly updated, DCW)

Coleridge is inviting us to acknowledge an experience, one that would make us cousins of the ancient Greeks. He is inviting us to remember what we may have lost touch with – an experience that perhaps must be forgotten, because we cannot entirely live with it, but which can also be transmuted into forms that ease its recovery. We may think here of poetic forms, particularly Greek tragedy. But the philosopher to whom Coleridge surely returns us by his invocation of the experience of being is Aristotle, who is first credited with making the study of 'being in its essence' into a distinct theoretical enterprise – one outlined in his *Metaphysics*. Does this exercise preserve the power of such a fundamental experience, or can it, on the contrary, block the way to what most moves us?

According to Hegel, most of us flee from the word 'metaphysics' as we would flee from a carrier of the plague. Since Hegel, its reputation has, if anything, deteriorated. Metaphysics has been associated with unverifiable, hence meaningless claims; it has been said to be committed to the illusory ideal of presence, and instead of preserving our connectedness with Being, it is judged to have actually encouraged the forgetfulness of Being.

To take metaphysics seriously would commit us to a systematic study of fundamental principles, which seems a most desirable goal. Yet there are widespread objections to this project. Kant warned us of the danger of applying a language adapted to everyday phenomena to the noumenal world that lay behind them. (It is worth adding, nevertheless, that the spatial and causal language of this very account seems to perpetuate the error he sought to discredit.) Nietzsche taught us to detect the *ressentiment* lurking in metaphysics' negation of our sensuous reality, and the desire for conceptual mastery over the world that haunts our 'will to truth'. Moreover, the idea of metaphysics as some sort of fundamental descriptive science falls foul of many contemporary views about the capacity of language – whether common or technical – to perform any such transcendental role. Many have concluded that the very project of metaphysics harbours a long discredited privilege that philosophy once claimed in relation to other disciplines: that of accounting for their very existence, of scrutinizing their basic concepts, and even perhaps conferring legitimacy upon them. Is it not proper that these grandiose pretensions have now been silenced? Should we not accept that philosophy's new destiny is to farm its own plot in reduced circumstances, contributing its small voice on equal terms with other participants in the conversation of the West?

To assess this claim we need to return to the earlier scenes of the conversation. It is not only that Aristotle's nest hatched the *term* metaphysics, but it is there too that we can find the kind of definition of metaphysics that would establish this priority and, hence, discredit metaphysics if such priority is no longer given credence. Aristotle tells us that 'there is a science which investigates being qua being and its essential attributes'. 'This science', he goes on, 'differs from all the so-called special sciences in that none of the latter deals generally with being at all.' Curiously, although in translation these remarks appear in a book called *Metaphysics*, in a section called 'The Scope of Metaphysics' and in a chapter entitled 'The Object of Metaphysics', Aristotle did not use the word metaphysics at all; he named this science philosophy. The integrity of the book *Metaphysics* is the work of unloved creatures – editors – as is the use of the word to structure the volume out of a collection of texts that Aristotle had written at various times. This volume reflects the position these treatises were given 'after the Physics' – *meta ta physika* – when arranged by others after Aristotle's death. If this arrangement was not exactly an accident, it was equally not the systematic unity often supposed. But if the origin of 'metaphysics' lies in the contingency of editorial decisions, might not the 'metaphysics' to which, as we have seen, such exception is taken also be a fiction of the imagination? David Ross, one of the most eminent of classical scholars, described Aristotle's *Metaphysics* as 'not a dogmatic system but the adventures of a mind in its search for truth'. Could anything be more attractive?

Aristotle, of course, understands philosophy as providing us with 'positive knowledge' about substance and about its essential attributes – genus and species, part and whole, unity and plurality, limited and unlimited, identity and difference. And it is as such (as positive knowledge) that it is distinguished from dialectic which, as he says, is 'merely critical'. The character of this 'positive knowledge' – which provides a map of the operation of fundamental categories of thought – is such that it would naturally serve a foundational role in particular academic disciplines, or 'sciences'. Aristotle's approach here is consonant with his concern as a logician for understanding relationships between propositions and between predicates. The dignity of philosophy is assured by being a distinct *science*, one exploring a fundamental dimension of the real world: Being, non-Being, and central philosophical categories, each well-displayed, functioning in the Greek language.

Today we are much less convinced about many of the assumptions Aristotle made. Our understanding of science is less essentialistic, less foundational, less modelled on those traditions deploying formal method. And except when making funding applications to agencies that demand such an account, we no longer feel the need to pretend that philosophy supplies a specific kind of positive knowledge. Philosophy certainly involves, requires and is entangled with knowledge of various sorts – textual, historical, formal, as well as scientific – but no more than medicine is it reducible to facts about a subject matter.

If philosophy does not supply a special kind of knowledge, how can it play a foundational role for science? Can it provide a foundation for anything: e.g. morality, politics or faith?[2] Powerful arguments in the name of pluralistic pragmatism, and postmodernism suggest that this role is now redundant. It is no longer assumed that providing explicit foundations is a prerequisite for *understanding* a subject. Many disciplines are sites of struggle to determine what *are* the fundamental concepts. Moreover, the role of foundations in legitimating science, or discourse in general, has been severely questioned. Is not legitimation conferred by productivity, results or performativity, rather than by origin or pedigree? And it is increasingly difficult to ask whether legitimacy should be conferred in this way, or even to articulate the question intelligibly.

We might give the name *nihilism* to this stage in world history – the epoch in which all transcendent values have crumbled. We might even suppose that it was the failure of philosophy to achieve its promise that has brought us to this sorry pass.

If we thought this, we would be echoing the words of Husserl, the 'father of phenomenology', who in the first decade of this century sought to remedy the apparently defective foundations of logic, mathematics and thinking in general, by relaunching the philosophical enterprise in a way that would provide access to 'the things themselves', to phenomena as they actually show themselves to us. He believed that the aporias of these formal sciences resulted from a failure to clarify their basic concepts. Intuitionists in mathematics and logic had been resisting the introduction of such concepts as infinity and 'i' [the square root of minus one] precisely because they lacked any intuitive foundation, and it was not difficult to see this as the source of some of mathematics' problems. In logic, the problems of axiomatization, and the theory of classes, seemed again to suggest that formal operations had lost contact with their intuitive foundations. At the same time, he diagnosed a 'crisis' in philosophy itself. Phenomenology was his response.

For the pre-Socratics, philosophy was bound up with a whole range of topics and approaches that we would now associate with distinct subject matters – cosmology, theology, biology, psychology and physics. The history of philosophy has seen the successive detachment of these fields as distinct disciplines. (Since then the modern university has recognized and even invented disciplines that philosophy never knew.) In the late nineteenth century Husserl, like Frege, was quite properly concerned that psychology, perhaps the last fledgling to fly the nest, would take the nest with it, that philosophy itself was being thought of naturalistically as none other than the empirical science of psychology, or part of it. Husserl wanted philosophy to be a *strenge Wissenschaft*, a rigorous science, and thought that it had progressed along that path very nicely until Kant and Fichte. 'Again and again', he writes 'research is directed toward new beginnings, decisive formulations of problems, and correct methods'.[3] But with Hegel, and with what Husserl thought of as romantic philosophy, the rot set in, and the weakening of the philosophical impulse led eventually to relativism, scepticism, *Weltanschauung* theory and naturalism. Husserl wanted philosophy to be a strict, rigorous discipline, not a natural science, for one simple reason. If it were a natural science it would not be able to deliver on what he called 'humanity's imperishable demand for pure and absolute knowledge'.[4] The vocabulary of philosophy is 'to teach us how to carry on the eternal work of humanity'.[5] 'The spiritual need of our time', he writes, 'has become unbearable.'[6] If philosophy were capable only of providing empirical truths that would have generality but not universality, or of articulating world views that would have only local and temporary validity, it would be wholly unable to satisfy this demand. Husserl follows Plato and Parmenides in supposing that philosophical truth is of a quite different order. Where he differs is in supposing that it can be accessed through a carefully controlled description of what intuition reveals about the structures of experience. The gist of his position is this: the truths of logic cannot just be ways we happen, as a matter of fact, to find it useful to think, because they have a quite different kind of necessity. Any serious attempt to argue about this issue would presuppose just such a privilege to logic. And the same goes for philosophy's capacity to clarify the concepts of other sciences. These sciences cannot, *essentially* cannot, provide their own foundations, they cannot lift themselves up by their own bootstraps. For a legitimation of their concepts, principles and methods, they require an approach of a quite different (= essential) order.

Husserl raises the stakes high. What is held in the balance is the future of the Western ideal of reason and truth. But again, he demands that philosophy be a 'strict science' with, of course, its own kind of rigour – a careful descriptive attentiveness to phenomena which, in its submission to what these phenomena 'show', would be without presuppositions.

Surely this approach is attractive, even compelling. It promises not just a place for philosophy, but a renewed understanding of its essence, and a therapeutic satisfaction of wider human needs and desires. It is not, however, without presuppositions, and most important of all is the belief that discourse, particularly that of science, requires and can be given an intuitive foundation. Husserl's vision is not new: it is a vision of spiritual devastation, a world of learning torn from its moorings by writing, by signs.

While the impulse to save philosophy from the slide into naturalism is still shared by many, Husserl's remedy has not been universally accepted. Many have argued that what seem like neutral methodological considerations are actually highly contentious, and subvert the prospect of achieving phenomenological salvation on Husserlian lines.

There are a number of difficulties with Husserl's position, some of which were recognized by Husserl himself – his thought did not stand still. Let me mention three.[7] First, intuitive access to transcendental subjectivity, the sphere of essential intuition, rests on being able to separate, bracket out, man's essentially mortal worldly embodiment. We could call this the problem of finitude. Secondly, access to a pure intuitive realm rests on the possibility of a pure interiority unsullied by signs, by language, by difference. Lastly, there is the problem of the Other, of the radical interruption of intentionality effected by the Other person. Each of these problems threatens the prospect of philosophy as a rigorous science. What does that mean for philosophy's relation to other disciplines, or to the natural sciences and humanities? Is the dream of philosophy's distinctive place in the academy over?

The history of philosophy is interwoven with the history of announcements of its demise; but, to borrow from Mark Twain, rumours of its death are greatly exaggerated. What has died, perhaps, is a naive, if understandable, sense that philosophy could only be respectable if it had a distinct body of knowledge to which it made progressive addition, or a rigorous method modelled on the natural or formal sciences. What has taken its place? If 'The End of Philosophy' confronts us with 'The Task of Thinking', what is this Thinking?[8]

The limitations of the Husserlian model confront us with the difficulty of moving beyond it. For Husserl, philosophy was faced with a threat to its very survival by the success of disciplines concerned with 'the facts', which undermined the true significance of the scientific ideal. His response was, in effect, to propose an alternative transcendental science of essences – essential structures and relations, accessed through a purified intuition. The logic of this move is analogous to the claim that facts presuppose concepts. Husserl adds, however, that concepts are not just the practically useful sedimentations of human practices in the conventions of a natural language; they are essences, the structure of which is available to a methodologically controlled intuition. Empirical science is, strictly speaking, *naive*. It believes itself to be dealing with hard facts, and is blind to its soft conceptual and experiential underbelly. If it does catch a glimpse of what sustains it, it is not equipped to reflect on it philosophically.

Why should that matter? Is it not precisely a feature of the best modern science that it is innovative, inventive, even daring – even to the point of supplying the grand formative ideas of entropy, catastrophe and chaos for which one might once have looked to philosophy? Isn't a creative, intellectual responsiveness to the phenomena better than any backseat-driver philosophizing?

While philosophy can bring conceptual and methodological clarity to other disciplines, the best historians, mathematicians and lawyers already wear philosophical hats on occasion. This, however, should not disguise the fact that there are still questions of intrinsic and vital concern to all who are engaged in teaching, writing and research – and many of these questions are never raised let alone adequately dealt with or answered within the disciplines. Working as we do in institutions founded on statements of principle and on the declaration of certain rights and values, do we continue to try to bring them to life, or to extend and deepen them? Do we think of a university simply as an administrative unity, or as one whose reason for existence lies in its fostering a certain quality of intellectual life? And for whom should it do this? What mode of insertion into the world is presupposed by my chosen field, or by *any* field of research? What does science really mean for us? Or the humanities? How can I make sense of *my* commitment to *this* field?

These questions can become pressing and unavoidable for those engaged in defence work, or genetic engineering, or medical research, where life and death concerns are close to the surface. Yet these obvious cases can actually serve as alibis for our own thoughtlessness; they can obscure the universal scope of the questions being posed. And for those of us engaged full-time in the kind of questioning we call research, the very possibility of an altogether different kind of questioning can be lost. Indeed it may be one of the attractions of a discipline that questions can be contained or limited, and indeed for the most part *must* be, before any progress can be made.

But neither wonder nor responsibility rises up in such domesticated forms; the sources of ultimate puzzlement do not come packaged into the special concerns of this science or that faculty, and when we lock the laboratory door, return the book to the shelf, or switch off the computer, we are eventually left with ourselves again, and with each other. We are thrown back onto what we could call the contingency and fragility of specific contextual determinations. This is not the moment to abandon the task of thinking.

Some 45 years ago, in a lecture on Metaphysics,[9] the brilliant but forgotten comedian Severn Darden – an ex-philosophy student as I recall – began like this, in a heavy German accent: 'Why, you will ask me, will I be speaking on the Universe rather than on some other topic? It's really very simple. There *isn't* anything else.' What is *wrong* with this answer is that if we are considering significant frames of reference, there certainly *are* other topics – family, friendships, and football matches, to name only a few. What is at stake is whether it is possible or desirable to treat 'the universe', the cosmos and, in that wider sense, the world as the ultimate frame of reference. In some sense, surely, physicists and astronomers already deal with it. But, as Aristotle put it, they deal with 'the whole of nature' only insofar as it is in motion, i.e. as the object of a calculative science, and not qua being. We have already suggested that there might be significantly different ways of relating to 'all that there is', but what can it mean to relate to it *qua being*? Every distinct discipline has a domain of inquiry only by delimiting an object, by the principles and methods constitutive of the discipline and sometimes by temporal or spatial limitation. Is relating to 'all that there is' *qua being* another such specification or limitation, or is it something different?

Nietzsche began his famous early essay on Truth like this: 'In some remote corner of the universe, effused into innumerable solar systems, there was once a star upon which clever animals invented cognition.' We may think of ourselves as important, yet, 'even the gnat swims through the air with the same pathos, and feels within itself the flying centre of the world'.[10]

Nietzsche here brilliantly injects into our relation to the cosmos the crucial question of its significance, posed in its simplest Copernican terms – namely, whether man is or is not the centre of the universe. The fact that the gnat is flying of course immediately brings out the way in which 'centre' exceeds any simply spatial sense – which implies that the world, too, is not just being thought of spatially. But equally, what Nietzsche points up is the danger of simplistic anthropocentrism involved in talking about man's relation to the world. It is all too easy to think of the world as what is 'out there', so that one's relation to it is reduced to a relation of an inside to an outside. The most cursory reflection on the status of our bodies shows that this model is conceptually deeply flawed.[11] But if Aristotle was right to describe the distinctively philosophical approach as one that thinks of being qua being, how do we pursue such thinking, and what does *thinking* involve?

In the remarks with which we began, Coleridge suggested we could break with our natural practical assurance, however necessary that may be for everyday life, and think of *being as such*, a thinking tied up with the experience of awe, wonder and what he called 'sacred horror'. Such feelings are to be understood not merely as the *objects* of local psychological inquiry, but as ontological, and as revealing being. They also open up philosophy to all who have experienced them. This word 'being' points to the possibility of grasping the pervasive consequences of our relation to the universe having an ultimate significance. There may still be resistance to the word 'being', and it is not without its own difficulties. Consider then the phrase 'ultimate context of significance'. I have tried to argue for the importance of being able to reflect on and expand frameworks of significance, so that our thinking and teaching can be informed by considerations other than those that formally constitute the discipline with which we are professionally engaged. I have implied that philosophy, or some improved version of it, such as *thinking*, might provide a distinctive facility for being able to make these moves; but how complacent should we be about the expression 'ultimate context of significance'? The question can be put quite simply: Does awe, or wonder or sacred horror provide a 'context of significance' at all? Perhaps these experiences have the power they do, not because they point to an ultimate context, but because they transform our understanding of what that might mean. 'That there is a universe' is not one fact among others. Consider Wittgenstein's 'wonder at the existence of the world'.[12]

A context is a frame of reference, one that makes possible the determination of meanings within it. It typically consists of intersubjectively shared assumptions often only tacitly understood. Contexts determine meanings, and possibilities; they determine what is appropriate, plausible, and, in the case of indexically infected propositions like 'it is sunny today', they even determine truth. Contexts are essentially mediated socially, culturally, historically and linguistically. But if we understand context like this, what becomes of the idea of an ultimate context? It would suggest that there was a widest or deepest framework which, when we reached it, would finally determine the significance of every other sub-context. Is that what the experience of sacred horror comes to? Surely it signals precisely the opposite insight: that the world is not a context of significance, but transcends all tacitly shared assumptions; that it is not a framework at all, but is beyond all frameworks – an abyss. It is an abyss just because it cannot supply final answers to ultimate questions; it can offer no guarantees and no assurances. It is in this sense that we might come to speak not of the universe or of the world, which seem still to name regions however vast, but of *being*. The association we have made between being and abyss already warns us what not to expect to be able to do with this word. For Aristotle the study of being qua being was to be undertaken in the spirit of a special, categorial science, to which the name 'metaphysics' was given. We, on the other hand, have distanced ourselves from that model of philosophical activity. I will now try to give some indication of how a thinking that took its clue from an abyssal sense of being might proceed. I will argue that this not only gives to philosophy a distinctive task, but an indispensable role both in the academy and elsewhere. Moreover, this account is sufficiently general to anchor many of the debates that rage within philosophy itself.

Insofar as the world is calculable, and boundaries are fixed, there is no place for philosophy. There would be accountants, cartographers, librarians, bankers but no philosophers. Philosophy first arose, and still survives, because even as the realm of calculation spreads, the need to think the incalculable becomes ever greater. By calculation I mean here the subordination of the world and one's intercourse with the world to determination, whether it be linguistic, aesthetic or economic, so that in a real sense, our relation to it becomes *a priori*. By the incalculable, I mean all that resists such determinations, even, perhaps, as it succumbs to them.

Calculation, in general, is neither avoidable nor a bad thing. It is however essential to be able to realize its limits, and to be aware that limitation can be thought without specifying the unlimited. Thinking of being qua being is, on this view, nothing but thinking the limits of determination. In articulating some of the forms of these limits, I will at the same time attempt to amplify the three dimensions of inadequacy that we distinguished when considering Husserl's phenomenological project: finitude, otherness and language. I will take language first.

The limits of linguistic determination appear at two quite different points, giving rise to two kinds of indetermination in my descriptive or expressive endeavours. Sometimes, even though I manage to speak, what I say is not adequate to its object, or to the occasion. There are times when we have what is called a *pensée d'escalier*, and think of the right words on the way down the stairs, when it is too late; but equally there are times when no words are adequate. Here we find indetermination in the form of *incompleteness*; there is a residual something not capturable by any words. But even when I succeed, as it appears, in finding the precise words I was looking for, the significance of my words can never be limited by the meaning I was trying to express. Here we have indetermination as *excess*.

The *possibility*, at least, of these forms of indetermination is universal. As soon as one enters language, by writing or speaking – even by certain sorts of thinking – one creates possibilities of understanding that exceed those ever intended. This is true for a number of reasons. The internal relationships between words and between sentences in any complex utterance will be irreducible to any single reading. The context, both textual and pragmatic, in which these words are uttered, can never be entirely specified or saturated, and hence the context of their apprehension can never be rigidly controlled. This is not to say that anything goes in interpretation, but it is to say that there is almost always more than representational adequacy at stake. The implications of this for the humanities in general are quite profound. Those disciplines concerned with the interpretation of what are already interpretations (texts, paintings, buildings) continually have to face both incompleteness and excess, each of which fuels the destruction not only of positivistic methodologies, but also of any hermeneutics deaf to the roar of the abyss. These claims, however, are not restricted to interpretive disciplines. Every science proceeds on the basis of idealization – a process that feeds on the calculable and excretes what it cannot conceptualize or quantify. I have already argued that the limits of any positive science reside in its constitutive incapacity to deal with its conditions of possibility, and these arguments still apply. My response to the scientific realist who takes a hard-nosed approach to representation would be to interpret both Gödel's theorem and chaos theory as confirming the indetermination of excess: that indeterminacy affects every science at a certain level of formal complexity of representation.

The point is not just a formal one, however. It ought to give pause to those of us who work in the humanities when we ape the jargon of hard science. And there are even more direct practical implications. Eminent computer scientists have collectively protested that the programs running the US National Defense are of an interactive complexity that renders them incapable of being debugged, making them so functionally unpredictable as to be at best useless, and at worst a serious threat to national security. A truly abyssal thought.

Perhaps incautiously, the point I have been making about both interpretive and positive sciences could be summarized as follows: the achievement of their avowed ends is limited in two ways.

1 Idealization, a necessary initial stage in any discipline, is at the same time a form of exclusion. It does not just exclude the raw stuff – the singularity of things – that cannot be taken up by idealization. It also excludes, or covers over, the possibility of other idealizations.
2 The very theoretical apparatus of any discipline will have implications and consequences secondary to their avowed ends.

The question of the limits of linguistic representation has presented us with the opportunity to draw consequences for the status of scientific discourse in general. Although this may seem a far cry from Coleridge, I do not think so, and if we now return to the other two topics mentioned – finitude and otherness – this will become clear.

I used 'finitude' to capture what I called our mortal worldly embodiment – such embodiment supplies a locus for a range of experiences that would root philosophy firmly in the human condition.
If thinking required the marking of boundaries between and around
the things being thought, then to think embodiment is to think the
unthinkable. As embodied I am *part* of the world 'out there', I move
around it and in it. Of course, when I say 'out there' I mean something
much more than beyond the surface of my skin. In a sense my body is
also out there, and I can even seem to occupy a vantage point on it.
Dualism is an ontological error, but it has phenomenological motivation. Embodiment is essentially ambiguous, and this ambiguity permanently resists and confounds determination or calculation. No
determinate boundary between me and the world can be drawn. As
a being acting in the world, the stage on which I act is part of my
action; as an observer, my very spatial form can seem accidental. With
embodiment comes an essential dependency on the world, as I breathe
it, chew and digest it, drink it, and in so many ways sense it. With this
dependency there also comes mortality. I can be pierced, torn open, or
ravaged from within. Indeed something of this sort is our common
fate. I can, of course, take precautions, buy insurance, and order my
affairs, but in a stronger sense I cannot reduce my own mortality to
calculative thought – not because the date and time are uncertain, but
because my own death is a singularity absolutely unthinkable to me,
and interrupts any economy of calculation. A veritable abyss.

It may be said, however, that this abyssal thought has its own
limitation. Does it not, as Levinas has insisted, privilege those neutral
ontological relations to being that invite wonder, consigning the
ethical relation, the relation to the other person, to secondary significance? Not at all. My relation to the other is an explosive interruption
of intentionality, of any recuperative, assimilative recognition of an
alter ego. Or, perhaps better, even if every relation to the other
involves some analogical transfer from myself to the other, it is
precisely in limiting that, and opening oneself to difference, that the
alterity of the other – the otherness of the other – is revealed. To
recognize that the object of one's recognition radically transcends any
determinate grounds for that recognition is the beginning of respect.
But what kind of transcendence is this? There is one important sense
in which the other is essentially indeterminable which I share with
him, or her. I can no more know myself completely than I can know
you (probably less so). However, there is a stronger sense in which the
alterity of the other has nothing to do with my understanding of the
other's qualities, and everything to do with the interruption wrought
by his or her very existence to a narcissistic world in which all needs

and desires are first mine. The shattering of that economy is the incalculable opening of ethics.

Surely we have returned to the spirit of Coleridge only to depart just as quickly. He asked, you may recall:

> Have you ever said to yourself thoughtfully, It is! heedless in that moment whether it were a man before you, or a flower, or a grain of sand...?

Is he not giving pre-eminence to an ontological experience that denies the specificity of the human other? But it is something of an illusion to suppose that the ethical dimension of thinking is to be found in its specific application to our relation to others. The implication of the understanding of philosophy articulated here – of a thinking that addresses the limits of determination, that marks and voices the abyssal, that thinks the unthinkable, that protects and preserves the experiences Coleridge and others have described – is *already* an ethical one that puts the response back into responsibility. Love and respect are perhaps not so very distant from wonder and sacred horror.

Philosophy cannot be reduced to experience, however revealing that experience may be; but it is inseparable from a thinking that preserves our continuing exposure to the power of experiences that shatter our maps, and remind us of their fragility. It is just this shattering potential of experience that has proved irresistible to those – such as Heidegger, Blanchot and Derrida – who had steered clear of its implications of humanistic integrity.

2

The Return of Experience

[I]s it possible that this displacing comes over human beings? Indeed. And that is the distress of the abandonment by being.... But this distress must still be *experienced*.[1]

The importance of concepts to ethical life is not too difficult to grasp. We owe to concepts like 'justice', 'rights', 'duty', 'virtue', 'good', 'responsibility', and 'obligation' our very capacity for ethical judgement. And yet the important work of clarifying and codifying the scope and significance of these terms is the source of another danger – the calculation of our responsibility, in which the ethical as an openness to the incalculable is threatened with extinction. In this chapter, I plot the way in which appeals to experience have staged an unlikely resurgence precisely because of its power to break with conceptual calculability, and despite the legacy of its humanistic and subjectivist associations.[2]

In his 'Letter on Humanism',[3] Heidegger tries to revive ethics as *ethos*, as abode or dwelling, and in an example which is truly exemplary, he interprets Heraclitus' location of the gods in his hearth as his way of thinking 'dwelling' as the preservation of the unfamiliar in the familiar.

In 'Eating Well',[4] Derrida describes the 'subject' as the principle of calculation, and it is for this reason that Heidegger's displacement of a certain topos of subject-hood in his essay 'Language' is presented in terms of a transformation of our dwelling in relation to language. Heidegger writes:

Language speaks. Man speaks *in that* he responds to language . . . It is not a matter here of stating a new view of language. What is important is learning *to live in the speaking of language. To do so* we need *to examine constantly* whether and to what extent we are capable of what genuinely belongs to responding...[5]

What we call the activity of a subject (speaking) is conditioned by something else – something more 'middle voice' than a passivity.[6] It is, however, important to realize that 'conditioned by' does not mean limited by, or undermined by. Quite the opposite. Heidegger is re-thinking authenticity here, not in terms of some restrictive sense of 'mineness', but in terms of an openness (or responsiveness), to an Other (language). The idea of responding to language is of course a strange one, employing a term (response) that would normally make sense within communicative *interaction* to illuminate a certain productive dependence. What is at stake here, is the way language *gives*, provides and supplies ways of thinking, seeing and being which we don't individually invent, but we do create from, and to which we do have to take up an attitude. To live in the speaking of language suggests maintaining the tension between given form and appropriating response. And it is important that he speaks of 'examining constantly' how far we measure up to the challenge of such a relationship. All this suggests an image in which, as Kierkegaard put it, the subject is 'constantly involved in relating itself to itself'. For we cannot adequately understand this self-relationship without recognizing a constitutive role for a mediating third term, what in *The Sickness unto Death* he terms a 'Power'. The structure of Heidegger's argument here, and Kierkegaard's in *The Sickness unto Death*, is identical. Kierkegaard claims we cannot understand the kind of despair in which, instead of giving up, we carry on 'desperately' (as we might say), without positing a constitutive role for such a power.

Kierkegaard is starting off from an experience and insisting on certain transcendental conditions for its possibility. Rather than being a proof of God's existence, this is a demonstration of the role being played by a certain deep structure of relatedness in making possible the experience we are undergoing. In Heidegger's case, the experience in question is not despair but another breakdown, the experience of not being able to find the right word – a rupture with the habitual.

Both Heidegger and Kierkegaard are here endorsing the implication of Derrida's account of the subject (and of experience), that we need to sever its link to naive self-presence, not the idea itself. Of course, the need for vigilance that Heidegger stresses when he describes our changed relation to language arises again, and at another level, when Derrida (in conversation with Jean-Luc Nancy) argues for the importance of not becoming too free with old metaphysical language.[7] I claim, however, that true vigilance would lead us to conclusions a little different from those of Blanchot and Derrida.

The issue of response, dependence and essential relationality is played out as I've suggested in both Kierkegaard and Heidegger. We can extend our discussion by reference to an important remark from Wittgenstein's *Notebooks*. He writes:

> we have the feeling that we are dependent on an alien will. *Be that as it may*, we *are* at any rate, in a certain sense, dependent, and that on which we depend we can call God.[8]

Wittgenstein *begins* here with an experience – a *feeling*. It is not a feeling in the sense of a twinge or a tweak. It is after all 'a feeling that...' – it has propositional content – and involves complex concepts such as 'alien will'. Wittgenstein then takes this experience and reflects on it 'Be that as it may...' and performs a phenomenological *epoché* on it – bracketing out any reference to specific other entities. He leaves himself with 'a certain sense of dependence', and then reinvents a pole for this dependence in the shape of God.

Of course Heidegger could locate this same dependence in our relation to language. Wittgenstein's sophistication comes in his self-conscious witnessing to the 'naming of God', in which the name and the projected entity are drawn back to the experience of dependence that gives rise to them. But while it explains the move to God, it does not necessitate it. After all – and he seems to admit as much – we could call it fate, or even chance. *What difference does it make what we call it?* Here I recall another of Wittgenstein's remarks, this time actually *on* Heidegger and Kierkegaard, which deals with a quite specific experience and says something extraordinary about it:

> I can readily think what Heidegger means by Being and Dread. Man has the impulse to run up against the limits of language. Think for example, of the *astonishment* that anything exists. This astonishment cannot be expressed in the form of a question, and there is also no answer to it. Everything which we feel like saying can *a priori* only be nonsense. Nevertheless, we do run up against the limits of language. This running up against Kierkegaard also recognized and even designated in a quite similar way (as running up against Paradox). This running up against the limits of language is *Ethics*.
>
> [Dec. 30 1929][9]

The *experience* in question – 'the astonishment that anything exists' – is, of course, not just any experience; it is one of *the* fundamental philosophical experiences. And the degree to which philosophers find, or do not find ways of sustaining the power of this experience is a good indicator of their philosophical seriousness. Consider what Wittgenstein says next. Despite the fact that for such a serious thinker as Leibniz the question 'Why is there anything rather than nothing?' was a deep and central question, Wittgenstein insists that this experience of astonishment 'cannot be expressed in the form of a question'. This seems to be plainly wrong – we've just done it, and so did Leibniz, Heidegger and many others. The clue to what Wittgenstein means comes in the second clause: 'There is also no answer to it.' It is the logical force of this clause that is doing the work. He is claiming that because there is no answer and could be none, what looks like a question really is not one. But what does it mean to say that this 'running up against the limits of language is *Ethics*'? And what does 'nonsense' mean here? There is a straightforward sense that would link paradox with the ethical, but there is also much at stake in how one works through these ethical implications. Blanchot and Derrida will not escape our critical scrutiny here.

Heidegger's 'Language speaks, man speaks insofar as he responds to language',[10] and numerous other remarks of his, are essentially creative transformations of language. The point of these transformations is to break up the habitual grammatical reinforcement of our sense of the subject as an active autonomous agent working on the passive world. And the point of that, as we have seen, is ethical – the transformation of an *ethos*, of a way of being in the world, the way we understand our relation to language. That is the point of those references to passivity, endurance, suffering, responding, etc.

The explicit references Wittgenstein makes are to Heidegger's discussions of Being and Dread in *Being and Time*, or just possibly Heidegger's inaugural lecture 'What is Metaphysics?' [1929]. When Heidegger tells us that 'Dread reveals nothing',[11] and 'Nothing is neither an object nor anything that "is" at all. Nothing occurs neither by itself nor apart from what is as some sort of adjunct',[12] we can read Wittgenstein's references to ethics and nonsense as some sort of response (*avant la lettre*), to Carnap's response to Heidegger in his essay 'The Overcoming of Metaphysics ...'[13], which focuses precisely on what Carnap thinks of as the logical howlers in Heidegger's references to nothing. Wittgenstein is *reminding* him (and us) that there is more at stake. This more, of course, is that Heidegger is not just making logical blunders, he is trying to analyse, or respond to, an experience. 'Only in the clear night of Dread's nothingness is what is as such revealed in all its original overtness: that it is and is not nothing.' The experience is that of recognizing that things exist – a variant of astonishment, in other words. Here we might say that, from the point of view of ethics, what is first at stake is the preservation of that potential for transformation of *ethos* that comes from acknowledging that things exist (and might not). Here 'God' would be someone to thank – it is perhaps not unconnected that Heidegger writes of thinking as thanking in his book *What is Called Thinking?*[14] The world of the grateful man lights up in ways that the ungrateful man's does not; think of the significance of grace at mealtimes. A whole rethinking of theology would follow from hesitating over the thought that we could discharge our debt by thanking God.[15] But there is a second ethical resonance in our very willingness to stay with our experience, to honour it, to ponder it. And if phenomenology has an ethical dimension, it is not its alleged foundationalism or its search for essential intuition, it is this patience with *experience*.

If, after Hegel, the movement from *naive* awareness to reflection might be called an experience, then what I am seeking to record here is an experience with experience. Experience is a thick and fuzzy concept, being not only a central player in so many philosophical schemes and arguments, but also mediating in so many ways between philosophy and its many others (religion, literature, psychoanalysis, common sense, politics and science). And as our understanding of experience develops, the *Methodenstreit* [the struggle over method] between phenomenology, hermeneutics and deconstruction is increasingly exposed as a mock battle. Moreover, these *mediations* are not ones in which dutiful experience reports back its foreign findings to the throne of philosophy, but rather ones that confuse, disrupt and disturb any and every demarcation between philosophy and non-philosophy. Labelling experiences religious or mystical ought always to be an issue for philosophy. Experiences do not herd obediently into these categories, and when philosophy thinks they do, something vital has been lost. Wittgenstein's discussion of the experience of the world as a bounded whole, or of the feeling of dependence, might already have come to be seen as exotic, but along with wonder, the astonishment that anything exists, the anxiety that everything is falling apart, the worry that there might be no certainty, many of what are called 'religious experiences' are the milk and honey of philosophy. The same obviously applies to what we call 'the everyday,' which not only supplies us with the *language* we play with, and sometimes try to regiment as philosophers, but, if the truth be told, with the intelligibility of most if not all of those critical practices by which we seek to transcend the everyday.

Experience then, both as a *concept* and as an *openness*, is a condition for philosophy's productive intercourse with what lies outside of itself – and indeed that very experience of separation and our overcoming of that separation is itself 'experience'! If negotiation with alterity is the locus of the ethical, 'experience' is the essentially contested marker of that site.

Just how experience provides philosophy with conduits to other disciplines and other areas of culture is distinctively and importantly marked in literature and the arts more generally. This is not surprising, because the objects and performances in question exist for no other purpose than to be experienced. The real challenge to philosophy lies in how to access the *complexity* of the experiences involved – which are in no way restricted to supplying natural knowledge – and how to assess their *significance*. Is the coherence of art a *substitute* for or a *beacon* for the realization of such unity in the real world? The challenge that art has always posed to philosophy is how to handle without compartmentalizing the force and complexity of aesthetic experience. The link between the teleology of art and of nature in Kant's third critique is a sign of this challenge, and without adjudicating on Kant's various accounts of experience, it is clear that a *version* of his concerns is still central, namely that which would try to distinguish in every experience between what was supplied by the object and what was supplied by the experiencing subject. I say a *version* of this because, after Hegel and his successors, it is clear that there is a category missing from this account, namely that of language and culture, the ways in which the coherence of our experiences is made possible by shared social practices and their symbolic mediation and interruption. If that *were not an issue*, there would be no crisis of modernism, no problem of nihilism. And it is clearly not just a problem for our experience of art but equally for our experience of social life, our relations with others, our sense of political community, etc.

As for such accounts of experience as we think we need to make sense of scientific knowledge, the revolutionary origin of these models (science appearing on the scene as the scourge of religious consensus) made it easy to ignore that this symbolic and social dimension permeates even scientific experience. Habermas' discussion of validity claims and consensus, and the ideal speech community, is one recognition of this, and Husserl's account of the ideal community of scholars working in harmony is another. But of course the downside of recognizing this third dimension (subject/object and language) may be that *experience* presupposes a certain 'form of life' or coherence in the public use of language that no longer obtains. If the transcendental conditions of the possibilities of experience may be thought to overlap with social, political, symbolic and linguistic ones, and if these are in principle historically fragile, then it is not impossible that experience may have disappeared, and ceased to be possible.

However, this is *not* so, and how and why it is not so demands a renewal of philosophy, one to which deconstruction makes a singular contribution. We can find in the movement of Derrida's writing an exemplary *development* of the problematic of experience; deconstruction 'itself' (and indeed the concept of 'responsibility' to which Derrida has given so much weight) are each nothing *other* than *experience regained*. Deconstruction is, if you like, the experience of experience.[16]

A false, but nonetheless plausible misreading of the development of experience in Derrida's writing would go like this: the early Derrida identifies *experience* with (self-)presence, with the central myth of phenomenology, which we have to abandon if we want to get anywhere. The concept of experience belongs to the history of metaphysics, and we can only use it under erasure. 'Experience' has always designated the relationship with a presence.[17] And yet the later Derrida talks, apparently freely, about 'the experience of aporia', 'an interminable experience', 'the [impossible] experience of death', 'the experience of the non-passage', 'the experience of mourning' and even 'the experience of what is called deconstruction'.[18] If experience here has anything like the dynamic Hegelian sense of a productive undergoing, then we can see how it is that each of these phrases, 'the experience of *X*', will have an objective and subjective genitive sense – the same bivalence that will so easily allow so many of those inversions beloved of Blanchot, such as experience of impossibility: the impossibility of experience. I will show shortly something of the 'dialectical' development that Hegel's account of experience has suffered in the transition to Blanchot (and Derrida) being plotted here, but before doing that I want to explain just why this account of the revaluation of experience in deconstruction is mistaken. There is much at stake here – not least the relationship between deconstruction and phenomenology. We know, of course, that Derrida's treatment of Husserl extends beyond *Of Grammatology* to *The Origin of Geometry* to *Speech and Phenomena*, and some other short essays,[19] but the general argument seems to me to be the same throughout, and surprisingly Hegelian it is too. There is a truth of experience, let us call it presence, that presence does not know – that presence (self-presence) involves a constitutive differentiation, bifurcation, and / or a relation to the other, one that it is not only not aware of, but that it may *be* the non-awareness of (as when we say that love is blind, and mean that love is made possible by a certain objective idealization).

Suppose we think of presence as self-presence, self-awareness, or what Derrida calls 'auto-affection'. We may think of this as simple identity, or as a *relation* capable of a certain development and complexity, as when Kierkegaard shows that *despair* rests on a self that relates itself to itself.[20] Derrida writes:

> Auto-affection is a universal structure of experience ... this possibility – another name for 'life' – is a general structure articulated by the history of life, and leading to complex and hierarchical operations.[21]

And how is this 'life' lived?

> Speech and the consciousness of speech – that is to say consciousness simply as self-presence – are the phenomena of an auto-affection *lived as suppression of difference*.[22]

Later he writes:

> Auto-affection constitutes the same as it divides the same. Privation of presence is the condition of experience, that is to say, *presence*?[23]

> Presence is experience (is differentiated, articulated, etc.) but doesn't know it. And of course the implication is not merely that 'presence' is *not itself* reflective, but that when philosophy itself does reflect on presence, it swallows its story of undivided innocence. And it is hard to see why one could not apply to this the words that Hegel used to describe the movement of experience: This new object contains the annihilation of the first; it is the experience constituted through that first object.[24]

These allusions, first to Husserl and now to Hegel's concept of experience, may seem wild. Am I going to make Derrida into one kind of phenomenologist after another? I do think that Derrida is a radical phenomenologist, and to keep the record straight I will briefly quote the crucial move Derrida makes. After talking about how far transcendental phenomenology 'belongs to metaphysics' he speaks of the need nonetheless to come to terms with the forces of rupture.

> In the original temporalization and the movement of relationship with the outside, *as Husserl actually describes them* [my emphasis], non-presentation or depresentation is as 'originary' as presentation. [...] *That is why a thought of the trace can no more break with a transcendental phenomenology than be reduced to it.*[25]

Husserl then actually *gives* us the material with which to bring about a deconstructive interruption of his own evidence. That he does not effect this interruption can be put down to his commitment to working with a certain *telos* of ideality for which, in a Nietzschean vein, Derrida will supply a further account.

Here idealization is the movement by which sensory exteriority, that which affects me or serves me as signifier, submits itself to my power of repetition, to what thenceforward appears to me as my spontaneity and escapes me less and less.[26]

I will not comment on the parallels with Hegel's account of experience here. At the same sort of period Derrida described deconstruction as infinitely close to, but absolutely distinct from, dialectic.[27] His claim about the trace shows why and how. Compare the idea of *Aufhebung* (both overcoming and preserving) with the idea that the thought of 'the trace can no more break with than be reduced to...' – it is the same thought inside-out.

In sum, the apparent contrast between Derrida's early and later remarks about experience may be more apparent than real. What *is* true is that he no longer seems to use the word experience 'under erasure'. There has been a kind of mutation in the presumption built into references to experience. If 'speech' or our consciousness of speech is, as he claimed, the 'suppression of difference', *that it is so* is not merely a truth discovered by theory or reflection; rather it is testified to by all experience – 'the experience of writing', 'the experience of mourning', 'the experience of the impossible'. In other words, Derrida is appropriating 'experience' in a way that strongly resembles Hegel, for a process productive of a certain kind of insight. To Derrida's claim that there has never been any 'perception' we might add that there has never *not* been experience!

However, the use of this word is not without its strategic risks – of which Derrida is always acutely aware. Consider, for example, (i) the connection between the ideal of 'experience' and that of the human 'subject' (it is hard to imagine one without the other) and (ii) his discussion with Jean-Luc Nancy ('Eating Well'[28]) on the admissibility of retaining that word 'subject'. Nancy[29] says he does not understand how Derrida can keep this word 'subject' without enormous misunderstandings. And Derrida admits the danger of 'reintroducing' precisely what is in question.

So we *might* suppose that he ought to be just as wary and just as cautious about 'experience'. We only need to turn for a moment to Blanchot to see why. In *The Writing of the Disaster*,[30] Blanchot repeatedly locates 'disaster' in terms of a *break* with 'experience', with the very possibility of experience. Blanchot writes of subjectivity as exile from the realm of 'experience'. He talks of 'the disaster, unexperienced... what escapes the possibility of experience', and he writes of a kind of passivity which 'escapes our power to test it, to try or experience it, and as interrupting our reason, our speech, our experience'. Whatever Blanchot means by disaster, he insists on a kind of allergic relation between disaster and experience, as if they occupied or structured the space of thought differently. Surely if Derrida were listening to Blanchot, he would not be so free with experience. But let us keep reading Blanchot. He writes:

> There is suffering, there would be suffering, but no longer any 'I' suffering, and this suffering does not make itself known in the present. It is not born into the present (still less is it experienced in the present)![31]

The moments at which the word 'experience' erupts in a text are often highly significant, but we do not restrict ourselves to tracking this word. When Blanchot mentions *suffering*, for example, that too is experience. In fact, when we dissect what he says about suffering, we see it is exemplary of the way in which 'experience' can itself undergo a transformation, an 'experience'.

On a Hegelian or a Christian perspective, 'suffering' would teach us something. We are deepened by the recognition of our vulnerability, our dependence, perhaps our mortality, by the recognition of the limits of autonomous selfhood. Undergoing suffering might put a certain sense of self or subject in question, but only in transition to a deeper sense. For Blanchot, suffering is an experience that demands, that forces a suspension of self. The 'I' that suffers is not thinking, synthesizing, making present. And in a more Levinasian tone, Blanchot goes on to write of 'the neighbour... opening me to the radical passivity of the self', and of 'subjectivity as wounded, blamed, and persecuted exposure'.[32]

These moves lead to a kind of ambivalence, especially in Blanchot, but also in Derrida's writing, between a recognition that concepts like 'experience' and 'subject' are instruments that we must preserve – even in their own transformation – and a sense that we need to effect or record a radical break with traditional metaphysical thought – an abyssal exposure of the *loss* of meaning, of any unity of experience, and of the very idea of the subject.

I will argue that the sense that both Blanchot and Derrida have of a kind of abyssal alternative to dialectic is itself in need of a certain deconstruction – that the idea of absolute loss is a kind of dialectical misunderstanding. It is a recognition of the interminability of dialectic, of the instability of any unity, and of the incompleteness of mourning, which is an important second-order truth about the teleology of thought. But this insight must never be allowed to spin free;

there can be no independent 'abyssal' realm. The experience of the impossible is nothing but the recognition of the impossibility of a certain *closure* of experience. In other words, abyssal thought is directly predicated on the value of *closure*. Without the effort at closure, and without the necessary failure of such closure (such determination of meaning, such completeness of identity, etc.), there can be no abyss. The abyss is derivative from the experience that it undermines. So abyssal thinking is essentially differentiated from, *and hence dependent on*, that recuperative negation that it refuses. That the fate of abyssal thought is tied up with that of recuperative negation would not be at all surprising if one saw it as something like a recognition of the limits of that recuperation. It is, however, a recognition that cashes out not as a new graspable truth, but as a *way*.[33] I want to argue shortly that all this comes to a certain problematic fruition in Derrida's account of *responsibility*, but I would like first to bring out an extraordinary and telling parallel between this strange displacement in Derrida and Blanchot of dialectical negation as a non-reconcilable negation, and Heidegger's reading of Hegel.[34]

In his *Hegel's Phenomenology of Spirit* [1930–1][35] and in his lectures published as *Hegel's Concept of Experience* [1950], p. 42,[36] Heidegger offers readings focusing on the introduction to the *Phenomenology of Spirit*. Heidegger compares Hegel's sense of experience with that of Kant, at least in the first critique – where 'experience means the totality of the theoretical knowledge of existing beings (nature).' I am not concerned here to defend Heidegger's characterization of Kant. Against the idea that 'Kant worked with an impoverished concept of experience', it is important to stress[37] the complementarity of the senses of moral and aesthetic experience to be found in the *Critique of Practical Reason* and the *Critique of Judgement*. His assessment of Kant's concept of experience is one of a number of foils in Heidegger's argument. Clearly it is Hegel's sense of experience as an undergoing that intrigues Heidegger. 'The Hegelian concept of experience', he writes, involves '*undergoing . . . something in such a way that this something is verified*, experiencing it as not being what it first seemed to be, but being truly otherwise.'[38] What Hegel understands as revealed by 'the experience that consciousness has of itself', Heidegger recognizes – in his own terms – as the being of beings. Heidegger treats Hegel (as he treated Kant) not as offering us an account of knowledge, but of being, or what it is for anything to be what it is. Now we might ask – where can Heidegger take this?

He concludes *Hegel's Concept of Experience* by various inconclusive speculations as to why Hegel dropped 'The Science of the Experience of Consciousness' as a title for *(The Science of the) Phenomenology of Spirit*. He surmises that Hegel may have been deliberately trying to free himself from the Kantian resonances of the word 'experience'. But it would not be too difficult to argue that Hegel's very project rests on a misrecognition of the character of his own discovery – that the *absolute* is not a kind of knowledge but (ultimately) a mode of comportment or recognition of the being of beings. And that Heidegger sees Hegel as, in this sense, transitional is borne out by the way in which Heidegger introduces the two central essays in *On the Way to Language*: 'The Nature of Language' and 'The Way to Language'.

Heidegger begins the first of these essays in the following way:

> The three lectures that follow bear the title 'The Nature of Language'. They are intended to bring us face to face with a possibility of undergoing an experience with language. To undergo an experience with *something*, be it a thing, a person, or a god, means that this *something* befalls us, strikes us, comes over us, overwhelms us, and transforms us. When we talk of 'undergoing' an experience we mean specifically that the experience is not of our making. To undergo here means that we endure it, suffer it, receive it as it strikes us, and submit to it. It is this *something* itself that comes about, comes to pass, happens.[39]

In other words, if in Hegel's sense, to experience something is to grasp its truth, for Heidegger that grasping has to take the existential form of being *in* the truth.

> If it is true that man finds the proper mode of his existence in language, whether he is aware of it or not, then an experience we undergo with language will touch the innermost nexus of our existence.[40]

The key to this 'experience with language' is to recognize the character of our relation to language – indeed *that* we *have* a 'relation' to language may be invisible in our everyday linguistic dealing with things (hailing a cab, talking to friends). But just as illness foregrounds our having a relation with our body, so the experience of 'not being able to find the right word for something that concerns us, carries us away, oppresses or encourages us'[41] allows us to reorient ourselves more generally to language, and consequently to ourselves. This is the same shape of example as Heidegger used in *Being and Time* to highlight the ready-to-handness of a tool – when it stops working. Instrumentality hides its own conditions of possibility. If Hegel's dialectic works by working through and working out false forms of the subject / object opposition, what is crucial to Heidegger's treatment, of course, is the recognition of the way in which our relation to language originally supersedes this distinction between subject and object.

We have remarked that, for Blanchot, the experience of *suffering* is not the experience of an 'I'. Heidegger's language here suggests a claim that is either subtly parallel to it or radically divergent. Consider first that undergoing an experience with language is elucidated via a series of passive expressions, 'something *befalls* us, *strikes* us, *comes over* us, or *overwhelms* us', and shortly afterwards Heidegger adds that 'we endure it, suffer it, receive it, and submit to it'. The point is that *erfahrung machen*, is not just of my *making*, but something (as Sartre might put it) being made of me. And the word 'passivity' is not quite right either, for this 'something' as he puts it, comes to pass, or 'happens'. The suggestion here is clearly that some sort of *recognition* of the significance of this structure of receptivity is part of what is meant by 'experience'. Heidegger seems to be saying that experience can be thought of as an appropriative recognition of our 'passivity'. Is this the death of the subject? If this is the same as what Blanchot means by 'suffering' then is it not incompatible with an 'I'? To draw them together, we would have to say that the 'I' that for Blanchot is incompatible with 'suffering' is one for which the only possibilities of transformation are thought in recuperative dialectical terms. If Heidegger is right, however, there *is* an alternative – one we discussed earlier in terms of a transformed ethos, 'dwelling', or 'inhabiting of language'.

Thinking of ethos in terms of dwelling is an ontological short-circuit of what Ricoeur calls the hermeneutic arc from interpretation to action, but it points to a certain way or character of human comportment. The import of many of Derrida's worries about Heidegger's repeated affirmation of the value of ownness, the proper, etc., is at the very least to question whether Heidegger has fully released himself from the grip of a recuperative teleology. But it is precisely Heidegger's reading of Heraclitus, for whom dwelling means locating the unfamiliar (the gods) within the familiar (the hearth), that disrupts this line of questioning. The unfamiliar is interruption as well as deepening. It is by following out such threads that we can eventually come to see Derrida's 'responsibility' as a way of reworking, reinscribing, repeating Heidegger's account of ethos.

The unfamiliar appears as the interruption of experience, both in the sense of experience as interruption and the interruption of a more domesticated sense of experience. I will now allow Derrida's own acknowledgement of this moment to emerge through a certain tracing of the course of 'trembling' through Kierkegaard.

The extraordinary virtue of Kierkegaard's philosophical thinking lies in his willingness to think the religious in terms of a certain mediated structure of subjectivity. This is not a simple displacement; rather it is an unending task, or *work* of experience – a kind of labour of the negative. But this passion for truth, for the deinstitutionalization and dereification of thought, must ultimately derealize God 'himself'. One could interpret the ambivalent importance of faith as a sign of such a consequence. Kierkegaard repeatedly in various ways says that objective thought concerns itself with the *what*, the subjective with the *how*,[42] and when he speaks of silence we discover it takes the form of 'indirect communication' where he emphasizes an 'artistic *manner*'. The knight of faith is a man (or woman) who returns to the finite, but always gets the infinite out of it. The ground structure of his dispositions has changed. What all this adds up to is this – that to the extent that he is successful, Kierkegaard translates religious belief into complexly mediated, and motivated ways of being and acting in the world. In this sense, at least, the religious is ultimately ethical.[43] The infinite is nothing but a certain kind of consideration brought to bear on action and thought. When Heidegger writes (as we have seen) that 'nothing occurs neither by itself nor "apart from" what is, as a sort of adjunct'[44] he is making a similar claim. We avoid confusion, ultimately, if we understand 'nothing' and 'being' as *modal* determinations of what-there-is, as *how* we can best see, grasp, understand what is. I am trying here to generalize the force of Kierkegaard's 'how' as a recursively applicable way of dealing with such objectifying projections as will continue to emerge. What I am saying here is not too different from Heidegger when (see earlier) he talks of 'examining constantly' the adequacy of our 'response to language'.[45]

There is no doubt that Derrida recognizes what I would call the phenomenological imperative – of staying with the experience, of acknowledging experience. For example, in *The Gift of Death*, after talking about Jan Patocha's references to the *mysterium tremendum*, and on the verge of introducing a discussion of Kierkegaard's *Fear and Trembling*, Derrida writes:

> As different as dread and fear, anxiety, terror, panic, or anguish remain from one another, they have already begun in the trembling, and what has provoked them continues, and threatens to continue, to make us tremble.[46]

Or again,

> In as much as it tends to undo both seeing and knowing, trembling is indeed an experience of secrecy or of mystery.[47]

Derrida introduced the term trembling as far back as *Of Grammatology* (making 'the value of presence *tremble*'), and I understand him to mean by it an experience in which the forces of difference constitutive of any and every identity or presence are activated, acknowledged and perhaps as such disturbed. 'Trembling' in this context might be thought in terms borrowed from Husserl as a kind of re-activation of difference. But, after Wittgenstein, to say that this coming up against the limits is ethical is surely to say that what is at stake in interpreting this experience, in 'appropriating' it, is the formation of certain dispositions, ways of remembering, bearing witness to, honouring the implications of these limits. In *The Gift of Death*[48] 'trembling' has come to mark the recognition of human frailty and finitude by contrast to an infinite and inaccessible God. In each case, we could say that 'trembling' is the experience of what escapes and perhaps subverts presence. Here the 'coming up against the limits of language' that Wittgenstein calls ethics, and his witnessing of an inexorable 'dependency', point in the same direction. If, as Heidegger would have it, we think ethics as *ethos* or dwelling, it suggests that the experience of 'trembling', when interpreted or (ex-)appropriated, would have to be translated into certain complex dispositions, ways of remembering, bearing witness to, honouring, acknowledging the significance of such an experience.

These dispositions are complex because their very enactment involves a renunciation of a certain model of fulfilment and success. In Derrida's writing, as in Heidegger's, there is a tension between the *terms* on which and with which we come to face alterity, and the complex dispositions, ways of proceeding and 'dwelling' (however problematized) into which these terms must be translated.

There is perhaps a change in the experience of the negative in the twentieth century. Should we treat what I have called *the loss of the law of the recuperability of loss* just as a logical discovery, as a discovery of flaws in the dialectic? Or is it something else? Consider Husserl for a moment. First, we find the emergence of the idea of passive synthesis[49] which requires a recognition of the power of cultural and linguistic formations over against the 'activity' of a subject. Second, there is his extraordinary supposition of the 'end of the world' (commented on by Levinas[50]) that the world might no longer make sense.

The crisis to which Nietzsche, and then Husserl, was responding, was one sensed first as a loss of a guarantee that through philosophical work we can attain salvation, and then the loss of the prospect of that salvation, what in another form Blanchot called disaster.[51] If mourning is the working through of loss, then, at best, we are mourning mourning, and working through the loss of the ability to work things through. But, of course, if confidence in the structure of working through has evaporated then perhaps we cannot be consoled with even this metamourning.

The story of this loss of dialectical confidence is not just a logical discovery – some flaw in the idea of absolute knowledge, or salvation, or emancipation – but also a historical and cultural crisis, of which the holocaust is the most potent sign, the indigestible experience that stops history in its tracks. What we think of as the displacement or deconstruction of the subject is the attempt to come to terms with the *failure* of that cultural formation – the autonomous individual – and to establish in its place a mode of being in the world that would recognize suffering, passivity, paradox and loss. However there is a danger in this, that of replacing one ideological or cultural formation (the autonomous individual) by another (the traumatized individual). The great achievement of the latter is to have brought back into the ethical domain some of the structures and economy of the religious, without the ontological (or onto-theological) baggage. But the trauma is being suffered *by* a certain cultural fiction of autonomy. In other words, there is a strange dialectical logic to this experience of trauma, and our task now is to translate traumatic loss into *ways* or *modes* of going on.

Derrida's recent discussions of responsibility reintroduce words like *infinite* and *absolute* – infinite responsibility, absolute singularity, absolute other – in ways that constantly threaten to cross the line between a *modal* truth, and a renewed mystification between recursive reminders and impossible prescription. The battle against good conscience is unending, not because duty calls us to an infinite task that we must fall short of, but because there is no finite response that exhausts our responsibility. Responsibility is not quantifiably (or even unquantifiably) *large*, and therefore is not a basis for guilt through failure to live up to it. It is rather a recursive modality, an always renewable openness.[52]

Derrida writes of 'an obligation to the other others I don't know, the billions of my fellows (... and animals)'.[53] He asks me how I can justify feeding *my* cat every morning, *and* allowing all the other cats in the world to starve. But the Good Samaritan for cats does not go searching for starving cats (or indeed starving anything or everything else); he would feed *any* hungry being that came along, and insist that every and any boundary of concern that one establishes is permeable.

Openness does not require that one leaves the door open, but that one is always willing to open the door. Responsibility then is the experience of that openness.[54, 55]

If the argument of this chapter is sound, the return of the centrality of experience to philosophy has made possible a reconfiguration of the ethical. Experience regained no longer shelters within conceptuality, or within the classical conception of the subject, but plots their limits, and in time breaks open each and every complacent demarcation. The ethical bearing of experience so understood is not, however, an infinite exposure but a way of comporting ourselves in our necessarily finite engagements, one in which the boundaries we necessarily set up are, as Heidegger put it, 'examined constantly'. Derrida's 'responsibility' inherits this legacy.

In the next chapter, we explore various attempts to subordinate experience to knowledge – notably in Kant – attempts that led Lacan to describe philosophy as the discourse of mastery. We argue, on the contrary, that philosophy is, at least in principle, the exemplary instance of a discourse that can stage our recognition of the limits of mastery.

3

The Voyage of Reason

The life of the mind has long been seen as a voyage of discovery, whether understood individually or historically, whether as the quest for scientific knowledge or for inner enlightenment. The birth of a new science has often been compared to the discovery of a new continent. But even as the analogy with exploration is sustained, this chapter[1] will explore the other voices that have been cautioning against epistemological naivety.

Almost exactly three hundred years after Columbus, in the course of inaugurating philosophy's Copernican revolution, Kant warned the sea-farers of thought not to be lured onto the rocks by the sirens; if they go too far, they will fall off the edge of the world of reason. His critique

> confines all our speculative claims rigidly to the field of possible experi-ence ... not by shallow scoffing at ever-repeated failures or pious sighs over the limits of our reason, but by an effective determining of these limits ... inscribing its *nihil ulterius* on those Pillars of Hercules that nature herself has erected in order that the voyage of our reason may be extended no further than the continuous coastline of experience itself reaches – a coast we cannot leave without venturing upon a shoreless ocean which, after alluring us with ever deceptive prospects, compels us in the end to abandon as hopeless all this vexatious and tedious endeavour.
>
> (*Critique of Pure Reason*, A395–6)

These remarks arise in the context of Kant's affirmation of the need to set philosophy on 'the sure path of a science', the model for which is logic that, since Aristotle, has not had to retrace a single step. The discovery that enabled empirical science to find this secure path – and he refers here to Galileo and Torricelli – was that while reason has to seek truth in nature it must 'adopt as its guide, in so seeking, that which it has itself put into nature'. (He compares the process to that of interrogating witnesses. (Bxiv))

Kant could be said to be engaged in sacrifice here. What cannot be known is abandoned as a lost cause, while philosophy is redirected towards more limited but achievable aims. Experience gives way to knowledge. But of course there is no real sacrifice, for we have nothing to lose but our illusions.

A more sceptical appraisal of this move, however, would judge it differently: that philosophy as innovation, discovery, openness has been sacrificed to philosophy as mastery. When Kant puts philosophy on the sure path of science he commits it to proceeding without error, without turning back, without accident, without interruption. In the midst, undoubtedly, of ravings, speculations and enthusiasms of all sorts, he commits philosophy to rigour above all else. It is then, perhaps, not surprising that Lacan two centuries later should diagnose the philosophical project as one of mastery.[2]

I will argue, however, that this is not a proper characterization of philosophy 'itself', but rather an issue with which philosophy is entangled, and which many of the best philosophers have resisted. Philosophy does have an important relation to mastery, one nicely prefigured in Kant's account. It is not mastery, however, but the *question of* mastery that preoccupies it.

I begin by discussing this question of philosophy's relation to mastery, starting out from what I take to be the attempt by psychoanalysis to distinguish itself from philosophy over this question, turning in the second part to the ideas of a domain of conquest, and of territory, implied by the value of mastery.

A discourse of mastery? Psychoanalysis and philosophy

In *The Ego and the Id* [1923] Freud describes as 'the first shibboleth of philosophy... to most people who have had a philosophical education, the idea of anything mental which is not also conscious is so inconceivable that it seems to them absurd and refutable simply by logic'. Freud offers against this philosophical prejudice the evidence of clinical experience, and in response to the philosophers' attempt to take account of the unconscious, he writes: 'to contradict them at this point would lead to nothing more profitable than a war of words' (p. 11) and speaks of 'endless difficulties of exposition' (p. 13). Freud's explanation of what is distinctive about psychoanalysis (which philosophers cannot deal with) is its recognition of powerful dynamic mental processes. He writes of an economy of forces, of repression and of resistance.

In this brief encounter, Freud sets psychoanalysis against the prejudices of the philosophers. There are three distinct aspects of his account. The first is that philosophy deals with concepts or words or logic, whereas psychoanalysis draws its evidence from experience; the second is that philosophers are dealing with a surface of static ideas, while psychoanalysis is dealing with deep dynamic processes; and the third is that psychoanalysis is a practice, indeed a technique (p. 12). I recall this example from Freud's work – there are many others – primarily to remind us that Lacan's description of philosophy as a discourse of mastery is a claim made within a broader history of the self-definition of psychoanalysis in opposition to philosophy.

Yet there is a deeper affinity than might be apparent between these two instances. If we identify philosophy with a commitment to the value of *presence* – a term wide enough to embrace consciousness, reason and intuition – then the subject-matter of psychoanalysis, the unconscious, is a plausible name for what threatens and disrupts such a mastery. The issue of *mastery* illuminates what is at stake in each of the three dimensions I identified in Freud's position. The attempt to work with schematic conceptual frameworks, rather than allow experiences to have a voice, is a symptom of the epistemological desire for mastery. The privileging of the static over the dynamic manifests the need for the mastery of time and the uncertainties and anxieties generated by its passage, and philosophy's confinement to abstract monologue rather than therapeutic interaction is at best authoritarian in its discursive orientation. We will return to each of these dimensions in the course of our discussion, when we will have occasion to correct the accounts they offer.

The relation between philosophy and psychoanalysis is not, however, my focus. Even if psychoanalysis were one thing and philosophy another, the relation between them would still be ambiguous and the complexity and diversity of each might suggest that nothing both interesting and clear could be said about this relationship. Positivists have attacked psychoanalysis as a science by questioning both its predictive success and its capacity to monitor success, and hence in their view the very significance of its claims. Other philosophers (such as Ricoeur) have argued that such an approach is inherently misleading – psychoanalysis is an essentially hermeneutic enterprise – both interpretive and therapeutic. For others, such as Sartre, Foucault, and Deleuze and Guattari, Lacan's verdict is precisely reversed – the discourse of psychoanalysis is itself inseparable from domination and power. (Both Foucault and Sartre have made the comparison with *confession*.)

The word 'ambiguity' is inadequate to describe the relationship between philosophy and psychoanalysis; something more systematically describable is occurring. It is perhaps worth repeating Freud's later remarks about Nietzsche – that he was glad not to have read him earlier as it might have prevented him from developing his own ideas. One thinks of remarks by Nietzsche, such as

> The unconscious disguise of physiological needs under the cloaks of the objective, ideal, purely spiritual goes to frightening lengths, and often I have asked myself, whether, taking a large view, philosophy has not been merely an interpretation of the body and a misunderstanding of the body... All these bold insanities of mastery... may always be considered first of all as the symptoms of certain bodies.[3]

In the case of Lacan one would need to answer the question about how he reconciles his diagnosis of philosophy as a discourse of mastery with his own enormous debts to philosophy – particularly Hegel, Sartre and Heidegger.

Surely something remarkably like 'mastery' is presupposed by claims about 'philosophy *as such*'. Our *objection* to such discursive gestures is not merely to point out the performative paradox in such totalization – which diagnoses mastery in another discipline while displaying it itself – but to claim that what it denies, suppresses, etc., is that *if there is* a unity to philosophy, it is the unity of a tradition held together quite as much by the radicality of its self-criticism as by any founding prejudice. This has certainly characterized what we call the *modern* tradition, beginning with Descartes, who sought to set aside all established principles and provide them with a new secure foundation. With the empiricist tradition, with Kant, with Hegel, and with Marx – *philosophers* have in each case written about the need to correct *fundamental errors* of philosophy, and have attempted to put it back on the right track. In this respect, philosophy is autophagy – feeding on itself. Should we not then treat the claim that philosophy is a discourse of mastery as another of these intraphilosophical moves, not substantially different from those by which philosophy has kept itself moving throughout the ages?

There is, in this account, both an important truth and the concealment of a problem. The insight is that philosophy thrives on change, on self-criticism, on self-transformation, and is perhaps inseparable from this. The problem concealed, however, is the possibility that these changes and transformations might nonetheless all be subject to a hidden agenda – that of mastery. (Cf. Nietzsche's talk about 'the invisible spell (under which) [the most diverse philosophers] always revolve in the same orbit'. He traces this to 'unconscious grammatical functions' and then to physiological valuation' (*Beyond Good and Evil*, section 20).) If philosophy is autophagy, the message is surely this: philosophy can be left to itself; it buries its own dead; it needs nothing else, it is self-sufficient *not* because it is complete, but because the significance of its incompleteness is something no other discipline is in a better position to thematize or deal with. It is not that there is no outside to philosophy, it is just that anything that mattered to philosophy would have to be able to be drawn into it. This is an important dimension to any story that would see philosophy as wholly autophagous. For it does not merely feed on itself, it continuously excludes, manages and subjugates other discourses. The relation to *science* is an obvious example – from Aristotle to Heidegger; … and the relation to literature – from Plato to positivism – is another. Philosophy is not an empirical discipline, it deals not with *beings* but with Being as such. Put another way, philosophy is concerned with thinking, not calculation, or mere 'reasoning'. If the place of science is important, philosophy guarantees it. If it gets too presumptuous, philosophy limits it. Plato banished the poets; but when Ricoeur reminds philosophy what a rich stimulus their products can be to philosophical reflection, even this judgement is a form of appreciative containment.

These claims, if true, would surely be enough to substantiate the view that philosophy was constituted by the project of mastery. Philosophy would be a discourse constituted by the exclusion and management of any other discourse that might compete with it. This conclusion would only be confirmed by looking at the specific cases we mentioned. Consider science. Whether we think of formal or natural sciences, philosophy is progressively faced with bodies of knowledge with very considerable deductive, predictive and explanatory power, which certainly seem to supply *truth* – surely the honey first promised by philosophy. Science here is competing for *mastery*; and philosophy can maintain itself only by measuring its distance from science, which it has done for 2000 years.

Literature is doubly problematic. It sometimes seems to compete for discursive mastery. And yet literature cannot be reduced to any sufficiently determinate relation to language. To the representational self-assurance of traditional narrative, one only has to oppose a poetic dissemination, in which any pretension to mastery is abandoned. Literary language as a distinct genre, then, both offers a competing discourse of mastery, from which philosophy must distinguish itself, and threatens mastery by problematizing the stability of mastery and the representational function of language. Also, as the literary is not confined to literature but is entangled with philosophy itself, the literary is both an inner and an outer danger to mastery. The project of the elimination of mastery from philosophy is a symptom of the recognition of such danger.

Does all this not suggest that if the model of philosophy as a self-reflexive, self-interrogating tradition is still plausible, it is not one to be opposed to the thesis of philosophy as a discourse of mastery, but precisely articulates the key mechanisms of that mastery? On this view, it would be naive to suppose that philosophical discourse was some sort of completed static cathedral of truth. Surely it is a discourse of mastery precisely in its capacity to manage its own boundaries by exclusion, appropriation and translation, and to transform itself by reflexion.

This picture is remarkably convincing at first glance, but we should nonetheless be cautious about accepting it. I have already suggested that the claim that philosophy – as such, in general, as a whole – is this or that, is itself in real danger of exhibiting the very defect it attributes to philosophy. My guess is that this claim is made convincing by the combination of two strategies. The first is to treat Hegel as the exemplary case of philosophy. If he can be shown to have taken philosophy to the limit, what is true of him is true of 'the philosophical project' as such. From the point of view of the analytical tributaries from the mainstream of philosophy – which for a long time steered clear of reading Hegel at all – this strategy might seem to be transparently implausible, serving at best as further evidence of why Hegel must be avoided. But even if we remain true to the broader Continental tradition, over whom the shadow of Hegel still falls – through critical theory, through existentialism, through Marxism, and indeed through most developments in contemporary thought – it would still seem to be a vulgar begging of the question to choose Hegel as exemplary because of his totalizing tendencies, and on that basis to attribute the project of mastery to philosophy as such. It would be much more plausible to treat Hegel as exemplifying a particular philosophical desire for systematization, or totalization. We could then line him up against other philosophies, and against himself.

This leads us to the second strategy by which philosophy is linked to mastery, which could be called the selective determination of the orientation of the struggle that is philosophy. Those who cannot remember railway travel before welded rails will have to watch *North by Northwest* for the sound, or invent their own example, but the characteristic sound of this train travel used to be tickety-tack, tickety-tack. The way I read this, and indeed punctuated it on the page, suggests the very illusion I would like to expose – that the dominant tendency is one of resolution. The drama of the rails is that escape is always thwarted (tickety-tack). And yet we could just as easily rejig the phrasing to hear tack . . . tickety, which says that every resolution is dissolved, broken away from.

If philosophy were a continuous struggle, a site of conflict, then reading it as the project of mastery would be the result of selective phrasing. There are many names for the protagonists of this struggle – the limited and the unlimited, identity and difference, order and chaos, perhaps death and pleasure. I may already be closing things off by reverting to binarism, and then to unity (one struggle, many names), but even on such traditional premises it is hard not to see mastery as the name of but one of the moments. Those for whom philosophy is essentially an emancipatory project would dispute the privilege of mastery in any political sense. And those for whom philosophy is the site for a renewed openness to experience, or to Being, or to the Other, would dispute the privilege more widely.

It is clear enough to me that, even if Hegel is a philosopher of mastery, he does not constitute the entire domain of philosophy, and to suppose that he does is to focus from the outset only on the moment of mastery, rather than dispersal, or dissemination. But even to read Hegel like this is suspect. That Hegel's is a philosophy of totality, committed to a teleological organization of the development of consciousness to self-consciousness to absolute knowledge, is not itself an example of philosophical insight but a cliché. Leaving aside Hegel's own insights into the continuing power and privilege of the slave in his account of the master/slave relationship, designating Hegel the philosopher of mastery seems to me to be open to serious methodological dispute. It may be that if we focus on Hegel's stated intentions, or on the surface development of the exposition of his books, we will typically find the drive to completeness, to 'mastery'. But to identify philosophy with the intentions consciously animating a text is not to discover mastery in the text, but to import mastery into the text as a hermeneutic presumption. If we assume from the outset that Hegel is in charge of his text, and then find that what he has produced is a discourse of mastery, our conclusion can be traced back to our original presupposition. If, however, we see Hegel's texts as exemplary stagings of struggle, then we have, perhaps, a better way of thinking of philosophy.

The claim that philosophy is a discourse of mastery has not, so far, been substantiated. The most powerful argument surely is still to come – namely, that the most important philosophers have themselves come to the same conclusion. I have already quoted Nietzsche on the unconscious domination of philosophy by physiological valuations. In terms of the thesis of mastery, of course, his is a complex claim. Mastery would seem to be only one option among a range of economic possibilities. But his association of philosophy with 'the revenge against time and its "it was"' suggests that the passage of time itself is understood as the object of mastery for a whole post-Platonic tradition. I will return to this shortly. But with Heidegger, Levinas and Derrida in particular we find philosophers who would surely endorse Lacan's claim about the link between philosophy and mastery.

The *locus classicus* of Heidegger's statement of the need to de(con)-struct philosophy is section 6 of *Being and Time*, 'The Task of Destroying the History of Ontology'. We find ourselves in a position in which, as he puts it, 'tradition becomes master... in such a way that what it transmits is made inaccessible' (H21). Here, however, it is not philosophy that desires mastery, but rather, being ruled and governed by tradition, it falls prey to unreflective tradition, i.e. common sense. Philosophy lapses into a condition in which there is a certain failure of questioning. Can this lapse be thought of as a search for mastery? As an original interrogative openness to Being, philosophy increasingly contents itself with its earlier answers and loses access to the fundamental question of Being. The desire for mastery manifests itself in its transformation into science, *Wissenschaft*, in which thinking is governed by rules, and in which there is an adequacy in the relation between words and things, what I earlier called epistemological naivety.

What corresponds in Heidegger to diagnosing philosophy as a discourse of mastery is the attempt at overcoming metaphysics. Heidegger tries to re-open what has been closed off and so destabilize those forms of assurance we call philosophy. To talk about the question of Being is precisely to talk about an openness prior to and beyond any ontic discourse or any traditional ontology. Openness to Being is an antidote to mastery.[4]

Levinas' agreement with the philosophy-as-mastery thesis can also be obtained. What is initially curious is just how critical he is of Heidegger, whose orientation to Being he, quite wrongly, associates with the philosophy of totality. For Levinas' concern is, in effect, with philosophy's subordination of ethics to ontology, or with the space of ethics to the closed space of ontology. What he clearly resists is the idea of simply making a topological change in ontology (openness to Being) and demands, instead, a recentring of philosophy on the ethical opening onto the Other, which would break utterly with the project of mastery, not merely at the level of institutions, but at the most basic encounter.

Do we not, finally, get confirmation of the thesis associating philosophy and mastery in Derrida's diagnosis of the commitment of the philosophical tradition to logocentrism, to the metaphysics of presence? Is not the value of presence in its various forms – consciousness, self-consciousness, reason, intuition – precisely that of mastery, of a containment and control that leaves nothing to chance? If, for Levinas, the other person explodes the intentional gaze, then, for Derrida, intentionality can be challenged from within even in its purest manifestation (e.g. in Husserl). If, as I am suggesting, Derrida's insistence on the constitutive significance of otherness, alterity, is consistent with the positions of Heidegger and Levinas, even as it digs deeper, do we not have an extraordinary measure of agreement with this thesis from the philosophical camp itself? Does this not close the case? Have we not turned the last page of this question?

Well of course we have not. For each of these philosophers makes his version of the charge of mastery in the course of a transformation of philosophical practice. Their confirmation does not, however, endorse the abdication of philosophy, but of the need to pursue it in a different manner. Indeed I would argue that for each of them there is a necessary entanglement in mastery even as we attempt something different; and for none of them is it necessary to take one's bearings from psychoanalysis, even if (particularly through Lacan's understanding of the unconscious) there are real parallels.

I have not so far defined the term 'mastery', not out of laziness or for reasons of difficulty – though such motives would certainly have sufficed – but because I am more interested in activating the range of senses and associations of the term, and exploring their interconnections, than in making a small clean contribution to the analysis of conceptual interconnections. Even so, as will become apparent, there are lines I have not pursued, such as the gendered nature of mastery. I do think, however, that it is worth distinguishing different aspects of mastery – even if we eventually have to conclude that it is not one thing – both to demonstrate the different levels at which the issue of mastery arises (which relates to the issue of entanglement) and to enable us to think more concretely about it.

I will take three different dimensions of mastery – language, time and the Other – and try to explain in more detail how understanding and undermining the desire for mastery is possible within philosophy.

The importance of language for the question of mastery is perhaps decisive. The ancient art of rhetoric was the object of philosophical interest and suspicion precisely because of the way it went beyond truth to persuasion and power. We are not here thematically concerned with rhetoric, but it is the condition of all philosophizing that it involves both writers and readers, or speakers and hearers. To speak naively we could say it involves communication, but, as Kierkegaard and Nietzsche made very clear, this claim is inherently problematic. The model of writing / speaking as communication is one that crystallizes the author and reader as the terms of a relation, in a way that closes off problems about the terms themselves. If the subject that speaks is always in dialogue with himself (or herself), and if the same is true of the listener or reader, what is speaking, what is reading? Kierkegaard identifies this condition with 'subjectivity' and insists that true communication bears witness to this and, thereby, awakens the subjectivity in the other, and is therefore emancipatory. This model is quite helpful, for it suggests that at the moment of speaking, writing (perhaps acting), there is a necessary resolution or determination, which we might think of in terms of a temporary ascendancy of one point of view or another, or at least a way of breaking into what Gadamer calls the soul's conversation with itself.

And if Kierkegaard is right, it is possible for us to talk of success, in the sense of successfully emancipating the other. It is said that Kierkegaard does manage to communicate this very thesis both directly (*Concluding Unscientific Postscript*) and indirectly (*Fear and Trembling*), but in each case there is an important sense in which the communicative success is based upon a free response of the reader, and this sounds like a model that avoids mastery. Given what I have said about entanglement, I am not so sure. To speak in such a way that those who understand you have to perform the very mental operations that will supply them with the evidence they need to confirm what is being said is quite close to manipulation, and hence not unambiguously free of the desire for mastery. (I have in mind here Lacan's *Discourse of Rome*.) And the reader's or listener's free response is a remarkably fragile concept. At the very least, the thematization of what is at stake in communication – even down to the suspension of the speaking subject's inner activity – brings out the deep structure of the question of communication, and hence the importance of posing the question of mastery in this layered way.

There is here an interesting meeting point between philosophy and psychoanalysis. The philosopher can insist that the dimension of power in a relationship is not adequately located until the identity of the participants is established and he can conceptually clarify the kind of relationships possible between self-mastery and the mastery of others. It nevertheless remains the task of a therapeutic discipline to propose and confirm the existence of certain actual mechanisms linking the two (e.g. that deficiencies in ego-formation lead to aggression).

The problems of mastery at the level of the pragmatics of language are thus both dialectical (e.g. persuasion requires free assent) and, let us say, transcendental, because the reflexive questions of mastery already posed by the identity of speaker / hearer, etc., are as much in play as any simple assessment of the given relationship.

While mastery *through* language is tied to the possibility of mastery *of* language, Heidegger and Derrida offer us two different but, I believe, compatible reasons for casting serious doubt on this possibility. When I first discussed Heidegger, the critique of philosophy as a discourse of mastery was linked to the destruction of ontology and the overcoming of metaphysics. But a thematically much more direct focus would have been his discussion of language, particularly in his later work. Heidegger's early account (*Being and Time*) of Dasein's thrownness is already a good indication of his position. The Cartesian subject enthroned like a god surveying his creation is a fiction. We find ourselves in circumstances, not of our own making, which we can never 'master'. The structure of this thought – which suggests a redirection of our thinking, not resignation – is reapplied to language. In various of his essays on language he is concerned to break any assimilation of the relation between speaker (or writer) and language to the already defective account of the relation between a subject and its intentional acts.[5] The psychoanalytical version of the necessary defect of a voluntaristic consciousness model of intention is clearly only one variant of a number of alternatives. The general version Heidegger is offering us is that our possibilities of linguistic expression, communication, intention, etc., are themselves dependent on our immersion in language.

At this general level Saussure's *langue* and Lacan's *symbolique* perform analogous displacements of the primacy of the subject. What is distinctive, perhaps, about Heidegger's account is that the recognition of the primacy of language over the subject is the moment for an invitation to an act of surrender. He writes:

> Language ... speaks. If we let ourselves fall into the abyss denoted by this sentence, we do not go tumbling into emptiness. We fall upward, to a height ... [and then] to reflect on language means – to reach the speaking of language in such a way that this speaking takes place as that which grants abode for the being of mortals.[6]

It would be too easy to say that Heidegger is simply inverting the master / slave opposition. That we are not masters of what we utter does not mean we are dummies for the ventriloquist of Being. In an important sense Heidegger is not contesting our ordinary capacity to mean what we say. He is saying, however, that it rests on conditions of possibility, the exploration of which is the proper business of philosophy – or 'thinking'. And this exploration is not simply the scientific documentation of a domain, but something like a recovery of Being. Heidegger is surely here breaking with Hegel's warning that philosophy should beware of wishing to be edifying. Mastery of language is, for Heidegger, an illusion, and one that blocks a therapeutic release. Heidegger talks of listening to language even as one speaks – an orientation particularly effective in his readings of the poets.

The position Heidegger is attacking is comically presented, of course, by Humpty Dumpty in Lewis Carroll's *Through the Looking Glass* [1896].[7] But there is more to Humpty Dumpty's account than is usually noticed.

> When I use a word, Humpty Dumpty said, in rather a scornful tone, it means just what I choose it to mean – neither more nor less.... The question is, said Alice, whether you can make words mean so many different things.... The question is, said Humpty Dumpty, which is to be master – that's all.[8]

This is pure voluntarism, the pure assertion of the possibility of mastery of language. What follows is less often quoted. For Alice, puzzled, does not reply. (What is there to say?)

So after a minute Humpty Dumpty began again.

> They've a temper, some of them, particularly verbs: they're the proudest – adjectives you can do anything with, but not verbs – however, I can manage the whole lot of them! Impenetrability! That's what I say.[9]

The pragmatics of this discourse deserve much greater attention. I would just point out that what happened is that the thesis of mastery is explicated not as total domination, but as management. It is important to know about the temper of different words. (And, of course, the word *temper* itself means, among other things, to manage, control, etc. – well-tempered scale, tempered steel, etc.) Of course mastery itself can have just this sense (e.g. mastering a skill) of combining power and discernment. Lewis Carroll is playing many games at once here!

I offer this interlude from the official programme of discussing philosophers because it brings us close to the slightly different versions of the problems or question of language and mastery offered by Derrida. As I said earlier, it is not difficult to see Derrida's whole position as the creative demonstration of the impossibility of linguistic mastery. One of the ways of glossing what he has called 'logocentrism' is the guiding philosophical presupposition of the transparency of language. This attributes to philosophy as a whole the belief that language is functioning properly only when it unambiguously expresses a meaning, or when it successfully refers to some particular state of affairs. There are different views about whether ordinary language achieves this end, whether a new technical language is required, or whether what is needed is a continuing clearing-up operation – conceptual analysis – which would give us guidance in our use of language. Language, on this view, is a mere tool, which works best when it is not seen, when it functions as a transparent medium. Language, in other words, is an ideal servant, that does not speak itself, but is a neutral means to an end. One way of understanding the move towards formal philosophy is precisely the withdrawal from essentially unimprovable natural languages, towards the meta-level, where order, clarity, etc. – and control – can be re-established.

On Derrida's view, such a model of language reflects metaphysical prejudice in favour of self-presence – of a simple given identity undisturbed by difference, which, when tracked to its lair in its most rigorously worked-out form (Husserl's phenomenology), is both implausibly solipsistic and in a number of key respects defective.

For all his interest in metaphor, and his suspicion of the project of eliminating it from philosophy, Derrida does not conclude of course that philosophy should simply give itself up to metaphor, to ambiguity, to slippage, etc. – a common misreading of his early 'White Mythology'. Derrida's position is perhaps best understood as translating Heidegger's 'listening to the speaking of language' into a discourse that registers awareness of the traditional figures of rhetoric, his own intellectual trajectory – through linguistics – and a different sense of the economics of discourse. Where Heidegger's tone is reverential, and almost mystical, Derrida's is one of negotiation; he does deals and accepts the necessity of getting one's hands dirty.

The first few pages of his 'The *Retrait* of Metaphor' illustrates this quite well. He begins this essay about metaphor by developing in a most exaggerated way all the traditional language used to explain metaphor – especially that of transportation. He begins to reflect on the methodological messiness of this, and suggests to himself (or to us) that he should stop:

I ought to decisively interrupt the drifting or skidding. I would do it if it were possible. But what have I just been doing? I skid and drift irresistibly. I am trying to speak about metaphor, to say something proper or literal on this subject, to treat it as my subject. . . .

[But] I cannot treat it without dealing with it (*traiter avec elle*) without negotiating with it the loan I take from it in order to speak of it. . .[10]

I can only here offer a flavour of this. Derrida's point is that there is an essential entanglement of all discourse – even philosophical – with what we call metaphor. But not only is this entanglement not reduction, the very idea of metaphor rests on the essentially metaphysical idea of the 'proper meaning'. The moral of this is that while philosophy cannot achieve mastery either of or through language, there is nowhere else to go – whether to found that project anew, to celebrate a newly acquired anarchy, or to negotiate with the enabling conditionality of language.

The theme of mastery, or rather of the necessary failure of mastery, is also central to Derrida's description of what is involved in a deconstructive reading, which plots just how, in each case, a writer 'writes in a language, and in a logic whose proper system, laws, and life his discourse . . . cannot dominate absolutely'. We discuss this at greater length in chapter 4, but it is important to note here that, for Derrida, it is precisely the impossibility of mastery that makes writing possible, and it is the demonstration of the shapes of desire spawned by this impossibility that fuels his own work.

From this brief discussion of Heidegger and Derrida I conclude that the association of philosophy with mastery is not confirmed by philosophers' radical attempts to confront mastery in their midst, for their very response shows that a philosophical response to this problem is possible, even if it is one that distends and extends philosophy.

The second theme I would like to pursue in the connection between philosophy and mastery is time. We do not need to be philosophers to find the passage of time disquieting. We do not have to be philosophers to find it difficult to understand how we can place so much value on any particular occurrence when it will soon be past, a nullity. And realizing that there must come a world from which one will be absent – in cosmic terms, very soon indeed – is equally a source of anxiety. Some engage happily in everyday activity, in what one could call temporal virginity, while others distract themselves from the horror of this abyss. In different ways, it could be said, religion and philosophy have made the mastery of time into a profession. And those who have thought of the history of philosophy as a series of footnotes to Plato must have had his quest for timeless forms in mind. It is Plato, we recall, who described philosophy as a preparation for death.

The relation between philosophy, mastery and death is exceedingly complicated. Hegel's account of the emergence of the self-conscious subject, which is also the emergence of the possibility of social relations between beings who respect each other as such, is described in *Phenomenology of Spirit* (sections 178–96 on 'Lordship and Bondage'[11]) – the life and death struggle.[12] This has to be suspended at the point of achieved mastery in a finite economy, precisely because *death is risked only up to a point*, and the commitment of philosophy to mastery is a commitment to a kind of seriousness and closure exceeded only by what he calls sovereignty.

The confrontation with the limitations imposed on philosophy by its attempts at the mastery of time, especially death, is a theme one can also happily pursue through other philosophers.[13] The structure of response we offered in the case of the mastery of language can be repeated – that while philosophy exhibits powerful tendencies in this direction, it also demonstrates an impressive ability to critically interrogate and respond to just such a claim. Neither Heidegger's Being-towards-death, nor his account of 'anticipatory resoluteness', is a denial or even mastery of death, but a recognition of the impossibility of that mastery. Is such a recognition another level of meaning? Clearly it could become one, but that is not how Heidegger presents it. Derrida first thinks death not as event but (through the condition of writing) as necessary possibility, in which the absence if not the death of the writer always figures.

But instead of pursuing these more recent philosophers, I will briefly consider the case of Nietzsche, for he comes closest to having claimed outright that philosophy is an attempt to suppress time, and comes closest to being an anti-Platonist, a champion of *becoming* over *being*. Nietzsche is repelled by the smell of fraud whenever eternal truths are presented. What he smells is consolation, sometimes revenge against time. He has the same attitude to teleological thinking, which, while it accepts the reality of time, subordinates it to an orderly development or realization of a goal. What other philosophers had claimed were necessities of thought, Nietzsche treated as incapacities and weaknesses. And what is his prescription, his remedy? Eternal recurrence. He presents this idea in many different ways and it can be read at a number of different levels. It can be treated as an account of the passage of time as such (the 'now' as eternally recurrent), or as an account of the strict recurrence of all events in sequence, or indeed as an imaginary moral test. Whichever way we treat it, it is an ideal that powerfully resists mastery. The response he seeks to this idea is not one of pleasure at its power to organize time for us, but a kind of exhilarated affirmation in which the desire for mastery would explode at the same time. Acceptance of eternal recurrence means accepting that there is *no resolution in time*, no ultimate purpose, no escape from time, just ... more of the same. Affirmation of this is not a new level of mastery, but rather an abandonment of that dream.

The last theme I propose to pursue is that of the Other. I will simply say that important as psychoanalysis surely is here, the history of our philosophical reflection on the Other is both a history of the exclusion and subordination of the Other to the same (e.g. Husserl's 'alter ego') *and* the confrontation, sometimes not even noticed, with the difficulty or even impossibility of this reduction. This is true both for that history of the self-other dialectic that one could date from Hegel's account of the master/slave relation, for the phenomenological attempts to deal with the other (in which I include both Husserl and Levinas), for Habermas' insistence on the emancipatory interest of philosophy, and for Lyotard's account of the *Differend*.

Philosophy is not *one* discourse, hence it is not a discourse of mastery. And it is precisely a condition of its continuing health that it can respond effectively to the challenge that it shows itself not to be such a discourse.

Is it wholly wrong to describe philosophy as a discourse of mastery? In my view it is less important to ascribe this feature to one discipline as to recognize the various forms of the danger it poses to any discipline, and indeed to our ordinary thinking. What is particularly heartening about some of the philosophers I have alluded to is that they have increasingly come to dramatize the interruption of the Other in their practice of writing, and this is a kind of general prophylactic against mastery.

Territorial ambitions

Where Kant insisted on the need for critique if philosophy is to be set upon 'the highway of science', we responded with a discussion of the value of mastery implied by his claim. In this second part we must further pursue the question of scientific knowledge and its proper terrain — a question that will make visible numerous aporias of discovery and of conquest.

To begin with it must be said that the model of *science* being appealed to is anachronistic. Particularly within recent philosophy of science, it has been the object of serious criticism, and for many people – scientists and non-scientists alike – discredited. Science may give us various more or less successful forms of *control*, and may help us to improve our knowledge, but it does not give us truth; it gives us hypotheses, theories, models. And every time we forget this, and become so comfortable with a new theory, basking perhaps in its practical or technological benefits, we are reverting to a renewal of the natural attitude with which science, and in a different way, philosophy, represents a break. Every time the latest scientific hypothesis becomes received wisdom, the true significance of science gets lost.

On this view, science is not knowledge or wisdom, but a process of critical investigation that continually questions all that we take for granted – a process in which new models, new theories are continually being thrown up, and the old ones discarded. On this model, science is not knowledge. It may contribute to eliminating error and complacency, but it does not deliver knowledge *per se*. On this model, science is permanent revolution. And if normal science does not seem like this, it is because the practice of science itself is vulnerable to the disease of complacency and institutionalization.

The model of science as a foundational construction – the sort on which it is possible to proceed without being 'required to retrace a single step' as Kant put it – can be given many explanations.[14] Before Kant it could have been described as metaphysical or even theological. Metaphysically, it would rest on the assumption of natural kinds, of a real world that in itself is organized in ways fundamentally open to mathematical description. Theologically, science would have at its end-point the discovery of the mind of God as revealed in his creation. Scientific knowledge would allow man's mind to converge with the ideas on which the universe was based. In Galileo, for example, these two views coincided.[15] With Kant, as we have seen, the basis of knowledge was redefined in such a way that philosophy could be included, and it was no longer God's mind that was to be interpreted but rather the *a priori* element that we ourselves have already contributed.

Against the view for which philosophy is a revolutionary practice, Kant's understanding of philosophy is thus anachronistic. For it to be a science, it too had to have a territory, a realm, which it would proceed to conquer. But it is not clear that the analogy with the natural sciences, for which the conquest of nature was often described in terms of inquisition, interrogation, of forcing nature to give up its secrets, is entirely appropriate.

For what I have called the revolutionary view of science I am drawing on a loose amalgam of Popper, Kuhn and Feyerabend, who, if they can be persuaded to share the same bed, will not spend the whole night together. We need not, however, suppose that science is nothing but revolution. There are stable periods (Kuhn's normal science) *within which* all manner of possibilities are tried out. There can be formal requirements for anything to count *as* scientific knowledge, as the proper object of a revolution. And there are paradigms that at any one time limit what may be treated even as an option. None of this commits us to Kant's transcendentalism, but it does suggest that there may still be life in the idea of scientific discovery and of science as engaged in the conquest of a domain of knowledge, even if all that has to be understood under a certain erasure. The central question we will be asking here is what happens to the values of mastery, conquest, discovery when the domain or territory in question is not simply there in advance, but in important ways constructed, constituted by the operation of knowledge upon it.

I will take my lead in this from Foucault. Foucault's discussion of sexuality in the nineteenth century takes a detour through the discourse of sexuality. By so doing he disturbs the complacency by which sexuality would be a natural phenomenon *subjected* to a repressive discourse. The repressive hypothesis, as he puts it, cloaks a naivety about the supposed object of repression, and it fails to consider the constitutive role of discourse. Whether or not one agrees with Foucault's particular conclusions here, his method is such as to replace our naive realism with a sophisticated series of questions about the contribution of discourse to the constitution of its own terrain. This epistemological shift can, as I have said, be traced back to Kant, to Husserl, and to certain contemporary philosophers of science. Without denying for one minute that knowledge is knowledge of the real world, our claim is that what we call scientific knowledge is necessarily couched in a discourse that *constitutively maps the world* in the course of its application to it. We might say that for science to come into being it must produce a certain order, a certain articulation of the real. Operationally, this will then take the place of the real, and become invisible. Geometry *seems* to apply directly to space; but we know, after Husserl and after Derrida, that that idealized space has its genealogy in a long history of geometrical discourses and practices. Geometrical space is a constitutive achievement, and not simply given. It is an achievement not merely because geometry is a formally successful discipline – we can prove theorems – but because it has synthetic power. Bridging rivers long ago; now ballistics – and always architecture, town planning, land surveying, road building – and with these applications, the constitution and the conquest of space go hand in hand. Geometry is not simply a repressive science. It is hard to see how there could be repression at all without science, without the articulation of a domain.

Maps of old countries record in sedimentary layers cross-cutting ways of constituting space. The Roman conquest of Britain is still visible in roads that cut straight lines through the earth and are heavy with traffic to this day. In America, the coming of the railway, the theme or backdrop of many a Western, allowed the 'opening up' of the West, and indeed the effective unification of the America that Columbus had 'discovered'. What the rule of law did for social relations, the railway (and perhaps the telegraph) did for communicative infrastructure. The railway, with all its violence, did not just cut through America, it knitted it together; it allowed a state to be constituted. The analogy, if successful, can be developed: the history of science involves not merely the discovery of new facts, nor even the throwing up of new hypotheses or new theories. It is the successive creation of new domains of inquiry, new articulations of conceptual/ discursive space. In the special case of geometry, the space of discourse is occupied by the discourse of space. In such articulations of space the line between the regulative and the constitutive, and between repression and production, is rendered mobile. The history of discovery and conquest, too, is governed by a logic in which the line between the regulative and the constitutive is repeatedly shifted. If we ask who 'discovered' America, the answer will depend on a complex narrative of discursive constitution and reconstitution (to which Henry Ford, John Wayne and Ted Turner have made one sort of contribution and Cavell, Baudrillard and perhaps Heidegger have made another).

We could imagine distinguishing two forms of discovery. In the first, the object is anticipated, even named, and perhaps searched for, and then eventually 'discovered'. The planet Uranus, for example, was deduced, then suspected, before being observed (Herschel 1787). In the second form, discovery obeys a future perfect logic shared with other forms of initiation and creativity. What has been discovered, indeed *that* there has been a discovery, is only 'discovered' later. And nothing finally privileges a particular date for judging this. If free-market capitalism of the type we associate with the USA were eventually benignly to spread across the entire planet, creating a new order of self-maintaining peace and prosperity, what Columbus discovered will have turned out one way. If the dollar collapses under the combined pressure of international counterfeiting and bad debt, and the American banking system follows suit, and the separate states of the United States regroup, with California and Texas, for instance, going the way of Estonia and Georgia, then what Columbus discovered might revert to being a continent rather than a way of being human, a way of being on earth. And, of course, it is a commonplace that he did not so much discover America as find it blocking his route to China by sailing west.

I have said there are two forms of discovery. The second succumbs to the fate of narrative and discursive reassessment and discontinuity. But it is important to realize that the same is true of the first. An anticipated event or object is never *exhaustively* grasped in advance, and this suggests that the future perfect logic of the second form of discovery in fact provides the frame of reference within which even anticipated discovery is ultimately to be evaluated.

If the analogy with the domain of a science has any plausibility – that by which Euclidean geometry projects Euclidean space, for instance – and if we are right to think of such domains in terms of discursive articulation (discourses that *constitute* a space as a domain rather than merely regulating it), then this future perfect logic could be said to be subject to two distinct, and even opposed, necessities. As a discourse develops, it will increase in complexity, allowing the precipitation of new features, the dissolution of others, the confirmation and disconfirmation of earlier projections. But equally, if discourses constitute domains, and if the identity of a science (and perhaps a historico-geographical ideality like America) is bound to the integrity of such domains, this future perfect logic may not always be the site for the indefinite deferment of judgement – waiting to see how it turns out – but also the site of the cessation and demise of a domain (a science, a nation) and of its discursive articulation.

This discussion itself begins to sound like the attempt to constitute (or reconstitute) a discursive field, to establish perhaps a meta-domain. What cannot be concluded, however, and what is not implied is that any of this offers ways of *deciding* on some particular occasion what, if anything, has been discovered, whether the party is over, etc. The way we have expressed it makes it sound like a higher order matter of fact, but there is no doubt that the nature of any discovery, at the time and at different subsequent times, can remain what has been called an *essentially contestable* matter. The terms in which I have tried to articulate the discursive (you could here substitute 'textual') dimension of the being of such entities as sciences, or nations, make it easier to see the shape and necessity for this essential contestability. The adequacy of a discourse either for practical needs or for the constitution of a domain is not something for which there are advance or general rules.

Such a discursive or textualist epistemology clearly has consequences for ontology. The relation between discourses and domains, if anything like that between geometry and 'its' space, is a logical one. Geometrical discourse *orders* space, masters it, not in the sense of

oppressing an alien territory or population, but in the positive, creative sense of giving rise, giving life to a certain *order*. Such an order is
a part of the real, not merely an idealization of it. It supplies rules for
actual engagement – interaction, communication, exchange – rules
which make possible engagements that would otherwise not have
been possible. (Think here of money markets, natural languages,
families, and even conferences.) To say that such orders are part of
the real is, however, to leave open what else there is, and indeed how
different orders relate to one another. When we play chess, the spatial
boundaries of the game are fixed and visible on the chess board. But
what we call the real is characterized by ambiguities as to the *limits of
efficacy* of what we have called *orders*, both between one order and
the next, and between order and what does not function as an order at
all. Conquest, whether economic or military, involves the successful
introduction of a dominant order: dominant both in the sense that it
dominates other orders and in the sense that it determines, as far as it
is necessary, the relation between that order and the real. It is
common, for example, to extract taxes from a population. This may
well require the introduction of a common currency, a way of assess-
ing income, and finally institutions of law enforcement. This, however, would have to replace or significantly displace existing forms of
economic organization. But to complete the task there is still the
matter of determining the relation between the new order (and indeed
any order) and what may lie beyond the order of discourse, 'the real'.
Here perhaps the role of religion in conquest becomes clearer, man-
aging transcendence.

This double concern – of domination (or co-existence) both between different orders (discursively ordered domains) and between
the domain of such orders and the real – takes on a very precise
significance for 'man's conquest of nature', importantly linked, of
course, to what has been called the march of scientific discovery.
Science, we could say, *establishes* the ideal domains; and technology
makes them real. The conquest of nature involves, then, the progressive *alignment* of an idealizing scientific domain with what is left of
nature, the real, etc.

Military conquest is notoriously unstable. Nations put under the
boot revolt. The same can be said of the conquest of nature, but for a
different reason, which we could call the ideality of truth. We have
talked of sciences as discourses that constitute domains, and in Euclidean geometry this seems straightforward enough. Such domains
have an ideal existence, but it is precisely this ideality that can enable
them to be realized – town planners, architects, navigators, all use
geometry, and through its *a priori* power the world comes to be built

in its image. But science does not just generate ideality; it is, as we have said, a profoundly subversive activity, ceaselessly inventing, testing and discarding hypotheses and theories. And if that were not enough to tarnish the image of ideality, it is equally clear that nature has no respect for the forms of its human ordering. The most powerful effects man has on nature are not found in the roads, the cities, the communication networks in which order is imposed, but in the resulting and unpredictable disorder elsewhere. Entropy bites back. What we call the environment is resistance to conquest.

Let me now draw the conclusions for which I would like to have provided the evidence. I first quoted Kant's account of how philosophy could become a science by abandoning ocean-going voyages of discovery and sticking to the coastline of experience. If we were to accept Kant's account, it would be hard to defend philosophy against Lacan's charge that philosophy is a discourse of mastery. I argue that far from being such a discourse in itself, philosophy stages the struggle for mastery in an exemplary way. And if mastery is mastery of a domain, or territory, or field, then there are profound epistemological issues to be resolved over the constitution of such domains, issues which render problematic any univocal sense to the conquest of nature, or even the conquest of territory.

There are many straightforward lessons that have long been learned from Columbus' discovery of the Americas: that history chooses strange heroes, or the power of serendipity, or of gold, for example. I have tried to suggest an analogy between the way a discourse constitutes its object (and does not merely regulate it) and the conquest of a territory. If conquest is the imposition of an order, it will have a constitutive and not merely regulative or repressive significance; it will open up possibilities even as it closes down others. The ethical and political issues that the course of history throws up here exhibit the same epistemological complexities as does the development of science.

There may not be a science that deals with being qua being, but there is a discipline whose resistance to epistemological naivety both prevents it being a discourse of mastery and enables it to stage in an exemplary way the temptations of mastery. That discipline is philosophy.

Our next chapter deals with the ambivalences that beset a philosophical writing that notices the gap between what it says and how it says it. If it fails to incorporate the implications of what it is saying for the way it says it, it surely falls into a kind of performative contradiction. If, on the other hand, it seeks a pure performativity, does it not reach out again for a kind of mastery?

Part II

Dangerous Intersections

4

Heidegger and the Challenge of Repetition

Many have clearly found it tempting to respond to aporetic moments in philosophy by supposing that these 'paradoxes' and 'difficulties' are to be eliminated and dispelled – the spectres of confusion. And it may be that on this question the path forks, and philosophers simply divide, marching in different directions or, better, marching in one direction and walking thoughtfully in the other. Such an aporetic moment is defined by Nietzsche when he says that he is not seeking 'followers'. We read these remarks, and may even applaud the sentiment. And yet we then find ourselves caught in a thicket, for our very agreement with Nietzsche would seem to be a kind of following. This problem could be resolved by distinguishing between different levels. When Nietzsche (following Pindar) tells us to 'become what you are', he means each of us to become what each of us 'is', as he has attempted before us. He does not want us to agree with his views on the English, or on vegetarians, nor is he suggesting we each acquire a bushy moustache, or write pastiches of Liszt.

But while this strategy points us, in some respects, in the right direction, any suggestion that it resolved the issue would be deeply misleading. First, it can be easily read as a (mere) existential admonition: Do your own thing, where the distinctly philosophical dimension of the quest gets eclipsed. Secondly, it is quite clear that moving to a second-order formulation (don't follow the specifics, follow the underlying idea or principle) is far from resolving the question. For there will always be a question about the level at which one's own autonomy is supposed to kick in, and there will always be an issue about how to construe a level, an idea, a principle, etc. What is it that is fundamental to a thinker's thought? What is it to be fundamental?

Perhaps these considerations simply set us a more challenging task – that of penetrating to whatever it was about a thinker that was fundamental to his[1] thought, or rather that space in which, without recommending a particular thought, or line of thought, we can still grasp what is distinctive and important about it.

But what could be expected to arise from this encounter? A grasp of a particular thinker's thought? Or his fundamental question? For what purpose? Is it like deciphering a treasure map, then voyaging to the distant island to find the treasure? I recall an old adventure story in which the explorers find the gold, but cannot spend it as they lose their boats in the process and can never leave the island. This story echoes those fairy tales in which the object of greed resists the desire that seeks it – the man who wishes that his wife be younger and ends with an infant in his arms. The moral of such tales can be stated crudely and empirically – be careful about what you wish for, as you may get it. And this caution extends no less to philosophy. The truth may set us free, but both truth and freedom can take the form of snares and delusions. Similarly, understanding another philosopher, following in his footsteps, is indispensable in becoming philosophically educated, as well as being educated about philosophy. What we are still unclear about is what it is to follow in the footsteps of other philosophers in the sense of doing what they did, by philosophizing. Can this be accomplished simply by understanding their philosophy?

Kant drew on the Platonic 'idea' to explain how we could understand someone better than he understood himself.[2] We could understand the Idea within which a thinker thinks better than he does. (It is curious that without directly mentioning this passage, Heidegger[3] gives Kant an F for his historical understanding of Plato's doctrine of ideas!) However brilliant someone else's exploration of a dark room, we will put many of his puzzlements to rest if only we can find the light switch. It is not necessary to follow a thinker completely (in the sense of understanding him) in order to follow him (in the disciple sense). Zarathustra's animals could repeat as a children's nursery rhyme (a hurdy-gurdy song) the doctrine of eternal recurrence, but only as a grinning mask might surround a jaw that mouthed the right words. To follow a thinker in a stronger sense, to continue his thought, or to depart critically from it, is it not necessary to understand him better than he understood himself? If following someone were a matter of completing his work, we would only be dealing with understanding. Given the architect's plans a new builder can complete the work of his deceased colleague. There have been many successful completions of Berlioz's unfinished symphony. I have been delighted on occasion to complete, with some revisions, the crossword puzzle started by previous readers of in-flight magazines. But it is rare that we speak of someone taking up where a previous philosopher left off. Mostly people start again.

Heidegger repeats Kant's own formulation about understanding a philosopher better than he understood himself with regard to Kant himself, in the course of proposing an ontological reading of Kant's overtly epistemological perspective.[4] Kant's concern is not simply with knowledge, but with Being, whether or not he himself can put it like this. And here perhaps we may have arrived at a curious question. If we can make Kant out to be an interpreter of Being, then we will have found a way of addressing him, of listening to him, perhaps with ears behind ears, in a new way. The most extreme form of the thought here is this: that the word Being in Heidegger's thinking serves, very precisely, to name the level at which it is significant to engage another thinker while at the same time promoting a model of thinking as a struggle within what I will call, neutrally, a 'space of significance' that one can never control.[5] 'Being' would name a certain structural and methodological imperative of reading, interpretation, etc. – namely, that one must reconstruct, reconstitute, or at the very least indicate or gesture towards what lies essentially unarticulated in the other's thinking. This would be to claim, in other words, that in some important respect, we can understand the meaning of Being in terms of the structure of our engagement with the other, what it is to *go to his encounter*. One consequence of this approach would be to undercut the complaint that Heidegger's concern with Being is an occlusion of the ethical. It would be precisely the opposite. At this precise point there arises both an opportunity and a danger. The danger, of course, is to understand this 'essentially unarticulated' in terms of a remediable shortcoming, which criticism would then put right. The problem here is that if there is something 'essentially unarticulated' about thought as such, then a critical, correctional approach will, precisely, be uncritical in a fundamental way because it will miss the opportunity to think this 'essential limit of articulation'. Heidegger's version of this can be found in *What is Called Thinking?* at the point at which he distinguishes between going towards the thinker's own encounter and going counter to it.[6] Polemics would be the extreme form of this. Paradoxically, it is hard to avoid making critical remarks about critique, not for its failures, but for its masquerading as the way to proceed. And there is no doubt that shallowness and depth operate here as selective criteria.[7] Going counter to a thinker, we may suppose, is precisely the move that turns away from the space within which the opposition is constructed, when it is just in thinking this 'space' that the way forward lies. If, however, we 'go to the other's encounter', we may equally be tempted to articulate a concrete specification of the structure of the other's dependency. This effort might be thought to mark the simplicity of this or that thinker's finitude. On this version, one would be able to give an account of both the fundamental enterprise of a thinker, and the conceptual space within which he was operating. Here we might locate Kant's account of understanding a thinker... in the Transcendental Dialectic. Such a reading, it has to be said, is a considerable accomplishment. And this perspective is incredibly powerful. Derrida provides a version of this when he writes that

> The writer writes in a language and in a logic whose proper system, laws, and life his discourse by definition cannot dominate absolutely. He uses them only by letting himself, after a fashion and up to a point, be governed by the system. And the reading must always aim at a certain relationship, unperceived by the writer, between what he commands and what he does not command of the patterns of the language that he uses. This relationship is not of a certain quantitative distribution of shadow and light, of weakness or of force, but a signifying structure that critical reading should produce.[8]

And when he suggests that

> Nietzsche himself did not see his way too clearly there. Nor could he, in the instantaneous blink of an eye. Rather a regular rhythmic blindness takes place in the text. One will never have done with it. Nietzsche too is a little lost there... Nietzsche might well be a little lost in the web of his text, lost much as a spider who finds he is unequal to the web he has spun.[9]

It dramatically deepens our critical capacities to come to see how a thinker was tempted, first in this way, then in that, to solve a problem generated by an invisible relation to an underlying schema.

On the view I am recommending, we may construe much of Heidegger's apparatus as an attempt to think through what it is adequately to inherit a tradition, to repeat without merely repeating, to recover the sites and scenes of our encounter with the *Sache* of thinking.

We may say, roughly speaking, that the pursuit of temporality as the horizon for our understanding of Being, the project of *Being and Time*, comes to be seen as at least too easily misunderstandable in terms of this second model of reading the other, inheriting the tradition, where the shape of this receptivity would come (down) to the reconstruction of a certain relationship between two levels. It will be my claim that what drives Heidegger is his sense that this dyadic relationship (self / other) is itself an inadequate principle of structuration. There is a third term, and this fundamental schema, which a thinker may never be able to 'dominate, control' or fully articulate, is itself a response. 'Being', if you like, is structurally recessive, withdrawn, not because it is a complex schema we cannot quite grasp, but because it is not a schema at all.

To put this structural transformation more simply, Heidegger is insisting that to go to the other's encounter is not merely to enter the closed space of his problematic, but to enter the open dimension of his encounter with Being. This suggests a refinement of our understanding of Heidegger's famous remark that disagreement between fundamental thinkers is like a 'lovers' quarrel'. The quarrel is between those who share a non-exclusive love for some third thing. Although his is importantly different from a lovers' quarrel, what is shared is the sense that what unites those who quarrel is far deeper than what divides them, if only they would see it.

In *Being and Time*, section 6, Heidegger speaks of the need to destroy the tradition, the need for a repetition, a *Wiederholung*, which would return us to 'those primordial "sources" from which the categories and concepts handed down to us have been in part quite genuinely drawn' (H21). This is not just one of the (many) things that philosophy needs to do. It is one way of approaching what philosophy must do if it is to avoid falling prey to the ever-present danger of scientism, merely representational thinking, positivity, etc. Inheriting the tradition is at one and the same time a necessity, a danger, and a challenge. It is a point of intensity for philosophical reflection because philosophy is nothing if not a tradition, but it is also a tradition of a thinking for which the issue of tradition itself is a point of contestation, something immediately visible when we reflect that the history of philosophy is a history of new beginnings, of repudiations and transformations of 'the tradition'. We might here say of the tradition what Nancy says of 'community'[10] – that it is a tradition of singularities – that what is shared, at best, is a certain limit on what can be shared, a certain requirement, one not restricted to Descartes' or Husserl's demand for reductive self-institution, for making one's own.

The reception and inheritance of tradition are inseparable from human mortality, from the cycle (and repetition) of birth and death, the appearance of new children with old questions, the passing away of old men and women whose questions have already been buried. The inheritance of tradition is the inheritance of the human struggle with meaning and mortality and in the very act and passion of inheritance it is marked with these concerns. We might suppose that Heidegger adds to this already potent brew a concern with the temporal horizons of Being. In fact he did not so much add something extra as intensify what was already occurring in that passing on of the baton of existence that we call thinking. It is hardly possible to decide whether in thinking we are satisfying our own deepest needs or honouring the memory of those who have gone before, or whether indeed these two options are really distinct.

Heidegger's understanding of the significance of time and the temporal for the thinking of Being can be understood somewhat technically via the recognition that on his view the opening up of the question of Being requires us to resist (then rework, repeat) the privilege given to the present in the model of time that typically informs our understanding and questioning of Being. In *Being and Time* Heidegger attempted to open up the question of that privilege by relocating both the present and any sense of presence, within an articulated and existentially grounded account of ecstatic temporality. Heidegger then found himself with a strategic dilemma, which can itself be formulated in terms of repetition – of whether the framework of *Being and Time* provided sufficient resistance to those reductive, interpretive repetitions that would make Heidegger's thinking into an existential humanism. It is well known that Heidegger's trajectory takes us to his thinking of time-space and *Ereignis*. I would like to try to show how what is at stake in this movement is intimately tied up with the question of (1) how to indicate the site of a thinker's (fundamental) encounter, i.e. how we might elucidate a non-contestatory level of engagement with another thinker; and (2) how to enact a (movement of) thinking that would perform the event or eventuation of philosophy.

I will attempt somewhat schematically to trace a certain movement through Heidegger's treatment of Nietzsche in *What is Called Thinking?* to his discussion of *Ereignis* in *On Time and Being*, and then raise the question of what might be involved in repeating or inheriting the tradition not just after Heidegger, but with Heidegger now 'part' of the very tradition. Are we not called on to 'repeat' repetition? Here, we might add, Heidegger is far from being unhelpful. First, we must stress, Heidegger's own thinking is a repetition of repetition, a working through of working through – indeed, in his displacement of overcoming (metaphysics) by a step-back, and by a letting-be, we can see that repetition is not just a site of urgency, but being actively reworked (or replayed) at the heart of Heidegger's thinking. In other words, to read Heidegger by inheriting his own thinking of repetition would already be engaging him in his own encounter. Secondly, the question of Nietzsche for Heidegger is, as we have suggested, an exemplary case of this repetition, even though 'exemplarity' is itself already in question when we think of repetition.

It will eventually be my claim that whether or not we can say that we have understood Heidegger better than he understood himself, we can nonetheless understand the ways in which others (such as Levinas and Derrida) have read Heidegger in terms of a certain motivated reformulation and loosening of Heidegger's own fundamental questions, and indeed 'responsiveness to what calls'. I will conclude by suggesting that if, as I think must be the case, questions of risk and strategy are all inseparable from repetition – and I think Heidegger's own thinking proves that they are – then the proper conclusion is that without risk there can be no repetition. And this inaugurates the thinking that goes under the name of interruption, transgression, etc. (with all its dialectical twists). Such a thought would still move within the sphere of the event.

Heidegger's return to Nietzsche

What calls for thinking? What calls on us to think? In *What is Called Thinking?* Heidegger meditates long and deep on Nietzsche's cry that the wasteland, the desert, grows. And then fastens onto Nietzsche's remedy for this situation, the need for 'deliverance from [the spirit of] revenge'. This is not therapy in a psychological sense. Indeed such a psychological limitation would itself be in need of therapy. Rather Heidegger pursues the fundamental metaphysical position that Nietzsche is proposing here. It is through the gates of this diagnosis that Heidegger enters the question of time and repetition, and in so doing 'repeats', 'retrieves', rethinks Nietzsche's problematic, and in so doing pursues the path of thinking. For Heidegger, in short, thinking is the repetition of repetition, the recovery, which is also a projection, of a way of encountering the thought of another thinker, which is itself essentially, and as such, a repetition.

Let us just briefly rehearse this first step in Heidegger's argument, a step which will take us to the point at which Heidegger comes to recognize Nietzsche within the metaphysical tradition of the philosophy of the will, and 'retrieves' in the most stunning fashion the dimension within which Nietzsche formulates both the 'problem' and its 'solution'.

We join the conversation in lecture VI. Near the end, Heidegger quotes the first and last framing sentences of Nietzsche's juvenile autobiography. The question contained therein – 'Is the ring that in the end encircles man the world? Or God?' – is still the question of his last years. But to understand this question we need to be willing to read. Nietzsche describes himself as a plant born near the churchyard. Heidegger is telling us that Nietzsche's life and thought are exemplary in the mode of singularity. Heidegger warns us against 'the purely historical view of tradition' as 'one of those vast self-deceptions in which we must remain entangled as long as we are still not thinking'. To hear and to read differently requires a certain acknowledgement and respect (*Anerkennung*) and this, he writes, 'consists in letting every thinker's thought come to us as something in each case unique, never to be repeated, inexhaustible, and being shaken to the depths by what is unthought in his thought'. Such an 'unthought' he continues is not a lack, but 'the greatest gift that thinking can bestow'.

In this formulation, however, Heidegger stresses something new, a different dimensionality of the repetition. Whereas in *Being and Time*, the language is one of aiming, destroying, staking out, purpose, achievement, etc., this formulation is marked by a turning: 'Acknowledgement and respect' [*Anerkennung*] call for a readiness to let our attempts at thinking be overturned, again and again, by what is unthought in the thinker's thought'. Heidegger calls for 'clarity in the manner in which we encounter' thinkers, which means becoming aware that everything hangs on this; we may, as he puts it 'go to their encounter' [*Entgegen gehen*] or 'go counter to them' [*Dagegen angehen*]. The former will magnify what is great, and allow us to enter 'what is unthought [*Ungedachte*] in his thought'. Heidegger is offering us a recipe for engagement in which, as a condition and as the ongoing shape of that engagement, the wilfulness and dominance of the subject has already been suspended, or rather displaced into a transformative receptivity, not merely a dialogue with the other, but a dialogue with an enhanced version of the other's silent dialogue.

Going counter to the other is precisely a repetition that fails to address the frame within which it constructs its inversions – an insight that Nietzsche himself of course captured when he described his own style as 'a dance, an overleaping mockery of symmetries'.

Heidegger's account of going to the other's encounter is presented in terms of respect and acknowledgement [*Anerkennung*]. This *Anerkennung* is an amplifying grasp of the space of any repetition or retrieval or *Andenken*. It is amplifying in that the event of this repetition is being opened up both in terms of a transformation of my relation to the other (from wilfulness to vulnerability), but also in terms of my grasp of the other as himself engaged in a certain structure of openness and concealment, which I can transform. This movement, similar to the way in which Nietzsche structures the space of friendship (*Thus Spoke Zarathustra*) is perhaps exemplary in understanding how the ethical opening to the other is always figured and then refigured. My respect for the other is a receptivity to his thought already construed as a response. We may, of course, wonder whether the question raised by Bentham with respect to the rights of animals is not relevant here: 'Not does it think? but does it suffer?' It is precisely with such considerations in mind that Nietzsche formulates the problem – how to 'overcome the spirit of revenge' with which Heidegger too is now grappling. It would be easy to dismiss Heidegger's metaphysical interpretation of Nietzsche's account of revenge as a repudiation of its ethical and psychological significance, but I cannot adequately resolve this issue here. That our suffering might be grounded in a metaphysical interpretation of Being does not lessen it; indeed it might make it more intense. But equally, this kind of reading opens up the possibility of being 'in pain' without feeling anything, the possibility that the absence of pain might be a symptom.

Nietzsche understands the deliverance from revenge as a bridge to our 'highest hope', to the possibility of our 'overcoming' man. Heidegger understands Nietzsche's formulation of this problem of transition as a fertile, indeed exemplary site for the reformulation of the problem of thinking *as* repetition, as a rethinking of transition, as an opening up of the possibility of thinking as event. The next step in Heidegger's reading of Nietzsche here consists in showing how both Nietzsche's presentation of the problem and his solution move within a certain metaphysical space. Importantly, of course, one of the reasons that Nietzsche is not simply making a mistake here, at least in his construction of the problem, is that metaphysics is not just a shape or limitation of thought into which we philosophers fall, it is a condition of the world and the culture we inhabit.

The spirit of revenge, we recall, is understood by Nietzsche, not just by Heidegger, as essentially connected with time, and with a specific way of construing time. If the horizon of time and temporality have been, from the beginning for Heidegger, the clues to understanding Being, it is hardly surprising that Heidegger should fasten on the section 'On Redemption' in *Thus Spoke Zarathustra* in which Nietzsche puts all this together. 'This alone is revenge itself: the will's revenge against time and its "It was".' With this clue, how can we 'go to Nietzsche's encounter' with thinking here? Although Heidegger's analysis is well known, it bears repetition. Or perhaps I should say, *because* Heidegger's analysis is well known, it bears repetition. First, consider Nietzsche's acceptance of the metaphysical tradition of understanding Being captured in Schelling's account of 'willing as primal being'. Such a will, however, confronts an obstacle in the past, in what has been, for while its orientation is to the future, it breaks its teeth on what it cannot change. Heidegger goes on to argue convincingly that when Nietzsche speaks of 'time and its "it was"', he is not speaking of a particular dimension of time (the past) but of time itself, construed as a passing away, as the transitory, that condemns every now to extinction. In other words, this is 'the representational idea of time...standard throughout the metaphysics of the West' (*What is Called Thinking?*, p. 99). And the will that is revolted by this is a will that is 'independent of time' and eternal, one that 'eternally wills its own willing' (p. 105).

At the end of lecture X, the last lecture of Part 1 of *What is Called Thinking?*, a strange mood falls over the argument. For while Heidegger has in effect reduced Nietzsche's position to a schematic representation, and has diagnosed the eternal return as a solution to the problem of revenge itself dependent on Nietzsche's inheritance of the Aristotelian conception of time as passing away, he stops short of concluding with such a triumphalist spirit, telling us that in various ways Nietzsche's thought still remains to be thought, remains veiled, etc. Or better, that this has only been a raid on Nietzsche's unthought, leaving much more to be explored. At the same time he even opens up the suggestion that, in pursuing the idea of eternal return as the being of becoming, Nietzsche might, as we have seen Derrida suggest in another context, have got lost in his own thought. In each case, what is in play, and what it brought into play again, is the scene of Nietzsche's encounter.

What does Heidegger's reading of Nietzsche teach us here? Without drowning us expositorily in levels and reflexivities of repetition, Heidegger nonetheless manages to construct through this reading of Nietzsche, an elaborately layered demonstration of what we could call an exemplary singular repetition of a singularity – a singularity whose own encounter can only be thought in terms of the problematic of repetition. And, we might add, all this for good reason. For the problematic of repetition is precisely the *fils conducteur* that interlaces and draws together both his reading of Nietzsche here, his subsequent moves in *What is Called Thinking?*, and his later account of time in *On Time and Being*. Allow me to note briefly some of the connections to be drawn here.

How are we to understand the discussion of thinking as thanking in lecture III, which expands outwards to embrace Pascal's thinking of the heart? I am tempted to respond in the following way: Heidegger's thinking is deeply bound up with the need to return to the Greeks, even if we then need to develop their thought. His method of philosophizing is tied up with an attempt to recover what other thinkers have unearthed. And for all his disclaimers ('technology is not the devil's work'), Heidegger clearly sees the pre-technological world as preferable.[11] When Nietzsche offers up 'Time and its "it was"' as the source of the will's revulsion and desire for revenge, it is not for Heidegger, I submit, just an interesting example of an attitude to time. Rather it is all too close to his own struggle. Heidegger's thinking may not be driven by nostalgia; it may not be an attempt to restore a broken order of things, but many people have found such a verdict hard to resist. And Heidegger does constant battle against such misunderstandings – repudiating the parallels with Spengler, insisting that he is neither pessimistic nor optimistic, etc. Part of what fascinates him about Nietzsche is that Nietzsche offers us a remedy for thinking of time as loss, namely willing the loss. Heidegger's way of following Nietzsche here is to try to solve the problem that Nietzsche poses not at the level at which Nietzsche poses it, but at one level further back. We would not need to overcome the revulsion with the past by willing the past (and future, etc., etc.), if we could rethink the underlying account of time that Nietzsche presupposes. This of course is just what Heidegger attempts. And if I am right, this requires us both to rethink thinking, as well as to rework time, not least because our thinking is itself bound up with an orientation to time. We can see this intimate connectedness, for example, when he says that he is not trying to get somewhere but for once to get to where we are already.[12] And in his pursuit of the links between thinking and thanking. Thanking certainly has the potential for an affective expansion and connectedness that will rule out taking thinking in any narrow calculative way. But, more importantly, it is one of the planks in a general strategy of resistance against dwelling on the past as a site of loss, even as Heidegger is articulating structures of withdrawal (as the withdrawal of Being). Indeed we could understand the demonstration that withdrawal is a necessary structure as another of these planks. As too the whole way in which for Heidegger we are 'called upon to think'. Answering this call is a responsibility, not lamentation or mourning. But I would particularly like to show how some of the account he gives in *On Time and Being*, of space-time, the *'es gibt'* and *Ereignis* succeeds in thinking of time in precisely such a way as will mitigate the sense of loss, mourning, revenge, etc., and the kind of thinking that follows from those fundamental evaluations.

What is Heidegger drawn to, or by, when he fastens onto the phrase *'es gibt'*?[13] At first, perhaps, it offers relief from the essentialist trajectories of 'What is?' But it soon becomes clear that the semantic space of 'giving' offers extraordinary possibilities of condensation and relational expansion as well as this initial displacement. Let us note just a few possibilities that come to mind.

'Giving' is central to Heidegger's problematization of the *phenomenon* in *Being and Time*. Husserl (as Heidegger quotes him in 'The End of Philosophy') had relied on givenness in defining the intuition central to phenomenology's 'principle of principles'. '"Intuition" is simply to be accepted as it gives itself out to be.'[14] But Heidegger writes: 'Just because phenomena are proximally and for the most part *not* given there is need for phenomenology.'[15] And he will soon write of the need for a grasping that is opposed to any naive showing.

Giving is tied up with the gift, with sending, with destining in such a way as to open up a space of dynamic relationality within which structures of withdrawal can be thematized. In this way, Being can be understood to be delivered over to a play of concealment and unconcealment. Heidegger is linking his thought to the framework of the gift in Nietzsche's *Thus Spoke Zarathustra*, which begins, of course, with Zarathustra announcing that, like the sun, he has something he needs to give.

The gift sets up a space in which thinking as thanking (gratitude, receptivity) can be articulated. Thinking Being as gift predisposes us against the thought of revenge, the thought of an original loss. Rather the gift proposes an original surplus.

Heidegger has already deployed the thought of the gift in describing the status of the thinker's unthought – this is his greatest gift. And his very thinking of the gift, through the *'es gibt'*, itself takes the form of gratitude – a response to a gift of language that it would be easy not to have noticed, not to have 'taken' as a gift.

But it is only possible for giving and the gift to vanquish revenge and loss if the underlying sense of time is changed. If we continue to think of time in terms of nows that pass away, mocking the will, giving would find no grip. What is significant about *On Time and Being* is that it is here that Heidegger provides an account of time as a horizon that in some ways fulfils the promise of *Being and Time*. What is perhaps even more astonishing is the way in which the accomplishments of the existential analytic – the description of the ready-to-hand world – in effect return in the form of a schema of relationality. Heidegger writes of time–space, for example, that it is

> The name for the openness which opens up in the mutual self-extending of futural approach, past and present. This openness exclusively and primarily provides the space in which space as we usually know it can unfold.[16]

Or again, he writes of past, present and future that they 'Belong together in the way they offer themselves to one another'[17] and 'Dimension...is here thought...as reaching throughout, as giving and opening up.'[18]

We might be tempted to say that Heidegger is deploying metaphorically a version of the space of our practical engagement with things and other people in these accounts of the interconnectedness of the dimensionality of time. At the very least it gives us a clue to how he might have hoped to have provided access through the existential analytic to an account of the temporal horizonality of Being. And in a rare glimpse back to that problematic, Heidegger tells us precisely that we cannot think of man either as the giver or receiver of time. Rather, 'he can only be man by standing within the threefold extending'. And 'there is only giving in the sense of extending which opens up time-space'.[19]

I want to suggest that these extraordinary descriptions – and I have not even broached here the discussion of *Ereignis* – provide us with a way of thinking about time and about the past that makes impossible a metaphysically driven sense of revenge, or nostalgia or loss. And for two sorts of reasons: First, the ground phenomenon of both time-space and *Ereignis*, is the language of giving, which suggests that any sense of revenge, *ressentiment*, or loss already presupposes a prior play of givenness. Second, the past, what-has-been is understood as a mode of absence, as manifesting itself as a mode of presencing. The implication is that it is not necessary to will the past for it to cease to resist my will. Pastness is already set within a structure and play of human receptivity to a space of givenness.

In other words, Heidegger has opened up an elaborate new articulation of our fundamental dimensionality, which functions as a general antidote to both the Aristotelian sense of time, and the identification of the past with loss.

It has been my claim throughout this chapter that the significance of this move is intimately tied to the temporality of our philosophical practice, precisely because that practice consists in a reading of great past thinkers, one which can only repeat the event of philosophy by 'going to their encounter', which will itself typically turn out to be premised on an unthought permeated by Aristotelian time. I am trying to suggest that Heidegger's own practice of philosophy – thinking – is driven by the desire to exemplify in its very movement the possibility of a more fundamental dimension of time. And in his performative reading of Nietzsche in *What is Called Thinking?*, all this comes together.

Performativity as repetition

Heidegger (and others follow him in this) is exploring, pursuing, the implications of the performativity of philosophy.[20] And perhaps this is the unthought in Heidegger, or rather the web whose further exploration he bequeaths to us: *The philosophical attempt to present truth as a showing is not only accidentally caught up in its own operation. When a phenomenology that thematizes an understanding of phenomena as 'self-showing' comes to understand itself as tied up with language in more intimate ways than had been suspected, then the relation to language itself takes on, albeit problematically, the weight of this self-showing.*

The critique of a teleological reason goes hand in hand with the sense that philosophy cannot satisfactorily be thought to be a mere means by which some independently valid result is achieved. It is not a taxi you can take to a conference and then dismiss.

Nor can philosophy, Heidegger comes to see, rely on a model of its own process in which the logic of development belies the end sought. The thought here is as follows: we may agree that in philosophy the end does not justify the means, and further that where the end is a certain understanding of the path or way of thinking, that a certain operational relation between means and ends can actually prevent the achievement of the end. But this also means that it is not sufficient to say, as Hegel did for example, that the truth is something we have to experience, or go through or undergo, because within this processual understanding of truth, there are further issues to be addressed. It is this that Heidegger is claiming when he speaks of setting aside all 'overcoming', and leaving metaphysics to itself. 'Overcoming', common property to both Nietzsche and Hegel, is a hard term to do without, not least because it is natural to invoke its power when contemplating going beyond it: overcoming overcoming.

It is tempting to think that Heidegger is just getting tired as he gets older, that ceasing all overcoming is a form of resignation. But that would be a mistake. Rather we need to see this as an imperative generated by a certain performative consideration, itself generated by the recognition that (self-)showing is not just a theme for philosophy, but a characterization of its own 'practice'. This is why Heidegger will write of the need to 'follow the movement of showing'.[21]

But there is a missing piece to this puzzle. Heidegger's meditation on the limits of overcoming, of a developmental approach, of process are deeply bound up with his reflections on time, history and tradition. For Heidegger, the Enlightenment sense of history as progress is not wrong because the alleged progress has not occurred. Heidegger equally resists the pessimistic valuation of history of Spengler. If anything, this very sense of the possibility of valuing the course of history is part of the problem; it is part of the problem of *any present* that fails to wrest itself free from it. Paradoxically, particular moments of history end up having greater or lesser value to the extent that they draw on the possibilities of their own time for transcending historicism. But such transcending is not towards some timeless realm. Rather it is a step back into the opening of time itself.

The problematic of performativity in philosophy is precisely what plagued *Being and Time*, and Heidegger's own subsequent assessment of it. The laying out of a fundamental ontology in this way, despite all precautions, seems bound to the time of representation even as it attempts to break with the representation of time. But is Heidegger's worry here justified? If I write a poem about a flower, it need not have the shape of a flower on the page. It need not be made of ink made from flower extracts, etc. Those who treat drug addiction need not be on drugs. The man who drives oxen need not be fat. Why should a philosophical exposition not deploy a similar distance between its own form and the content it describes?

It is here that, as I see it, the significance of repetition is to be found. If we hold that philosophy is at least at one level an essentially historical activity, in the minimal sense that it involves reading and dealing with what our predecessors have said and thought about the same subjects, and if we also think that this is a condition of our being able to say anything interesting, then the question of repetition comes into centre stage. For philosophical activity becomes tied to *how* we repeat (exposition, critique, commentary, etc.) our predecessors. And this condition, this fate, is not one which began with us. It is precisely one of the questions we ask those very predecessors. How did they deal with the question of what it is to begin again, to learn from the past, to cope with being in this position? And of course, this position – of creating ourselves anew in the light of an inheritance that functions as a *pharmakon*, as both a nurturing opportunity and an overwhelming danger – is not just the situation of philosophy; it is at base what is distinctive about human existence – that we are not complete as natural beings and that it is only by acquiring culture that we become human. Part of the point of *Being and Time* was to show that what is critical about this process is how it handles that uncircumscribable part of our natural condition that we call mortality, and that we somehow need to perform our mortality, not merely represent it.

But how does this answer our question? It cannot be enough to say that because philosophy is a human activity, it must conform to whatever we think is best practice. But this may not be so far wrong. Philosophers' discussions of the fundamental concepts of *praxis, poesis, techne, theoria* are not simply designed to provide helpful analytical classifications, but to help us in particular to think about the ways in which ordinary practical activity is both illuminating in itself, and yet further illuminated by other activities (poetry, philosophy) which are not obviously practical. What is distinctive about these other activities is the way in which they are ends in themselves. But for an activity to be an end in itself is precisely for it to exhibit a temporality quite unlike that of practical life. Is this not then divorced from practical life? Not at all. For although particular calculative actions have a means/end structure, life itself does not. The frame that human activity itself occupies is precisely that of being an end-in-itself, even though it occupies time, and is stretched out in time. But being an end in itself does not mean that we realize an extratemporal end in time. Rather it means that we embody a responsive relation to the impossibility of such completion – to the absence of grounds, to the Other, to death, to the unrepresentable dimension of space–time in which we live and move and perhaps have our being.

I have tried to show that Heidegger's reading of Nietzsche in *What is Called Thinking?* is performative in a way that philosophy cannot help trying to be once it realizes it cannot suspend the accomplishment of philosophy without subscribing to a model of time which it has already rejected. It performs a repetition of Nietzsche's own repetition of the act of philosophical renewal, a repetition that Nietzsche cast in the form of eternal return, in other words, or repetition. But of course, Heidegger's foray here into Nietzsche interpretation is not his first. And I would like to conclude by showing how it is itself a reworking of his treatment of Nietzsche's *Augenblick* in his 1937 Nietzsche course.[22] The version of eternal return which Nietzsche offers us in the chapter 'The Vision and the Riddle' in *Thus Spoke Zarathustra* is centred on a gateway, to which Zarathustra comes, with his dwarf on his shoulder. In Zarathustra's second phase of his questioning of the dwarf, he *seems to understand* the situation, one in which the future and past extend infinitely in both directions. But in his book *The Glance of the Eye*, Will McNeill reminds us that what Heidegger homes in on here is the crucial demand placed on us to move from the standpoint of the spectator to that of participant, 'taking up a position of one's own within the *Augenblick* itself, that is, within time and its temporality'.[23] Heidegger understands this standing-within or dwelling in the moment to be prior to distinctions between theory and practice, thinking and doing. Thinking becomes a manner of dwelling in the moment in such a way as to decisively project a future and respond to the past.

Heidegger's subsequent discussion of time-space and *Ereignis* will be precisely a repetition of these formulations, a repetition that reworks his account of dwelling in terms of a response to a structure of givenness, rather than the language of decision and decisiveness. In each case, the crucial move that Heidegger makes is to draw out the implications of his setting aside the whole representational stance. And it is this move that enjoins us as philosophers, or perhaps now as thinkers, to ponder the dimension of the performative, that is, of the necessity of drawing into our thinking that the event and eventuation of philosophy has always (already) begun.

For all the interest of *What is Called Thinking?* for the question of performativity in Heidegger, it only prepares us for a final extended discussion of these issues as they arise in *Contributions*. This will occupy our final chapter: 'The Performative Imperative'.

5

Heidegger's Reading of Hegel's *Phenomenology of Spirit*

Is the 'presence of Hegel' thinkable without considering Hegel's account of presence, of presentation, of appearance?[1] What could it be for Hegel (is this a name, a man, an author, or a series of texts?), to be present 'in' contemporary thought? Where are we to locate what haunts us? What account of time and history licenses any sense to 'contemporary'? For the *OED*, contemporary means: 'Living, existing or occurring together in time.' But what if philosophy had weaned us off this 'in time', or taught us that it was not fundamental. Who then would be our con-temporaries?

And who believes in *thought* any more? Even Heidegger insisted on *thinking*. Can we still speak of *thought* after Derrida, after Foucault, or even after the collapse of idealism? Does *thought* mean philosophy? Does it suggest the continuing reign of ideas? If we had to understand the title before we proceeded, we could I suspect go no further. I hesitated, however. Perhaps the title just appeared on the scene with few credentials, and seemed appropriate at the time. Perhaps it was a mere instrument or contrivance, a device to lure people together. But if it was so ungrounded and unthought, would it not all the more deserve our care and attention?

The topic I had already proposed was not, however, so easily jilted, and in homage to some of the issues raised by the title I will try to show how Heidegger's reading of Hegel helps us pursue them.

But why read Heidegger on Hegel now? Let me offer five general reasons:

1 Critical Theory's debts to Hegel make a comparison between Heidegger and Hegel vital to any assessment of the attacks of Adorno and Habermas on Heidegger. With the collapse of East European Marxism, and the subsequent narrowing of political alternatives to liberal democracy, this debate seems increasingly urgent.

2 The revelation of the details of Heidegger's Nazi involvement provoked, among other things, a reassessment of his place in German philosophy. His willingness to deploy the apparently metaphysical language of spirit in his Rectoral Address, and in subsequent writing, forces a re-examination of his relation to Hegel, from whom he claimed to have distanced himself. Derrida's *Glas*, and more pointedly *Of Spirit* pursue these issues on a wider canvas. And Hegel's account in his *Lectures on the Philosophy of History* [1837] of the creative amorality of the world-historical individual might explain what Heidegger saw in Hitler.[2]

3 Despite the real and imagined obstacles to taking Hegel seriously (especially his philosophy of history), particularly the logic of the self-development of spirit, there is if anything a greater awareness of the power of history today than there was in the *Differenzschrift* [1801] when Hegel himself was talking about the 'need for philosophy'. We may have little time for simplistic stories of historical necessity, but the historical sweep of Hegel's thinking is hard to ignore. Heidegger is not alone in having us think that reading Hegel could still be profitable. And Heidegger's own historical sweep meets for once some real competition. To some sensibilities, Heidegger will make Hegel come alive again.

4 Heidegger's treatment of Hegel is critical for our understanding of the problem of time, and of the possibilities of rescuing it from its 'metaphysical' determination. In Heidegger's view, Hegel had not significantly progressed beyond (or beneath) the account of time presented in Aristotle's *Physics*. The constant return of the spirit to itself demonstrated a continuing commitment to a circular teleology. And yet for Derrida, Heidegger's own position has an analogous deficiency. It is arguable, moreover, that this claim by Derrida (that Hegel too falls back into the very metaphysical space from which he seeks to escape), *itself* deploys this very model! This is no mere academic problem; it affects our very participation in the real, our very *existence*, as Heidegger would put it.

5 Finally, more simply, as far as Heidegger is concerned, his reading of Hegel is an occasion for authentic philosophizing, or thinking.

As usual, everything is at stake, including the practice of reading itself.

Heidegger's reading of Hegel's *Phenomenology of Spirit* spanned many years, many seminar courses, and although he claimed to have entered the womb of Hegel's thought, his reading remained incomplete, at least as far as published texts are concerned. Allow me to fill in some of the bibliographical details.

References to Hegel are scattered throughout Heidegger's writing, but there are a number of places at which he deals with Hegel in depth.[3] The first brief encounter is *Being and Time* [1926], section 82, entitled 'A Comparison of the Existential–Ontological Connection of Temporality, Dasein and World-time, with Hegel's Way of Taking the Relation between Time and Spirit'.[4] After Derrida's treatment of this passage, we will be testing the neutral tone of the term *comparison*, and asking what this tells us about Heidegger's understanding of his relation to Hegel.

In *The Basic Problems of Phenomenology* [1927] references to Hegel are numerous, though dispersed.

In 1930–1, published as vol. 32 of the *Gesamtausgabe*, Hegel gave a seminar course on *Hegel's Phenomenology of Spirit*, now translated into English under that title.[5] It is actually a discussion of about 50 pages of Hegel's text, leaving aside the Preface and the Introduction, focused almost entirely on the first section, on Consciousness, with a brief mention of Hegel's introduction to the second section on Self-Consciousness, and exactly falling short of the discussion of *Lordship and Bondage* and the *Freedom of Self-Consciousness*. In other words, it discusses just over 10 per cent of the book.

In lectures in 1942–3 (published 1950 in *Holzwege*), Heidegger returned to the *Phenomenology*, this time concentrating wholly on the *Introduction*, subjecting each section to minute analysis, exegesis and commentary. These lectures, published as *Hegel's Concept of Experience*, he described as his 'interpretation of Hegel's metaphysics'.[6]

In 1956–7 he gave a seminar course on Hegel's *Science of Logic*, which he elsewhere describes as 'an attempt to begin a conversation with Hegel...[on] the matter of thinking'.[7] His final lecture in that course, which is a very useful and in many ways accessible account of his reading of Hegel, 'The Onto-Theo-Logical Constitution of Metaphysics' [1957], is available in a bilingual edition of *Identity and Difference*.

Finally in 1958 (published 1960) Heidegger gave a lecture on *Hegel and the Greeks*, in which the Greeks serve as the origin and Hegel as the achievement of philosophy. This was published as part of a *Festschrift* for Gadamer, who himself subsequently wrote an essay on Hegel and Heidegger dealing with Heidegger's response to Hegel's *Science of Logic*.[8]

According to Heidegger, reading another philosopher involves bringing to that reading the power of an illuminative idea. At the very least a problem or a question might be thought to be useful. The idea that formed the original horizon of this chapter was born from reading Derrida's *Of Spirit*, turning back to section 82 of *Being and Time* and concluding that Derrida was mistaken in supposing that Heidegger had refused the concept of *Geist* in *Being and Time*. In fact Heidegger, in this penultimate section, establishes the basis for a translation of Hegel's claim that Spirit falls into time in terms of a relationship between everyday and authentic temporality, and effectively licenses himself to deploy the term *Geist*. The complexities of Heidegger's assimilative reading of Hegel are themselves obscured by overconcentration on the entrance and exits game of scare-quotes. The book targeted for our discussion falls precisely between *Being and Time* and the 'Rectoral Address', and I hope to make something of what goes on there.

The deeper theme suggested by *Of Spirit*, signalled by references to flames, ashes (and indirectly the idea of sublimation), could be said to be the ontology of conflagration, destruction, burning up – in which we could say a primitive form of time, substance and activity and death are all combined. Heidegger pursues the possibility of a pre-Christian *Geist* in this context through his reading of Trakl. I do not deal with this as such but I do look at the broader issues of working through, going through, and destructive reading in the light of the question of what is left behind, the question of residue, of ash, and what overcoming is. I begin here with the assumption that what makes a certain sort of philosophy possible (one that we might call metaphysics and in which many would include both Hegel and Heidegger) is *ontological penetration*. I mean by this the capacity to think about the totality of beings as such, in the belief that the considerations that arise at that level penetrate or pervade every other level.[9] The forms that such penetration takes are many – military logic, technology, and religion to name but three. Capitalism, understood as the unrestrained reduction of man and earth to mediated exchange relations, is perhaps the supreme example. Penetration means in each case that no dependent or intermediate formations can be guaranteed protection from a reductive and ultimately destructive scrutiny. The question that exercised Levinas, and exercises friends and critics of Heidegger and Hegel alike, is whether the kind of ontological penetration so powerfully provided by both Hegel and Heidegger paves the way for those forms of exploitation and even genocide, albeit unintentionally? Does not philosophy, or a particular style of philosophy, facilitate mass violence and exploitation in a way not dissimilar to the impact of the railway on the American Indians, or ranching (and now gold-prospecting) on the native people of Brazil? When philosophy raises matter to the level of the concept, or thinks of individual human beings in terms of their relation to Being, does not such detachment yield theoretical profit only by sacrificing concrete individuality? And does this not *actually* facilitate real elimination, extermination? (We know, for instance, that the rewards of heaven facilitate military heroism.)

Now Heidegger's political speeches do indeed make reference to sacrifice. There is a eulogy to Schlageter, a resistance fighter who died a hero. And Heidegger in effect pressed into service his account of anticipatory resoluteness in *Being and Time* by allowing that authenticity could involve identifying oneself with the aims of what looked like a radical and revolutionary movement.

The significance of this is not unequivocal. Heidegger does not use the language of duty, and does not buy into the idea of obeying the moral law, which, as it seems to install autonomy, equally accommodates chains of command and responsibility. There is nothing unique about the susceptibility of Heidegger's discourse to a political deployment.[10] What is special is the enormity of the error, and the consequences this might have for our assessment of his philosophical position.

The power of ontological penetration may be such that the attitudes and intentions of the philosophers that wield it may count for little when it comes to controlling its use or misuse. But the case of Heidegger is strangely poignant in that he has bequeathed to us ways of thinking that would challenge the very idea of effective political deployment. It might be said that this reserve is largely the product of his own more sober reflections in his later work. But the issues we have raised were clearly ones that deeply concerned Heidegger from the beginning, and his reading of Hegel is an ideal site for investigating them.

I have suggested that the idea of 'going through' is of great importance. If 'going through' means leaving something behind, what is the status of that left behind? Plato said there was no *form* of dirt. We might wonder whether dirt was actually the name of what was created by the production of *form*, what cannot be recognized as such, what must be eliminated. If 'going through' were a form of exclusion, of rejection, of elimination, the philosophical move away from the everyday, whether it be called bracketing out, reflection, meditation, etc., would always raise the question of the status of what has been left behind. Is it only left behind 'in its partiality' while being raised to a new level? Kierkegaard, for whom partiality (in the form of subjectivity) was the defining characteristic of an individual, clearly felt he was being treated like dirt.

Heidegger's reading of the history of philosophy is perhaps a good site for exploring his own understanding of working through, and thinking through. And his reading of Hegel could not be more appropriate, as it is in just such terms that he defines dialectic, which is one of the first focuses of his lectures on Hegel's *Phenomenology of Spirit*. I will turn to it shortly.

The question of *Geist* (and, for Derrida, *geistig, geistlich*) to which we have already alluded, has its own map and trajectory. But in fact the issues it raises are remarkably close. *Geist*, as Heidegger comes to employ it, both unifies and excludes. It reads like the mobilization of ontological penetration to specific historical ends, which is hard to separate from German nationalism. In each case, what is opened up are precisely the questions Heidegger wants to open up: of the relationship between time and being, history and event; and the role and responsibility of philosophy.

Heidegger's reading of Hegel is best understood in the light of his account in *Being and Time* of the destruction of the history of ontology. That destruction has as its aim to recover possibilities of thinking that the tradition has covered over or sedimented. It does not so much aim to think what the other thinker thought once again, but to think the unthought in his thought, to think what he did not or perhaps could not think. Whereas Hegel, he wrote, would enter into the force and sphere of what had been thought by earlier thinkers, he seeks an unthought from which what *has* been thought receives its essential space.[11] Only two years later in *Kant and the Problem of Metaphysics* [1929] he talks about what Kant uncovered but was unable to clarify or develop, and about what Kant intended to say about the use of an illuminating idea that 'entrusting itself to the secret élan of a work ... to [thereby] get through to the unsaid and to attempt to find an expression for it'.[12] There are, I am sure, important differences between Heidegger's various formulations. But what seems to persist is the claim that previous thinkers have opened up things they were not able to develop, and failed to raise certain questions that are taken for granted by the tradition. Either way, Heidegger defends a certain violence, while equally insisting on the need for care, respect, detailed discussion. The general implication of this double demand is very positive, although it raises further problems. What it suggests is that this tradition (Western philosophy) is, at least for us, essential, even if it is equally vital that we learn to read it with a certain critical violence. If so it poses a key question for our reading of the later Heidegger. Are we to read his essays on language, for example, in the light of his earlier work, as the outcome of his struggle to work through the history of philosophy? Or can we stand on his shoulders and avoid the labour ourselves. I am convinced of the first alternative, and that Heidegger is quite as convinced that there is no royal road to truth. But that doesn't mean that he shares Hegel's road.

The peculiar importance of Hegel as an object of Heidegger's concern is that this very relationship is one thematized by Hegel in such a way that should exclude any such critical alterity, and that Hegel himself is something of a model for Heidegger as a philosopher who values tradition. When Heidegger reads Hegel he has to go through going through.

In *Positions*, Derrida writes that deconstruction produces an infinitesimal and (yet) radical displacement of Hegel's dialectic, and the impossibility of going through going through without somewhat changing the game explains immediately why Heidegger cannot repeat Hegel's account of the dialectic.[13] Derrida's account of Heidegger's treatment of spirit leaps from section 82 in *Being and Time* [1927] to his 'Rectoral Address' [1933]. It is as if Heidegger went on a long walk in between. But in 1930–1, as we have noted, he gave a seminar course on Hegel's *Phenomenology of Spirit*. The published version of it is in two parts, a substantial part dealing with Consciousness and a very slim part that looks at the beginning of the Self-Consciousness section. These are preceded by an Introduction devoted to 'The Task of the Phenomenology of Spirit as the First Part of the System of Science'. This introduction is an awkward but interesting mixture of bibliographical remarks about the various titles of the *Phenomenology of Spirit*, about the place of the *Phenomenology of Spirit* in the System of Science, about misreadings of the *Phenomenology of Spirit*, remarks about the meaning of science and remarks about the point at which absolute knowledge appears in the text. Heidegger is concerned to locate the *Phenomenology of Spirit*, so that we approach Hegel's text in a very specific way, one in which it will be seen to be addressing a recognizably Heideggerean question. He seems to be setting the scene for what Werner Marx would describe as an assimilative reading while presenting it as an immanent reading. For Heidegger, Hegel's *Phenomenology of Spirit* is fundamentally addressing the question of Being. But let me lay out something of the path that Heidegger takes in this introductory section. When the *Phenomenology of Spirit* first appeared in 1807, it was under the title *System of Science, Part 1, The Phenomenology of Spirit*. But Part 2 appeared as the *Encyclopaedia*, where the phrase was subsequently incorporated as a sub-section.

If the *Encyclopaedia* could have the shape it did because the *Phenomenology of Spirit* had already been written, a phenomenology of spirit could be said to be both a foundation for and a part of the system. How can that be? Heidegger will claim that it shows us something fundamental about this book. The first clue lies in the word 'science'. Heidegger lumps together Descartes, neo-Kantianism and Husserlian phenomenology as giving a very specific sense to philosophy as a science, namely that it would ground the other sciences, it would be foundational. But Fichte, Schelling, Hegel and German Idealism generally are driven by impulses more radical than that of grounding knowledge; they are concerned with *overcoming finite knowledge and attaining infinite knowledge*, i.e. they are concerned with how philosophy unfolds itself as Absolute Knowledge. As he will argue in 'Hegel and the Greeks', Hegel's significance lies in his attempt to bring to completion the inaugural problem of ancient philosophy: What is a being? According to Heidegger, Hegel's answer is that a being as such, 'the actual in its genuine and whole reality', is the idea or concept. But this, he says, is 'the power of time', i.e. it allows time to be annulled. And with the annulling of time, the problem of being can appear. Heidegger's aim is to struggle free from the obligation on philosophy to be science in either the neo-Kantian way or that favoured by German idealism. Philosophy should ally itself not with science, but with the 'matter itself', in the form of the renewal of ontology. But if we are to pursue the way Hegel took up and, in a sense, completed the fundamental question, we have first to ask what absolute knowledge meant for him. Heidegger traces it to the power of relative knowledge, knowledge given over to its object, to ab-solve or detach itself from that dependency. And what is true of consciousness is also true, finally, of self-consciousness. At each step, the object detached from or ab-solved is not abandoned but *aufgehoben*, preserved by elevation. Science in Hegel's sense is the unfolding of this sequence of detachments in the form of a system. Here Heidegger is writing largely exegetically, taking care to absolve *us* from any confusion between Hegel and a neo-Kantian approach to philosophical science. With this reference to *aufheben* he has begun to think through thinking through. And these same concerns direct his discussion of *Erfahrung*, experience, as it arises in the *Phenomenology of Spirit*, a book Hegel had once called his *Science of the Experience of Consciousness*. This is an undergoing, a going through, not a mere intuitive confirmation, but more a discovery that something is other than it appeared. And what does one learn about? Heidegger reads 'the experience of consciousness' as a subjective genitive. Experience is a movement that consciousness undergoes with itself, and in this self-relatedness, consciousness grasps the necessity of this movement. In relation to relative knowledge it grasps itself as absolute. And as Absolute Knowledge aware of itself as such, it is spirit, an 'absolute restlessness' in which being-alongside itself returns to itself in becoming something other.[14] So it is that Hegel offers us a *Phenomenology of Spirit*, in that by this process what *shines forth or appears* is spirit. And the *Phenomenology of Spirit* is also interpreted as a subjective or explicative genitive. Anyone who has read section 7 of *Being and Time* will begin to recognize the language Heidegger begins to use here. He writes:

> Experience, properly understood in Hegel's sense, as *having-to-undergo-an-experience-with-oneself*, means appearing as a self-showing of knowledge which comes forward as what *becomes-other-than-itself* by coming to itself.[15]

I emphasize the Hegelian language because it marks, I would say, a level at which Heidegger is prepared, even eager, to translate Hegel's thinking into his own. This issue will return when we examine Derrida's treatment of Heidegger's account of *Geist* in *Being and Time*.[16]

Heidegger concludes here that this explains the place of the *Phenomenology* [*System of Science*, Part 1] in relation to Part 2 [*Encyclopaedia*]. Spirit prepares itself for the element of knowing by a kind of elementary performativity or self-exposition.

> Thus the exposition of spirit as it appears in its character as movement, itself reaches the point of being actual, absolute knowledge. In and through its character as movement, the exposition becomes *itself what it is to be exposed*. The exposition and what is to be exposed coincide, not by chance but necessarily.[17]

An encounter with this position must avoid three errors, Heidegger insists. The *Phenomenology of Spirit* has nothing to do with Husserl's phenomenology, or with a typology of *Weltanschauungen* (the forms that consciousness takes, a reference to Dilthey), nor is it an introduction to philosophy (e.g. a ladder from natural consciousness to speculation). What is it? Phenomenology is the absolute self-presentation of reason (*ratio*; *logos*), whose essence and actuality Hegel finds in absolute spirit. It would be easy to suppose that Hegel's problematic has been surpassed today, says Heidegger. His account of how we must read Hegel is drawn from Hegel himself, from the

Differenzschrift: 'If the living spirit which dwells in a philosophy is to be revealed, it needs to be born through a kindred spirit.'[18] And for Heidegger of course being kindred does not mean agreeing with him at all, but being 'committed to the last and first necessities of philosophical inquiry arising from the matter'.[19] Reading Hegel means for Heidegger working through his own staging of the field of inquiry in such a way that the original philosophical project of the Greeks can be discerned.

As we know, Hegel wrote that philosophy arises out of need. But how is Absolute Knowledge a response to that need? Heidegger poses the problem of the kind of finitude that Hegel's infinite sublates as another way of broaching his own concerns. If the finite is indeed sublated, then Heidegger's approach in *Being and Time*, which begins and remains with radical finitude and treats the infinite as derivative, must fail. But if there is another more original finitude than Hegel took up, his own trajectory could be rethought. And this is indeed Heidegger's position. This finitude he calls 'the innermost distress' [*Not*], one that belongs to Being itself not just human being. Its reality is no mere fact to be disputed about but a reality manifest in the necessity of philosophical commitment to which it gives rise. Philosophy is a calling not a talent.[20] And this *Not* has nothing to do with subjectivity. Here Heidegger promises, I would suggest, a substantially different mode of going through than Hegel. Responding to, listening to, staying within the finite, seem to be dedicated to a preservation without elevation, and without surpassing. There is an extraordinary sympathy here between Levinas's infinite, and Heidegger's finitude in that each represents a need that forbids totalization.

This long *Introduction* concludes with an explanation of the claim that Hegel begins absolutely with the absolute, and helps us see why it is not an introduction to philosophy. For Heidegger, the *Phenomenology of Spirit* is written from the beginning from the standpoint of Absolute Knowledge, continuing the level reached by 'philosophy in its passage from Parmenides...'. This level, he says, is *effective* and yet hidden from us. The collapse of Hegel's philosophy after his death (as he elsewhere remarks about German idealism in general) was actually a collapse of seriousness on the part of the public in meeting the demands it placed upon us.

Finally, Heidegger distinguishes his use of the term 'Being' from that of Hegel. Hegel restricts the term to a specific region and mode of being. Heidegger is concerned not only with 'what something is, but how it is, its manner of actuality'.[21]

I cannot here offer a detailed reading of the whole of this book. Instead I would like to fasten on the problem of *going through*, and in particular on Heidegger's discussion of the dialectic. This will have a further impact on our understanding of Heidegger's treatment of Hegel on time. That these matters are all closely connected is clear from Heidegger's account of Absolute Knowledge in terms of absolvence.[22]

Heidegger is developing a non-Hegelian sense of what it is to know absolutely such that we can begin to bring the subject-matter of philosophy into view, in order that we can begin to read the *Phenomenology of Spirit*. It does not involve a process of taking up what is one-sided and so on. Rather it involves letting go. But the acceptability of this model will depend on how Absolute Knowledge is thought to be actualized. We might suppose that Absolute Knowledge would have to 'be present in its unfolded and developed absolute fullness'. Not so.

> It is not the absolute fullness and absolute presence that is required but rather the character and way in which the absolute is, the *absolute restlessness* of mediation, which alone can be absolutely immediate.[23]

He describes the being of the restless absolute as *absolvent*, or involving perpetual detachment. The importance of this is that Hegel is both reintroducing a dynamic element into the absolute, and also withdrawing from it a sense of a temporally locatable point of teleological completion. The absolute is a level of restlessness. And dialectic can be thought of precisely through the idea of a restlessness of the logos. When Hegel introduces the speculative dimension into the subject–predicate proposition, Heidegger describes it as introducing the 'absolute restlessness of absolvence', and declares that 'The whole work of his [Heidegger's] philosophy is devoted solely to making this restlessness real.'[24] But it is the last section in the main part on sense-certainty that he devotes to the dialectic.[25] Here we will witness Heidegger working through Hegel, perhaps working him over, on the topic that most approximates this very going through.

For sense-certainty what is true and essential is the object. But this truth is thrown back, expelled from the object, and, as Hegel put it, driven back into the I. Sublation only occurs when experience has given its verdict on what has happened. How are we to think of experience? Heidegger can now say that

> [E]xperience is absolvent self-releasement into what appears in the light of Absolute Knowledge. This experience shows something to 'us', but not as those who happen to be alive and are registered as students or employed as teachers in this university. Rather, this experience

shows something to us who know absolvently, who are actual *in spirit*.[26]

Who is speaking here? Is this Hegel, Heidegger, perhaps spirit itself? Who is saying *spirit*? If it is Heidegger, is he using the word, or mentioning it, or something wholly different? Heidegger is here addressing issues *as Hegel has set them up*, but in the light of the question of Being. He goes on, for example, to describe 'the experience we undergo with the now... [as] an *exhibiting (Aufzeigen)* ... not an immediate knowing, but a movement, a mediation'.[27] This language of self-showing, exhibiting, is Heidegger's language, planted in Hegelian soil. There was no necessity to use the word *Geist* had he felt uneasy with it. Heidegger was not uneasy. What Derrida, in *Of Spirit*, pinpoints in 1933 was already in place in 1930.[28] In fact what Derrida describes as Hegel's *avoidance* of *Geist* (and other terms) in *Being and Time* came to an end in section 82 itself. For all its interest, Derrida's focus on avoidance is inadequate as a framework in which to deal with the extraordinary game of investment and disinvestment that Heidegger's readings of other thinkers require. *En passant*, Derrida's conviction that Heidegger's work is, in the last analysis, the most powerful defence of presence also seems shaken by this text.

But we digress. Heidegger's discussion of the dialectic proceeds through a return to the question of the finite and the infinite. Is Being essentially finite or infinite? If it is essentially finite, how does finitude register within philosophy in a fundamental way, rather than an accidental one? Or, conversely,

does the infinity of Absolute Knowledge determine the truth of being, and in such a way that it has already sublated everything that is finite into itself, so that all philosophising moves only in this sublation and as such a sublation in the sense of dialectic?[29]

Heidegger will soon describe the unhappy consciousness not as awareness of a disagreeable condition, but as 'knowing's restlessness, the disruption of not being able to achieve happiness', and again as 'the being of self-consciousness'.[30] This confirms the direction of his answer to this question. Finitude is fundamental. That it is fundamental can in part be stated in terms of the restlessness of absolution. But Heidegger is indecisive about whether the term 'dialectic' can be redeployed to capture this restlessness, or whether it must be abandoned at the threshold of Hegel's own inquiry.

At the end of this book, most hurriedly, and without preparation, Heidegger suggests that after all there is a new concept of Being in

Hegel's *Phenomenology of Spirit*, one that can be found in the introductory part of the chapter on 'The Truth of Self-Certainty', in which
being is described as inhering-in-itself. This new concept is actually
'the old and ancient concept in its most extreme and total completion', but it enables him to conclude that '*the phenomenology of spirit
is nothing other than the fundamental ontology of absolute ontology,*
or onto-logy in general. The *Phenomenology of Spirit* is the last stage
of a possible justification of ontology.'[31]

Heidegger cuts off the story only a short way into Hegel's text with
the assurance that the rest just unfolds what has already essentially
been exposed. I have left out far too much to dare to repeat that move.
Instead I will end my discussion of this book with what looks like a
paradox. Heidegger's method is what he elsewhere calls a 'step back'
(*Schnittzurück*), which he contrasts with Hegel's *Aufhebung*, which
goes onward and upward, negating, preserving, elevating. And yet,
Hegel's concept of time has essentially to do with the past. And this he
relates to the ontological claim that 'a genuine being is what has
returned to itself', 'understood absolvently', as he puts it. This
means that 'being is what has already occurred, in the face of which
nothing can be earlier'.[32] Strikingly, he claims that Hegel's understanding of the time of history, and even of the spirit, is formalistically
drawn from the philosophy of nature. The privilege of the circle
allows Heidegger to assimilate Hegel's conception of time to Aristotle, and the reference to being allows Heidegger to set up a fundamental opposition between himself and Hegel: 'For Hegel, being
(infinity) is also the essence of time. For us, time is the original essence
of being.'[33] With this remark, another huge topic beckons: the meaning of 'time' for Heidegger. Already the privilege of the future announced in *Being and Time* is a fading memory. And 30 years later in
On Time and Being, not only does Heidegger's sense of time become
more spatial, it also seems to have become more ontological, which
would make it harder to draw the contrast he wants.

What are we to conclude from this foray into Heidegger's Hegel? I
began with what I called the problem of ontological penetration: that
the power of ontological discourse is such that it is not implausible to
claim that its totalizing and idealizing operations can pave the way for
mass war and genocide, not to mention the continuing horrific destruction and exploitation of animal life in general. But Heidegger's
resistance to Hegel's operation of *Aufhebung* – his insistence on
patience, on the restlessness of Absolute knowing, his refusal to
subject the finite to the infinite – might best be understood as a kind
of inoculation against such consequences. Heidegger's 'penetration' is
not one that determines beings in their particular being (or lack of it).

In principle, it is a receptive, and responsive openness to being, an openness predicated on need, distress, etc.

The argument from Derrida's side is that Heidegger's recourse to the language of spirit demonstrates a limit to his anti-metaphysical resolution, and perhaps worse – the return of all that was most dangerous about ontological penetration. This is another story, which we take up again in chapter 7. But I would like to repeat that Derrida's own insistence elsewhere on the centrality of strategy at the 'end of metaphysics' is no guarantee against failure, even tragedy. And certainly the language of spirit has in principle universalizing possibilities that the biologistic racism he was attacking would not have appreciated.

Heidegger's treatment of the temporality of Absolute Knowledge raises important questions about time and the illuminations of experience, which will give point to our persistence with the question of going through, or undergoing. An overschematic representation might suggest two broad ways in which Absolute Knowledge can be actualized: 1. It can be actualized as a transcendence of the world, ongoing and radiant to itself, in which all the steps are preserved. Undoubtedly there are both mystical and rational versions of this. 2. It can be actualized as a being-in-the-world for whom the un-thought, the *Abgrund*, is not always present, but never far away, and for which that fact is embodied in a certain reserve, patience, or negative capability.

The illuminations of *Erfahrung* can be continuously actualized or can be dispositional. It would seem that the virtues of patience and tolerance would be more likely to accompany the latter than the former. Being *in* the truth, as Lukács put it,[34] seems much more dangerous than having access to it from a less elevated position, when at least questions can be raised. And indeed there might even be room for doubt, hesitation and discussion. The difference between permanent presence and dispositional access (or vulnerability) looks to me like the difference between a metaphysical illusion and a more subtle temporal modality.[35]

Are we now, after all that we have gone through, in any better position to think through the topic of the conference: *The Presence of Hegel in Contemporary Thought*? I will concentrate, for brevity, on 'contemporary'. For all the rhetoric, Heidegger has some useful things to say about this – both sceptical and bracing.

> Every genuine philosophy is unique and only as such has the power
> to be repeated and to be effective again in a particular time and in
> keeping with the spirit and power of that time. But never in such a way

that – sooner or later – it becomes something that belongs immediately to everyone, as, for example, in the *Kantgesellschaft* and now in the 'International Hegel Society'.

We protect the uniqueness of Hegel's work only when we take the trouble to confront it thoroughly. This means we introduce into the discussion the question whether and how this confrontation finds its necessity, that is to say, arises from the inner grounds of Dasein and thereby from the matter of philosophy itself.

In philosophy there are neither predecessors nor successors...every real philosopher is contemporaneous with every other philosopher by being, most intrinsically, the word of his time.[36]

Heidegger says that he has chosen to renew the question of Being by reading Hegel not for any extrinsic or personal reason, 'but rather on the basis of the necessities of *our* Dasein itself, in which that history of the problem of being is *actuality*' (G60; E41). I take it he is describing the condition he finds us all to be in – the darkening of the world, the flight of the gods, etc.

The implication of these remarks is clear: any ordinary chronological sense of *contemporary* is unimportant; to be *with* those who are our con-temporaries in thinking is to share their commitment, and the capacity to respond to the need of their own time. And if we can learn anything from Heidegger's commitment to thinking of being as fundamental event, his critique of teleology and of the history of progress, then his step back might just offer a way forward.

6

Heidegger after Derrida

The phenomenon of uneven development is no better illustrated than by conversations with friends about the philosophers who inspire them. With the occasional exceptions of Levinas and Nietzsche, no figures have been more salient landmarks in these conversations for me than Heidegger and Derrida. And when dyed-in-the-wool Heideggerians say they are moving away from Heidegger towards Derrida, you know something is happening. But the event of 'moving away from' is itself worth taking note of. As philosophers, we do not normally articulate our attachments to the figures we enjoy reading in ways that pass muster philosophically. And yet we are not shy of speaking like this. Lyotard [1973] wrote of drifting away from Marx and Freud, and Levinas spoke of the need to move away from the atmosphere of Heidegger's thinking. The uneven development is apparent when one's friends set sail from shared islands without warning. But it is apparent even more dramatically when you meet someone actively travelling in the opposite direction. The open water between Heidegger and Derrida has for years been congested with people travelling in both directions. And, of course, there are people sailing off to quite different shores.

But is it really possible to think of oneself as 'moving from Heidegger to Derrida' (or vice versa)? In what respect? And from what impulse? And what could be meant by this extraordinary conversion of names into landmarks or destinations? At the very least, one would surely have to acknowledge that these names stood not merely for positions, but for methods/ways/directions of...thinking, writing, etc. And even then, what happens to one's recognition that any interesting thinker does not merely develop a single project in predictable ways, but goes through transformations, reorientations, turns?

One could attempt to construct the space within which it would be possible to move from Heidegger to Derrida, or vice versa, by an elaborate consideration of their distinctive projects. I prefer to intensify our initial focus and orientation by fastening on a small quotation from Derrida in which at least one very general version of his relation to Heidegger is spelled out. In *Positions*, with all the reservations of an interviewee, he said (and then wrote):

> I sometimes have the feeling that the Heideggerian problematic is the most 'profound' and 'powerful' defense of what I attempt to put into question under the rubric of *the thought of presence*.[1]

In the face of those who would assimilate 'grammatological deconstruction' to 'prefabricated Heideggerianism', Derrida explains how he has repeatedly departed from the Heideggerian problematic over such concepts as 'origin', 'fall', 'time' and the value of the proper (*Eigentlichkeit, Eigen, Ereignis*). He continues:

> Wherever the values of propriety, of a proper meaning, of proximity to the self, of etymology, etc., imposed themselves in relation to the body, consciousness, writing, etc....I have attempted to analyze the metaphysical desire and presuppositions that were at work.[2]

The real difficulty in talking about 'moving from Heidegger to Derrida' or 'from Derrida to Heidegger' is that it constantly underestimates the importance of the movement of Heidegger's own thought – which even phrases like 'the Heideggerian problematic' tend to obscure – as well as the movement of Derrida's own thought and, in particular, his thought about Heidegger. Surely, for instance, Heidegger's own thought exhibits a progressive questioning of so many of those concepts Derrida mentions – of origin, of fall, of time as transcendental horizon for the question of Being, and indeed of authentic self-relatedness.

The question I would like to pose is this: Derrida has often acknowledged the fecundity of Heidegger's writing – it is 'a novel, irreversible advance all of whose critical resources we are far from having exploited'[3] – and he only ever criticizes Heidegger from another position within his own writing.[4] In the light of such remarks, is it possible rigorously to defend the reduction to a central project that Derrida perhaps casually offered us – 'the most "profound" and "powerful" defense of...the thought of presence'?

If I have doubts about this, and I will explain why, they are doubts that owe almost everything to Derrida. A couple of sharper questions would follow close on their heels: if it is wrong (as Derrida asserts) to confuse grammatological deconstruction with a 'prefabricated Heideggerianism', is it the 'prefabrication' or the Heideggerianism that offends most? Might not the progressive uncovering of Heidegger's own problematizing of 'the value of presence' suggest perhaps that Derrida had prematurely circumscribed the tools and resources of phenomenology, or would it show that Heidegger himself had already taken phenomenology beyond itself? How far, one wonders, does the series of Derrida's readings of Heidegger exhibit any sort of development about the possibilities of another kind of writing? It is a long time since Derrida claimed that there was no possibility of doing without metaphysical conceptuality in deconstructing metaphysics. This suggests that such a structure of reinscription and transgression is itself the limit, the final possibility for anything like philosophical thinking. But, if so, the case of Heidegger would then be one of an exemplary performance; and were such a structure unavoidable, then the fact that Heidegger had indeed confirmed, even re-established, the value, say, of the proper, might well not be his project, but only a local strategic necessity. So, again, is there not an important difference between the claim that Heidegger's project is ultimately a defence of the thought of presence, and the claim that this or that motif had, for strategic purposes, to be sacrificed on the altar of metaphysics to further the cause of transgression?

I will now simply mention a few of the places in which Derrida has discussed Heidegger, and comment on the moves being made.[5]

In 'Linguistics and Grammatology', Derrida defines his position in relation to Heidegger in terms of the distinction between discourse and intention. In discussing the case of 'trace', he writes

> Reconciled here to a Heideggerian intention, ... this notion signifies, sometimes beyond Heideggerian discourse, the undermining of an ontology which in its innermost course has determined the meaning of being as presence ...[6]

This formulation might seem problematic, for 'intention' has an ascendancy over discourse that it must be difficult for Derrida to defend. More importantly, however, it points in the opposite direction to the claim in *Positions* that treats Heidegger's work as a defence of presence. It is hard not to be fascinated by the role of intention in Derrida's writing, for it is in the very next sentence that he unifies his own *Of Grammatology* (which unity he elsewhere questions) under the guise of an 'intention'.

To make enigmatic what one thinks one understands by the words 'proximity,' 'immediacy,' 'presence' (the proximate [*proche*], the own [*propre*], and the 'pre-' of 'presence'), is my final intention in this book.[7]

I take it that a reference to a 'final intention' is being made ironically. Yet, strangely enough, the sentence is sufficiently plausible when read straight. And if we were to take the level of discourse (the words 'final intention') with a pinch of salt, we would be doing so only because we thought we knew what was intended at some other level. In other words, our capacity for reading the words 'final intention' lightheartedly most naturally rests on a capacity to set aside 'mere words', and understand what is meant more deeply. That, however, leaves us precisely where we were, totalizing a work through an intention, and even if there were a way of eliminating such a reference from Derrida's self-explication, intention is not replaceable in the reference to Heidegger's own writing. So, my puzzlement here stems from the fact that Heideggerian intentions are elevated above Heideggerian discourse, whereas, elsewhere, it is his underlying project that is claimed to be metaphysical.

In the previous chapter of the same book, 'The End of the Book and the Beginning of Writing', Heidegger's position is presented in a far more complex and sophisticated way. What is fundamentally in question is whether Heidegger's deployment of the term, or concept, of Being anticipates, confirms, or falls short of the deconstructive potential inherent in modern linguistics. Derrida's strategy here is to introduce this question at a critical moment in his assessment of Nietzsche, and particularly Heidegger's intra-metaphysical reading of him. It is a strategy dominated by a double reading. The first presents Heidegger as defending, reinstating Being as a transcendental signified whose source lies outside language. The second discovers a movement of transgression in Heidegger, a movement here associated with the work that followed his *An Introduction to Metaphysics*. Heidegger's situation is said to be '*ambiguous* . . . with respect to the metaphysics of presence and logocentrism . . . at once contained within it and transgressing it'.[8] Derrida advances much evidence to show that Heidegger's moves all point in the same direction – renouncing both the project and word 'ontology', the necessary dissimulation of the meaning of being, 'its occultation within the blossoming of presence', the intimate dependence of the history of being on the logos – all of which shows 'that nothing escapes the movement of the signifier'. These are, of course, (translations of) Derrida's words, and in these two vital pages Derrida carefully presents Heidegger's developing thought as one whose movement and economy are elucidated more effectively within his own discourse. Yet the work of explication is not always so different from Heidegger's own self-reflection. That 'the opening of fundamental ontology' is a 'necessary yet provisional moment' is something Heidegger himself said about *Being and Time*;[9] and Derrida's reading of Heidegger's practice of crossing out the word 'being' in *The Question of Being* is one with which Heidegger could concur.

Derrida's real contribution here is to have drawn our attention to the double movement in Heidegger's thought, to have drawn together the strands of each movement, and then to have presented these two movements as intimately conjoined. What he then does is to place in a most delicate way his own thought of *différance* ('not within but on the horizon of the Heideggerian paths, and yet in them') as a way (a) of coming to see 'being' always as a (historically) determined trace, (b) of grasping that 'all is not to be thought at one go', and (c) of giving radical integration to Heidegger's various moves.

The lesson we are to learn from this exemplary reading is what one might call a deconstructive reinscription or translation of the movement of dialectic – that the moment of erasure requires the prior moment of determination. Not only can everything not be thought 'at one go' but it is essential to take certain routes. I will come back to this shortly in relation to the place of phenomenology.

I began by suggesting that one problem in any idea that one might move from Heidegger to Derrida (or back again) is that each is himself 'in motion'. In this passage of which we have just offered a schematic representation, the movement that is brought into focus is that of Derrida's own reading of Heidegger. Is there not a danger that Heidegger's own movement has been reduced to a structure in tension, and that the real development in his work merely supplies evidence of both sides of this tension? Surely it is not only we and Derrida who pass through determinative inscription and erasure (in relation to Heidegger) – it is Heidegger's own practice. The issue would then be: how distinctively productive is Derrida's displacement of Heidegger's later language, which is itself, clearly, a discourse that already works on the other side of erasure? To discuss this, I will turn to Derrida's *Spurs: Nietzsche's Styles*, but precede that with some further thoughts on the last section of 'The End of the Book and the Beginning of Writing': 'The Written Being/The Being Written'. The order of presentation of the two readings does not seem accidental. The intra-metaphysical Heidegger seems to be more than counterbalanced by the post-metaphysical Heidegger. If Derrida's endorsement of Heidegger's 'opening of fundamental ontology as a necessary yet provisional moment' can be taken as the rule, then we have a clear victory for the transgressive over the regressive. Surely this is not consistent with Derrida's declaration in *Positions* (cited above) about Heidegger's fundamental defence of presence?

I have suggested that Derrida stresses 'structure in tension' in Heidegger's thought rather than its own (albeit not wholly continuous) movement of self-effacement. We now turn to *Spurs: Nietzsche's Styles*, and to Derrida's discussion of the value of the proper. For if Derrida were to offer a single argument for the unity of Heidegger's thought, the insistence of this family (of *Eigentlichkeit, Eigen, Ereignis*) would be a strong candidate. Derrida called it 'perhaps the most continuous and most difficult thread in Heidegger's thought'.[10]

I would like to raise one or two doubts about the use of this etymological chain as the basis for a unification of Heidegger's thought. First, it does not seem to me sufficient to treat the movement from *Eigentlichkeit* to *Ereignis*, say, as one of displacement, in which 'the same' concern is being handed on from word to word. That does not seem to account for the radical dropping of the term *Eigentlichkeit* after *Being and Time*, nor for Heidegger's own account of the provisionality of his formulation in *Being and Time*. In fact even the notion of authenticity has such an abyssal dimension in *Being and Time* as to disturb rather than confirm or sustain any form of self-present self-satisfaction. The term is nevertheless dropped, and it is open to question quite how seriously to take an etymological chain. The word '*Ereignis*' in *Contributions* and in *On Time and Being* seems to me to operate at a rather different level and in a different way. In saying this, I would like to paraphrase (I hope, not unjustly) Derrida's important clarification (in *Positions*) that there are no metaphysical concepts as such, but rather metaphysical deployments of terms in texts. It is this that permits erasure, which is, of course, not a dimension of a word's appearance, but rather its textual articulation. The value of an etymological chain would then be tested by seeing whether it led to the discovery of such articulations. In the case of *Ereignis*, however, I still need convincing.[11]

It is not difficult, for example, to find sentences, even paragraphs, in *On Time and Being* which would seem to support the idea that the value of the proper lives on and indeed flourishes. Thus:

> Because Being and Time are there only in Appropriating, Appropriating has the peculiar property of bringing man into his own [*Eigen*] as the being who perceives Being by standing within the time. Thus Appropriated, man belongs to Appropriation [*Ereignis*].[12]

Here we almost have the return of *Eigentlichkeit*, with the interarticulation of *Eigen* and *Ereignis*; but we surely have to ask something about what Heidegger is doing here, and how we are supposed to take these sentences, for there are certain overarching textual intentions that we must not ignore, and which would undermine any simple assimilation of Heidegger's use of this family of terms to 'metaphysical desire'.

1 One guiding question is this: Given that we cannot talk any longer about Being or Time, how can we understand their interrelation? Here it is important (a) that in some respect *Ereignis* is a new word whose fate will depend on how it is used and (b) that it has both the senses of 'appropriation' and 'event', but no ordinary sense of event.

2 That this whole lecture is governed by both general and specific warnings about the dangers of misconstruing its point ('The saying of Appropriation [*Ereignis*] in the form of a lecture remains itself an obstacle of this kind. The lecture has spoken merely in propositional statements') is a general warning. An example of a more specific one will be found below.

3 If Heidegger is explaining 'how man is brought into his own', this is as far as it is possible to be from constituting some sort of secure self-identity, no more, indeed, than is created by saying that 'presence is an effect of *différance*'. For *Ereignis* is understood in terms of withholding, withdrawal, denial, temporal extension, and expropriation. *Ereignis* cannot be placed 'in front of us', or 'opposite us', or 'as something all-encompassing'. One only comes into one's own by being radically outside of oneself, in 'time', as much as in 'space'. When Heidegger talks of *Ereignis* as 'the extending and sending which opens and preserves', we cannot fail to hear something more than a simple reinscription of the value of the proper.

We said that a proper understanding of authenticity as far back as *Being and Time* would bring out this same movement of a radical opening onto, radical extendedness, radical exposure, even dissolution. The tri-ecstatic analysis of temporality is one sign of this; the primacy of Being (outside oneself)-in-the-world is another, so it should not surprise us that in a treatment of Dasein's embodiment written shortly after *Being and Time* he should talk of Dasein's embodiment as a 'primordial *Streuung*' (bestrewal) 'which is in a quite definite respect a *Zerstreuung*.'[13] Embodied Dasein is dispersed and disseminated in time, in space and in its throwness and

entanglement in things, in nature, and it 'belongs essentially to factical dissemination that thrownness and captivation remain deeply
hidden from it'.[14] We could pursue this further – in particular it offers
an interesting example of Heidegger's use of the phrase 'essential
belonging' – but it is important to take stock. Heidegger's use of
Ereignis in *On Time and Being*, we claim, betrays so much dependence on extension and dispersion that we must resist the supposition
that any simple value of propriety is being reasserted.

We must now return to our recent point of departure, at which, in
fact, we never *arrived* – *Spurs*[15] – to consider Derrida's treatment of
this whole question of the proper. Again, I feel compelled to say
something about context (even if one of the main thrusts of *Spurs* is
to destabilize any such hermeneutic necessities). Derrida introduces
the question of the proper (belonging, appurtenance) in the framework of another defence of Nietzsche. Heidegger's claim that
Nietzsche's 'will' ultimately 'belongs' to the history of metaphysics
is broken open at the word 'belonging'.

Derrida's argument is this: that Heidegger's assimilation of
Nietzsche to the history of metaphysics rests on the plausibility of
attributing a univocal sense to 'belonging' which the word lacks, and
which Heidegger's own deployment of the word (and its cognates)
demonstrates. I agree with Derrida completely about reading
Nietzsche, but I am less convinced about his reading of Heidegger.
His account goes roughly like this:

(a) Derrida restates the claim about the continuity from *Being and
    Time* to *On Time and Being*, from *Eigentlichkeit* to *Ereignis*.
(b) He claims that this is unavoidable: 'A certain valuation of the
    proper and of authenticity – which is valuation itself – can never
    be interrupted.'
(c) He claims that what begins as a valuation of the proper in
    Heidegger's thought leads each time to 'the abyssal structure of
    the proper', which structure he says is non-fundamental.

Given that Derrida has cited Heidegger's persistent valuation of the
proper as an instance of his continuing commitment to the value of
presence, we may perhaps be forgiven for supposing that Derrida is
claiming here that this abyssal movement is something that befalls the
proper, that Heidegger finds the bottom constantly dropping out of
his attempts to find substitute ways of talking about Being. I would
put matters differently. Heidegger is so much aware of this abyssal
dimension that were it not an essential dimension of the proper, the
proper would have to be abandoned. Why does he use this word and

its cognates so persistently? He talks about the belonging together of time and being, and (in *What is Called Thinking?*) of thought and being, to stress their connectedness in each case. More generally, however, his concern, I take it, is to reactivate our grasp of identity, of the self, of our fundamental extendedness in the world, by fastening on a term of process (or event) by which those would be achieved – one that transforms our sense of what those terms might mean. If there is a valuation it is (residually) to a kind of hermeneutic reconstitution and repetition of unities of sense that continue to function, if only as rafts rather than fixed landmarks. But what Derrida said positively, affirmatively, about Heidegger's posing the *question* of Being, that

> incessant meditation upon that question does not restore confidence. On the contrary, it dislodges the confidence at its own depth[16]

is equally true of his abyssal understanding of the proper.

In brief, while I agree that Heidegger is too fast in claiming Nietzsche for the history of metaphysics, this does not suggest to me any failure to grasp the necessarily abyssal understanding of the proper, it is simply a failure to apply it at that moment to his reading of Nietzsche.

In 'Ousia and Gramme'[17] Derrida shows how the questions of time and presence that occupy him are being worked through within Heidegger's thought. *Being and Time* left these questions open on its last page, and Heidegger never lost sight of them. The essay's explicit point of departure is a footnote in *Being and Time*, so it is not surprising that the concepts of time and presence do not appear here in their fully developed form. Elsewhere, as we have suggested already, Derrida floats the possibility, perhaps even necessity, of reading Heidegger not from some exterior position but from another place in his interior. A more subtle response to the question of whether Heidegger's thinking is or is not committed to the defence of presence, belongs or not to metaphysics, would be to drop these big words that seem to force us to come to decisions, and concentrate on the particular possibilities of thought closed off and opened up by Heidegger.

I would like, here, to suggest a reason for valuing some of these very aspects of Heidegger's thinking that do not directly contribute to transgression – some of those aspects that might seem to be residual commitments to presence, or to be evidence of the partiality of his success, however heroic, in having broken free of metaphysics.

One of Derrida's most powerful and repeated moves has been to demonstrate the ironies of reinscription in the course of an attempted exit. The most radical attempts to escape metaphysics have typically repeated, at a deeper level, its fundamental motif. When he calls Heidegger's commitment to presence 'profound', this is not an honorific title but a reflection of the way Heidegger, as is typical, has dug deeper to struggle free. Our very word 'radical' has those implications. Perhaps, however, there is an inverse danger – that of prematurely supposing one has exhausted the possibilities of a thinker's thought – and of course the two dangers are linked. If I feel a certain hesitation in proposing that Heidegger has suffered this fate, it is because, in a way, Derrida's repeated return to Heidegger's texts would seem to confirm rather than contest the importance of avoiding this latter danger. What I am not clear about is whether we constantly underestimate the power of phenomenology to shake 'presence', or whether it is Heidegger's own transgression of phenomenology that has given him that power. When Derrida says we must go through phenomenology to avoid falling back into naive realism and vulgar empiricism, it is assumed that, however tricky, it is possible to go through phenomenology. That would allow Derrida to agree with me about the continuing resources of Heidegger's thought only by supposing that Heidegger had himself gone through phenomenology. Clearly Heidegger, no less than Derrida, has defined himself over and against the problematic of intentionality, phenomenological reduction, and transcendental subjectivity, but it is arguably his remaining within the space of problems opened up by phenomenology, while effecting a radical transformation of its formulation of problems, that is Heidegger's real strength. So I now offer a few reasons for continuing to see Heidegger's working with the limit *as* the limit, for not having Derrida's reservations about his attachment to presence. My general claim is this:

1 Heidegger's later thought, particularly as evidenced in the words in which he chooses to advance it (calling, giving, opening, clearing, granting, lightening, thinking, dwelling, concealing, preserving, sheltering, withholding, letting be, etc.), has the peculiar power to awaken in us the most profound possibilities of transformed relatedness for which we would otherwise lack a language.

2 By virtue of their essentially problematic metaphoricity they block any naive treatment of them as just another idiom. Their privilege is that they themselves shelter and preserve – and allow us to think – the most fundamental questions of language.

3 The extraordinary double span of these words – designating on the one hand some of our most primitive activities or conditions and,

on the other, the most profound philosophical insights – has a most powerfully integrating effect. Philosophy (or post-philosophy) produces vertical integration by repetition.

4 These terms have a capacity to deepen, without offering transcendental grounds, our reading of more traditional philosophy. A particularly good example would be Heidegger's discussions of the need to think natural light, the light of reason, in terms of *Lichtung*, and to understand lighting itself as requiring a reference to opening.

In short, I endorse thinking of reading as repetition, a repetition in which an old matrix is rethought and reveals new possibilities. My general claim about reading Heidegger is that it would be hard to overestimate the power and persuasiveness of the moves by which Heidegger himself persistently distances himself from affirming the value of presence and all its cognates.

Addendum

This has been a review of some of Derrida's early engagements with Heidegger, but there is nothing to suppose that the pattern shifts in his later work. *Of Spirit*, for example, could be said to be haunted by the mirror games of recognition / misrecognition, and even the recognition of misrecognition, as in Derrida's imaginary conversations between Heidegger and theologians, which might be read as projective transformations of his own relationship with Heidegger. The particular structuring supposition – of the privilege of the *question* in Heidegger, and his extended retraction of that supposition in an enormous footnote – is perhaps emblematic of Derrida's readings of Heidegger over the years.[18] Nevertheless, in trying to think through what is at stake for us, for philosophy, for reading, in this series of encounters, it is tempting to suppose that the struggle over the abyss will always, and quite impersonally, generate certain seemingly exotic patterns and strategies of reading. When we ask ourselves, for example, whether Heidegger can really allow himself to look into the abyss, or whether he will always turn away, there is a good chance that we are here using Heidegger as the fall guy in a game we are playing with ourselves. If *abyss* means something like the recognition of limits to thought, to reason, to language – limits that may well appear in a quite singular form, such as a traumatic event, immeasurable pain, the inassimilability of the other – then there will be inevitable failure in the way we witness this. We may treat Heidegger's particular failure as something to be avoided. But equally, if we began from the necessity of failure, we could treat Heidegger's response as an exemplary failure, and it is not out of the question that the structure of the abyss actually infects our capacity to read the other as such, and hence our (and Derrida's) reading of Heidegger. When Heidegger recommends the kind of reading that 'goes to the other's encounter' rather than 'going counter to the other', he is surely offering us a hint of how we might maintain the abyssal moment in our reading of the other. In this respect, Derrida's readings over the years are themselves exemplary – not each one of them, but the pattern of return, recognition of misrecognition, reworking, etc. In this, the most fundamental question that would bring into play psychoanalysis, both as itself an object of abyss-slaying desire and as a companion in arms, would have to do with whether we could ever do without the illusions of projective engagement by which we 'read' the other. And whether there is any good answer as to how to respond to the necessity of such illusion. What Derrida wrote about Heidegger's fundamental commitment to presence is reiterated very well, for example, by Chris Fynsk:

> In *On the Way to Language* the abyss appears precisely under the name of *pain*, which Heidegger relates to abyss. But the abyss is that by which difference folds upon itself and speaks, and the question would then be, 'What exactly is the nature of that tearing or articulation?' It is a joining and a tearing at the same time. Late in one of the essays he talks about the problem of the sounding, of the silent call of difference, about the necessity of a certain noise, which is introduced by human speaking; and the question becomes just how fundamental that noise is, just how fundamental that tearing of the abyss is which allows difference to fold upon itself and to speak.

The problem with Heidegger is this:

> One has to work terribly hard in each case to bring out the dispersal, the dispersion, or the dissemination...[I]n each case my sense is that one has to work against enormous resistance; and, in that sense, I would be more inclined to stress the kind of structural tendency in Heidegger towards reconstruction of the *same*. It is still one thing, in itself, still a certain oneness, or a certain privileged unity, which is reaffirmed from beginning to end.[19]

Fynsk could be right about this, but perhaps what we think of as the privilege of the same, of unity, of presence, is not the privilege of some autonomous value, but the privilege of a certain minimal framing on which even the appearance of abyssal moments is dependent. At stake here, of course, is both the difficulty of thinking abyss *without all that it constitutes a falling away from*, but, just as important, the question of strategy which inevitably follows the recognition that *abyss* is at no level exempt – as sign or signified, or just a trace – from difference, relationality or dependence.

7

The Actualization of Philosophy: Heidegger and Adorno

From avoidance to deployment

Heidegger's 'Rectoral Address' represents, it has been said, a betrayal of an original project, perhaps a betrayal of philosophy itself. In a way perhaps symptomatic of a deeper failure, Heidegger has forgotten his earlier careful avoidance of the metaphysical–humanistic language of *Geist*. Do we not have here a problem of memory, fidelity, in the face of temptation?

Derrida quite properly introduces the expression *an economy of avoidance*;[1] but who is it that avoids? What if Heidegger was himself asking this very question in these same years? We know that part of Heidegger's strategy involves selectively displacing certain terms, certain enchainments, certain resonances, but what if the place of the philosopher, the thinker of these thoughts, were essentially unthought? What if that problem threatened the very capacity to think 'avoidance', etc.? Who avoids the words subject, consciousness, meaning...spirit? What if this 'avoidance' were itself a ruse, not of a particular author, but one required by history? Who then avoids? Might it not be spirit itself? It is clear that Heidegger was not alone in his worry over such words. Even his self-declared opponents shared it.

On 7 May 1931, as his inaugural lecture to the philosophy faculty of the University of Frankfurt where he stayed until 1933, Adorno gave a paper entitled 'The Actuality of Philosophy', which is most intriguing from our point of view, not least for its timing and its topic. He claims there is a 'moment' prior to the question of Being – and it is 'the function [of] eternalizing the present condition' of reality. For

Adorno, 'the fullness of the real, as totality, does not let itself be subsumed under the idea of being'.[2] Although this is presented explicitly as an objection to Heidegger, the parallels to Heidegger's own caution about the term Being at the beginning of *Being and Time* are extraordinary. Adorno is, in effect, refusing to accept or endorse Heidegger's careful attempts to reopen the question of Being. Adorno's central critical aim seems to be a reprise of the argument in Marx's *German Ideology*, extending the charge of idealism, albeit transcendental, to Husserl and of vitalism and subjectivism to Heidegger. He further charges Heidegger with having ontologized time, that is, of having avoided the question of history by treating abstract temporality as the essence of man.

More positively, Adorno proposes a philosophy of interpretation, one which would abjure the big problems: 'the text which philosophy has to read is incomplete, contradictory and fragmentary, and much in it may be delivered up to blind demons.' The idea of a deep hidden meaning is illusory.

In the context of the thematics of the primacy of the question in Heidegger, and that of avoidance (of *Geist*), I would like to quote Adorno's hesitant series of suggestions towards a new programme. In the light of 'the collapse of the last philosophical claims to totality' he supports 'the liquidation of philosophy', and this would require of us 'the strict exclusion of all ontological questions in the traditional sense, the avoidance of invariant general concepts, also perhaps the concept of man, the exclusion of every conception of a self-sufficient totality of spirit (*Geist*), or of a self-contained "history of *Geist*"'.[3]

Curiously, it is with *Geist* that he ends: 'For *Geist* is indeed not capable of producing or grasping the totality of the real, but it may be possible to penetrate the detail, to explore in miniature the mass of merely existing reality.'[4]

Let us get our theme into focus. Adorno is arguing for the exclusion of ontological questions, and the avoidance of concepts like man and *Geist* – and he identifies Heidegger as the opposition. Is he right? Does he adequately articulate their disagreement? The answer to the second question is clearly 'No'. He makes the same kind of mistake as Levinas in identifying Heidegger as a philosopher of totality. Suppose we ask: Can [philosophy] 'produce or grasp the totality of the real'? Does Heidegger really suggest that we can do this? Or does he very precisely deny this? Listen to his inaugural lecture:

> As surely as we can never comprehend absolutely the ensemble of beings in themselves we certainly do find ourselves stationed in the midst of beings that are revealed somehow as a whole. In the end an

> essential distinction prevails between comprehending the ensemble of beings in themselves and finding oneself in the midst of beings as a whole. The former is impossible in principle. The latter happens all the time in our existence. No matter how fragmented our everyday existence may appear to be [boredom, joy, and *Angst* give us a rather different access to the whole].[5]

The difference between Adorno and Heidegger here is that Heidegger believes in some residual access to the whole, one which is not a grasping (or a producing), while Adorno, assuming that these latter are the only options, charges Heidegger with totalizations, and opts (after Benjamin) for focusing on fragments that Heidegger also acknowledges. Adorno argues against general concepts, and includes Being in this prohibition. Even in *Being and Time*, Heidegger had argued against all traditional ways of understanding Being as 'the most universal concept'. Later in his work, perhaps conceding the difficulty of maintaining this proscription, he subjects Being to crossing-out, displacement and rearticulation. Adorno argues against the primacy of big questions. Clearly, in *Being and Time* Heidegger asks a big question, one reworked in *An Introduction to Metaphysics*. It is quite true that Heidegger gives a central role to questions and questioning, but neither Heidegger nor Adorno abolishes the form of the question – they each privilege and then displace the question. For Adorno, questions become localized, historically determined, socially responsive; for Heidegger they are ways of opening up a 'path of thought'. If anything substitutes for the dialectical method in Heidegger it is the recursive opening power of questioning. Yet, for each of them, questioning, however crucial, is not primary. We may suppose that whereas it had been primary in *Being and Time*, it gave way to the *Zusage* in *On the Way to Language*. But there are earlier indications of a limitation of this primacy. Derrida points, for example, to the 'call of conscience' in *Being and Time*; but we can find an acknowledgement of the embeddedness of questioning in the very first pages of *Being and Time*, in which Heidegger is outlining 'The Necessity, Structure, and Priority of the Question of Being'.

> As a seeking, questioning needs prior guidance from what it seeks. The meaning of being must therefore be available to us in a certain way.... From this grows the explicit question of the meaning of being and the tendency towards its concept.[6]

Heidegger's account of *Angst* in 'What is Metaphysics?' [1929] makes it very clear that questioning is not even the primary movement, let alone an activity without conditions.[7] For Adorno, philosophy is an experimental and inventive response to the problems posed by concrete situations, the success of which is measured by 'the disappearance of the question'.[8] Adorno mistrusts grand narrative, and sets a new agenda committed to the reality of fragmentation, the absence of predetermined solutions, and the value of fantasy and invention. Heidegger attempts a different move from a similar initial position, but for him it is a matter of understanding philosophy's break with totality via openness to Being rather than the pursuit of therapy and the arrangement of fragments. Heidegger renegotiates our relation to totality so that it ceases to be a possessable ideal. Adorno seems to be left with the same desire to comprehend, while adjusting his sights to the essentially fragmentary real. It is not clear to me that these ways of proceeding are incompatible, unless each insists on being the true bearer of the flag of philosophy. It is important that Adorno did not, at this time, understand Heidegger. If he heard the news from Freiburg that Heidegger had been lecturing that winter on theoretical biology, it would have confirmed him in his view that Heidegger was lapsing into vitalism. It would be a mistake to base avoidance or rejection of Heidegger on Adorno's diagnosis here. But surely, it might be argued, such misunderstandings pale into insignificance when we consider the subsequent trajectory of Heidegger's work? Fortunately (or unfortunately) the choice is not so convenient. Adorno's post-metaphysical fragmentology did not prevent him from favourably reviewing a song-cycle in a way that saluted the consciously National Socialist nature of the poems of Schirach on which it was based.[9] Clearly, then, the question of the question is not exclusively Heidegger's, nor is the thought that terms like man, spirit, etc., are best avoided, or that new philosophical strategies are required. Leaving aside this concrete instance of its failure, Adorno, even in this lecture, recognizes that he cannot straightforwardly succeed even in this attempt to formulate his programme.[10] He resorts to the defence of 'the necessity of transition'. Here we have the opposite of avoidance: complicity. He is saying what Derrida would say forty years later: that we cannot dispense with metaphysical forms in the attempt to deconstruct metaphysics. Complicity is unavoidable. Nietzsche knew this well, and so of course did Heidegger, and if we single out the most powerful terms for specific avoidance, the critical work must still be done by others. Heidegger's *Being and Time* is a most extraordinary effort at avoidance, replacing and displacing every vestige of the 'subject' – understood both ontologically and grammatically. Strategic considerations alone would justify the retention of a privilege for questioning, despite its supposed attachment to an essentially autonomous subject.

As we have seen, however, even this cannot be sustained. The simplest version of one of the questions Derrida puts to us in *Of Spirit* is how Heidegger's 'Rectoral Address' affects our judgement of him as a philosopher. Given such a question, the comparison of the containment of *Geist* in *Being and Time* and its active liberation in the 'Rectoral Address' is ambiguous. We might suppose that the 'Rectoral Address', for this very reason, is not to be taken as a serious philosophical text, which could redeem Heidegger's philosophy if not his judgement. Or we could suppose that the language of the 'Rectoral Address' can precisely be understood in terms of Heidegger's own philosophy, which would seem to make matters worse. I will try to argue that matters are indeed worse, but not because Heidegger's is a Nazi philosophy, but because the 'Rectoral Address' reveals the vulnerability of Heidegger's discourse to a military transposition. What we need to do is not to demythologize Heidegger so much as to isolate the short-circuits in his thinking that led to this performance.

An adequate consideration of the movement of Heidegger's thought from the avoidance of terms with such a metaphysical legacy as *Geist* in *Being and Time*, through to its re-emergence in 'Rectoral Address' and its flowering in *An Introduction to Metaphysics*, would have to bear in mind the following:

1 In section 82, the penultimate section of *Being and Time*, he is quite as much grooming *Geist* for redeployment as censoring it.
2 As we saw in chapter 6, his lectures on *Hegel's Phenomenology of Spirit* [1930–1] find Heidegger using the term *Geist* in his own voice. This occurs before the 'Rectoral Address' – that is, outside the particular connection to the German nation, the university, etc., and outside the political theatre.
3 We have seen considerable evidence in these lectures of Heidegger's willingness to translate or ingest Hegel into his own language – even as he criticizes him – to the point at which Hegel and Heidegger are not clearly distinguishable. Indeed, we cannot fully understand Heidegger's 'Rectoral Address' without thinking through his relation to Hegel: in particular, on the relation between time and Being, between *Geist* and Time, and between *Geist* and leadership.
4 We can understand the resurrection of *Geist* specifically in the 'Rectoral Address' in terms of the structures of vertical integration – between students, the sciences, the university, Germany, and destiny – that it seems to facilitate.
5 In doing this Heidegger in effect reintroduces the structure of dependent Being that he attributes to the mediaeval doctrine

of substance. Such a subject has an essential or constitutional vertical relatedness to a higher being.

Of Derrida, Heidegger and spirit

In *Of Spirit*,[11] Derrida sketches out the reasons for Heidegger's avoidance of the term *Geist* (and soul, ego, consciousness, ego, reason, subject, life, man,...): they 'block any interrogation of the Being of Dasein'.[12] Nonetheless, Heidegger does not entirely dispense with *Geist* – it plays crucial roles in the book, even if guarded by quotation marks.[13] The non-Cartesian spatiality of Dasein is elucidated by reference to the 'spiritual',[14] and Heidegger has at least to *deal with* the concept of spirit when discussing Hegel's concept of time. What is at stake here is the question of how spirit can take a sensible form, how it can appear in time, how it can, as Hegel puts it, 'fall into time'. Heidegger argues that this way of putting it confirms the view that Hegel is working with the 'vulgar concept of time', and, to make clear what Hegel is claiming, in effect translates Hegel's claim that spirit falls into time, into a claim about the relation between an original temporalization and the time of the world 'in the horizon of which "history" as intratemporal happening can appear'.[15] Spirit, as Heidegger puts it, exists as originary temporalization, and the falling characterizes, then, the inevitable falling away from this originary temporality on the part of our factical existence.

Hegel accomplishes this relation of spirit to time by establishing their kinship through 'the negation of the negation'. Time, for Hegel, is, formally speaking, 'the pure self-external', the continual 'negation' of every now, while this 'negation of the negation' is both that which is 'absolutely restless' in the spirit and also its 'self-manifestation'. In its 'progress' Spirit has to battle continually to overcome itself. It falls into time in that this spiritual progress is actualized in world-history.

What is Heidegger's view of this in the last two paragraphs of section 82? Two vital points stand out. First, Heidegger distinguishes his position from Hegel by their respective starting points: 'Hegel's "construction" was prompted by his arduous struggle to conceive the "concretion" of the spirit.'

[Whereas] our existential analytic of Dasein, on the contrary, starts with the 'concretion' of factically thrown existence itself in order to unveil temporality as that which primordially makes such existence possible.

What is all this leading to? Derrida writes that: 'Heidegger does not take up as his own the word "spirit"; he barely gives it shelter', and then adds (is this a withdrawal?): 'At any rate, the hospitality offered is not without reservations.'[16]

Derrida first quotes Heidegger correctly: '"Spirit" does not first fall into time, but it exists as originary temporalization',[17] but on the next page, this has been worn down to 'spirit is essentially temporalization'.

In my view, Derrida is massaging things in one direction, while Heidegger is grooming *Geist* in another. Put simply, if 'Spirit' does not first fall into time, but exists as 'the primordial temporalization of temporality', this analysand is workaday Heideggerian prose. He has displaced Hegel's *Geist* by this translation, but he has also groomed it, and licensed it for subsequent deployment.

And this is really as far as Heidegger gets in *Being and Time*. The next section (83) is shutting up shop, exposing the ragged ends, confessing incompleteness and inconclusiveness.

In Derrida's theatre Heidegger's *Geist* walks unannounced onto the stage of history in 1933. Not only has Heidegger prepared us for this in *Being and Time*, but we can find places in his 1930–1 lectures (on *Hegel's Phenomenology of Spirit*) in which *Geist* is again on his lips, in his own voice. In these lectures, of course, *Geist* is on every page, but these uses can, broadly speaking, be sorted into different categories. There is quotation from Hegel, paraphrase, immanent commentary, rewriting or translating Hegel, and finally 'external' judgement. In each category the discourse of *Geist* persists.

Working through the section on sense-certainty, we discover that 'experience is absolvent self-releasement into what appears in the light of absolute knowledge' and then that '...this experience shows something to us who know absolvently, who are actual in spirit'.[18] But if this is translation, after claiming that the later Hegel had not entirely avoided the danger of doing dialectic by imitation, he goes on to say that

> Every serious philosophy is unique and only as such has the power to be repeated and to be effective again in a particular time and in keeping with the spirit and power of that time.[19]

The 'Rectoral Address' to my ears echoes with the ghost of Hegel, and not just in the appropriation of some of his language. It is not obvious what status to give to Hegel in Heidegger's thinking after *Being and Time*, but this 1930–1 lecture course is no accident; nor is it the sole instance. In *The Basic Problems of Phenomenology*, he writes of the

> overcoming of Hegel [as] the intrinsically necessary step in the development of Western philosophy which must be made for it to remain at all alive.[20]

In these Hegel lectures, Heidegger distinguishes his position from Hegel by saying that whereas Hegel thinks the essence of time in terms of being (infinite), for him, time is the original essence of being.[21] Heidegger claims that Hegel consequently finds the essence of time in the past, allowing the fulfilment of a being by it having returned to itself. On Heidegger's reading

> Hegel's explication of the genuine concept of being...is nothing less than leaving time behind on the road to spirit, which is eternal.[22]

It is very clear that whatever else concerns him about Hegel's having ontologized time, Heidegger is increasingly concerned with the problem of how to think in a time of crisis. Heidegger had already reached an account of the history of metaphysics by which he had inaugurated a radical dismantling of the tradition, but the years leading up to 1933 must have been experienced as a mounting crisis. There are many extraordinary features of this 'Rectoral Address', but what is most extraordinary is that it is more truly an inaugural lecture than his 'What is Metaphysics?' [1929]. Heidegger is not God, nor the founder of a nation, but this lecture is intended as the inauguration of a new age. In the past, things have been so; hereafter, they will be different. He offers not suggestions, or ideas, but proclamations. As he wrote in the Hegel book: 'transitions have to be entered into, and as long as we stay on one or other shore and talk back and forth, transitions can never be achieved.'

The language of the 'Rectoral Address' is the language of a transformation not just in time but of time, one whose legitimacy is defined by the idea of renaissance, 'recapturing the greatness of the beginning'.[23]

The 'Rectoral Address' is the most extraordinary instance of the attempted actualization of philosophy. That this was one of Heidegger's central concerns is made clear two years later in *An Introduction to Metaphysics*, where he writes, perhaps in sober reflection:

> All essential philosophical questioning is necessarily untimely...because philosophy is always projected far in advance of its time...

> Philosophy... cannot be adjusted to a given epoch but on the contrary imposes its measure on the epoch.

Yet he continues,

> What is useless can still be a force, perhaps the only real force. What has no immediate echo in everyday life can be intimately bound up with a nation's profound historical development, and can even anticipate it. What is untimely will have its own times.... This is true of philosophy.[24]

The language of spirit, then, understood as the temporalizing of temporality, as originary temporality, is being deployed by Hegel in the service of the actualization of philosophy as a reinauguration of a lost origin. There is, however, a second crucial function of spirit, which takes us into the heart of the matter.

The prohibition and avoidance of the long series of terms in *Being and Time* was in the cause of a systematic displacement of both substance and subject, and their central features of self-subsistence and self-presence. Dasein, mortal, temporalizing Being-in-the-world, is understood essentially through its openness to Being – an openness pursued philosophically through a questioning thinking and, later, listening. Faced with history, with actuality, with events sufficiently momentous as to have the direst consequences for the 'world' in which such openness is played out, the question of institution arises, for an analysis of individual Dasein is insufficient. What spirit and the spiritual achieves for Heidegger is a way of thinking concrete institutions (university, state, leader) while maintaining Dasein's openness to Being. Spirit has an essentially coordinating function. The model here is this: that the necessary participation of the student, worker, academic, etc., in this new movement, is presented as a chain of dependencies, in which the truth of each is found in an openness, attunement, not just to Being in the abstract, but to a particular Being (a leader, a community, a nation) which is itself essentially attuned to Being.

Spirit, as Heidegger defines it, 'is primordially attuned, knowing resoluteness towards the essence of Being'. Leadership, then, is obedience to one attuned by his vision to the (German) nation, which is itself attuned to its distinctive destiny, which is to be attuned to Being. True community consists of parallel vertical attunement, a close cousin to what we earlier called ontological penetration.

The application of management (or military) logic to spirit is not new. It is, in fact, an extraordinary reprise and extension of the structure of the very mediaeval ontology to which Heidegger had traced the Cartesian concept of the subject. How could this have happened?

If it would be too facile to see this move as marking a split between left and right Heideggerians, the link that Derrida makes to questioning (and then its own limitation) is surely vital. The spiritual organization Heidegger outlines rests on the possibility that questioning be itself subordinated to an end – the attunement of Dasein to a higher Being naturally attuned. Questioning would be complete when the recognition of this necessity of attunement had been realized. If this is so, listening, attentiveness to the *Zusage*, the grant, is not radically different. What in either case matters is whether there are resources within or outside of Heidegger for resisting this regimentation of the spirit that, as we saw in chapter 5, Heidegger describes as an 'absolute restlessness'.

One inaugural lecture. One rectoral address. It is clear enough that Adorno did not understand Heidegger, but equally it must be doubtful whether Heidegger himself understood the implications and echoes of the logic to which he subjected *Geist* in the 'Rectoral Address'.

Jacquesgillian :: Gillianjacques. Extremes meet?[25]

If the relation between Adorno and Heidegger clearly reeks of misrecognition, it cannot be reduced to that structure. And if the possibility of misrecognition is close to being a condition for a powerful reading, that does not lessen the need for specific explanations in particular cases. In the hope that drawing yet another line of interpretation may help to fix our object, I propose now to puzzle out something of the same structure of misrecognition reverberating through a more contemporary reprise of Adorno's response to Heidegger, one which nicely crosses Derrida's strange critical palimpsest of a reading of Heidegger in *Of Spirit*. I propose to discuss here a book by a contemporary independent spirit, strongly influenced by Adorno, and the author's strange difficulty in reading Derrida.

The book in question is Gillian Rose's *Judaism and Modernity*, subtitled *Philosophical Essays*.[26] This was one of the last instalments in the working out and working through of one of the most singular and forceful philosophical agendas in current thought. Gillian Rose's work was a persistent demonstration of the possibilities of critical and political reflection – a reflection covered over in modern, and particularly post-modern, philosophy. Strongly influenced by Adorno, her pervasive intuition is that the Kantian antinomy of necessity and freedom restated, but never completely resolved in Hegel's account of the diremption, the forced separation of law and ethics, abstract right and personal morality – that the history of nineteenth- and twentieth-century philosophy, and of the pronouncements of the end of philosophy, are all to be thought in terms of this fundamental split. This split has been institutionalized, if that is not a misleading word, in the modern state to the point at which it is invisible, and philosophy's critical emancipatory role is emasculated by its failure to understand the great fault-line on which it is inscribed. Gillian Rose, to use the jargon, has a grand narrative. She may suppose, not without reason, that its justification lies not only in the power of Hegel's original thought, but in the interpretive power it still offers us. Her work is a sustained illustration, and continuing proof of the potency of this premise: that we dwell, blindly or otherwise, in a broken middle ground with, at best, a dream of some unification of the personal and the political and, at worst, the utter loss of that horizon.

It is not difficult to agree that Hegel has suffered a certain misrecognition in this century. To think of Hegel simply as the philosopher of totalization, whose work completes, and hence kills philosophy, is to have forgotten how to read. The lesson we all need to learn is the seductive ease of misrecognition. One of the persistent motifs of Gillian Rose's work is the insistence on the need to maintain the philosophical categories of reflection, critique, truth, etc., at the point at which some *reduction* is being planned. *Hegel contra Sociology* is the repudiation of sociologism. Social and political categories are not just part of the descriptive apparatus of an academic discipline, they are, or can be the critical and reflective instruments of human history.

What is truly *philosophical* about Gillian Rose's position is her alertness to the dangers of philosophy's self-repudiation. If only philosophy could become a science..., if only philosophy could open itself to the thought of the Other... each of these thoughts, she claims, encodes a fatal desire. And in *Judaism and Modernity*, she diagnoses, I think correctly, the seductions of projecting onto Judaism a pure ethics of otherness that can supplement or complement a reason otherwise destined to blind totalization. One error is being 'corrected' by another. In fact, as she shows in her discussions of Levinas, Weil, Buber, Strauss, Rosenzweig and others, Judaism is not one thing. In his *Gay Science*, Nietzsche, describing woman as an action at a distance, talks of men gazing upon 'woman' as upon a sailing ship silently gliding past on the horizon. In fact as every woman knows, as we get closer to the ship itself, the noise, the clamour of voices grows ever louder. Gillian Rose thinks the same about Judaism. In particular, in the tension between Judaic ethics and law (*Halacha*), diremption remains. This is not to deny that there may be resources within Judaism that may help us in rejuvenating philosophy.

I would like to defend something of the spirit of Gillian Rose's project and position, while posing certain questions to that project from within a different tradition. Perhaps I could begin by an observation on the Derrida affair (or was it the Cambridge affair?), finally concluded with a vote in May 1992. There was considerable pressure against giving him the honorary doctorate that had been proposed – opposition led by leading lights, or perhaps one should say leading shades, of the Cambridge philosophy department. Leaflets were printed accusing Derrida of all sorts of things – but in particular the traditional English objections to French and German philosophers – that he was the high-priest of irrationalism, a mesmeric charlatan who corrupted the young, etc. – charges, first laid by Mill, by Russell and Popper against Hegel. Clearly there was hysteria and a witch-hunt. If it had been claimed that Derrida drank blood, it would only have raised eyebrows a little further. In all the hysteria it was important to remind oneself that if those things were true of Derrida, they would be right to protest. The question that needed asking was how they came to project those fears onto Vlad Derrida: a problem, in other words, of recognition, misrecognition.

At a completely different level, something of this same problem also flows through Gillian Rose's treatment of Derrida, to whom she devotes a chapter ('Of Derrida's Spirit') in *Judaism and Modernity*. What I would like to argue is that there are some extraordinary parallels between her own agenda and that of Derrida, and that in her critical engagement with Derrida in particular, there are chapters yet to be written.

Without wanting to dwell on chapter 8 of her *Dialectic of Nihilism*, 'Law and Writing: Derrida', which deals with some of his early works, I would like to draw attention to the logic of recognition governing Gillian Rose's reading. Derrida, on her reading, 'reconstructs while claiming he is deconstructing and closes questions while claiming he is opening them'.[27] In other words Derrida is doing the opposite of what he says or thinks he is doing. Derrida misrecognizes his own project. What is Derrida really doing? 'It will be a matter of arguing', Gillian Rose writes, 'that Derrida's [...] "positions: scenes, acts, figures of dissemination"...revive...a Fichtean act of positing.'[28] Whether we agree with this or not, what is clear is that the method being deployed here is that of *reduction to a recognized antecedent, whose place in the story, and hence limitations, are predetermined.* The problem with this is that it is ahistorical and even, dare one say it, abstract. The concreteness and specificity of Derrida's text threatens to be lost under a law of reading: find the antecedent.[29]

In her chapter 'Of Derrida's Spirit' in *Judaism and Modernity*, the drama of identification and (mis-)recognition is extended. Derrida is described as offering an *apologia* for Heidegger. Heidegger is at least 'consistent in refusing the conceptuality and conflicts of modern political theory'. 'His *oeuvre* is haunted... by the unacknowledged but evident diremption which he refused from start to finish, from origin to origin, to think.' But 'Derrida's *De l'esprit* has [she writes] a special dishonesty'.[30] I will not quote all that follows. The special dishonesty flows, as I understand it, from the level of reflective authorial control that Derrida exercises over his writing, while still refusing to recognize the truth of the diremption of law and ethics. But this whole approach – imputing refusals, and then dishonesty – is an *imputation* to Heidegger and Derrida of the author's own agenda, misconstrued. What if Derrida, for example, was not dishonestly refusing to do X but quite honestly doing Y? When Rose writes, in the previous chapter, 'From Speculative to Dialectical Thinking: Hegel and Adorno', of Adorno's remorselessly judgemental tone and style of writing, it is striking just how far this is a temptation she herself falls into. What Rose is perhaps caught up in here are the snares and labyrinths of recognition that Hegel has taught us so much about. I should say that I do not entirely excuse Heidegger or Derrida from methodological worries on this score. The problem with all diagnostic reading is that it reads to confirm and illustrate what it already knows, and the immense power of Rose's approach is not unconnected with this. Why, then, in the specific case of her treatment of Derrida, is there so much laying down the law, so much judgement, so much, dare I say it, anger?

My suggestion is this: that Rose's approach to Derrida is governed by a double difficulty. On the one hand, there are a great many *formal* parallels between Derrida and Rose, parallels that make establishing a clear distance difficult; but on the other, Derrida's philosophical *formation* is one that arises from certain traumatic displacements in twentieth-century philosophy that Rose, rightly or wrongly, has recognized from afar, and refused. Most particularly I would mention what has been called the linguistic turn, which for Rose is to be understood within the history of our modernity, of spirit's diremption, while for those thinkers touched not just by the structuralism of the sixties, but also by Husserl's transcendental turn, and Heidegger's renewal of ontology, it is the very possibility of the language of that assimilation that is in question.

Let me begin by mentioning some of the parallels. *Judaism and Modernity* 'challenges the philosophical presentation of Judaism as the *sublime other of modernity*'.[31] In the introduction, talking of what she calls *new ethics*, Rose attacks the contemporary focus on 'the Other' as in effect an empty abstraction, void of both personal or political content, and links this directly to Derrida, without naming him, thus: 'If "difference" has become the hallmark of theoretical anti-reason, "the Other" has become the hallmark of practical anti-reason.'[32] Even so, it is difficult to see why it is necessary to describe the thought of *différance* as anti-reason. What it represents more than anything is a willingness to think the limits and the conditions of what we have come to call reason, without presupposing that we know in advance the shape of the resulting package. For such a thinking, the very opposition between reason/anti-reason would be suspect. Returning to the Other, I agree with Rose that it is all too easy to think of Judaism as the sublime Other of modernity. A pure absence is no better than a pure presence. Derrida would agree, but it is precisely the complexity of the linkage between philosophical universality and its specific Greek determination, or the late eighteenth-century German insistence on its Greek determination, and the increasing interest in the construction and deconstruction of that legacy, that allows Judaism an entry, not as the sublime Other of modernity, but as what Wittgenstein would call a reminder. Rose does not, to my knowledge, discuss at any length Derrida's 'Violence and Metaphysics', his longest early essay on Levinas, though I may have missed this (there is one reference to it in *The Broken Middle*). But she would find there a very similar treatment of Levinas by Derrida himself. He writes, for example:

> But if one calls this experience of the infinitely other Judaism (which is only a hypothesis for us), one must reflect upon the necessity in which this experience finds itself, the injunction by which it is ordered to occur as logos, and to reawaken the Greek in the autistic syntax of his own dream.[33]

And, of course, Derrida ends this essay with a quote from Joyce's *Ulysses*: 'Jewgreek is greekjew. Extremes meet.'[34] Rose's reference to *new ethics* seems to elide Derrida and Levinas in their treatment of Judaism when what is more salient is precisely Derrida's suspicion of a Judaic salvation for philosophy. As for the specific treatment of the Other, again, it is the *parallel* between Derrida and Rose that is so striking. For the purity of Levinas' treatment of the Other is precisely one of Derrida's main difficulties with him. It is precisely Derrida's point that the ethical force of references to 'the infinitely other' not only is not compromised by, but actually requires, the recognition that this infinitely other is not an absolute other, that the other is in some respects like me. It is precisely here, we might say, that the concrete questions of community – who is my neighbour, who is my friend (including the question of the status of 'other' animals) – can arise.[35] What Derrida is doing to Levinas is reminding him of aspects of Husserl's analysis of my relation to the Other in *Cartesian Meditations*, chapter 5, the force of which Levinas seemed to have missed.

> Levinas *in fact* speaks of the infinitely other, but by refusing to acknowledge an intentional modification of the ego – which would be a violent and totalitarian act for him – he deprives himself of the very foundation and possibility of his own language. What authorizes him to say 'infinitely other' if the infinitely other does not appear as such in the zone he calls the same...[36]

Derrida's disagreements with Levinas here are crucial, but Rose's designation of *new ethics* presupposes that these differences can be elided. If they cannot be elided, then it is the very account given of *new ethics* itself that lacks concreteness. Rose writes that '*new ethics* amounts to the crisis of representation and modern law'.[37] There may be some truth in that; but my way of unpacking it would be to show that the very idea of 'the crisis of representation', far from being a docile and pliant *explanans*, is the most contested expression in contemporary thought.

Let me briefly mention one or two further ways in which, as I see it, Jacques and Gillian are closer than she thinks. Rose is to be applauded, I think, for refusing to allow philosophy to fall into the hands of any sort of reductive discipline, including sociology, even if we can learn a great deal from Weber and Durkheim about the antinomies of the modern secular world. Proponents of the end of philosophy are then lined up as the enemy, as modern irrationalism, as soldiers or generals in the cause of the destruction of reason. But what self-respecting philosopher would not go through the thought that philosophy had come to an end, or should be brought to an end? Kant agreed, Hegel thought this, Marx ditto, Nietzsche, Russell, Husserl, Heidegger, Levinas, Derrida. End as completion, end as exhaustion, end as goal – there are many ends to philosophy, and many senses of the philosophical project and its limits. The true test of a philosopher is the depth at which he or she engages with this question, and I cannot think that Rose would want to disagree with this. In many ways she is herself an exemplary figure in this respect. But this is equally true of both Heidegger and Derrida, and although it is hard to think of anyone more ferocious than Derrida in his refusal of any simple *step beyond*, his willingness to take risks with the determinability of philosophy's limits has frequently led to misunderstandings. Habermas,[38] for example, thought 'White Mythology'[39] was an argument for the reduction of Philosophy to Literature, when a central claim was the *impossibility of that reduction*. For the very distinction between the literal and the metaphorical is shot through with philosophical conceptualization. And it is also, I think, of considerable interest to read Derrida distantly echoing Hegel's insistence in the Introduction (and the Preface) to the *Phenomenology of Spirit* on the need *to go through* philosophical positions to understand their importance and limitations. Derrida says exactly this about (Husserl's) phenomenology. Much of Derrida's readings are best thought of as working through in this way.

Of course, Rose might well agree with this, but dispute the vision, the philosophical spirit that informs this working through. Here I ought to enter the final phase of these brief remarks, which could be called: *On the difference between the Rosean and the Derridean philosophies.* For it is my thesis, as you will recall, that it is the combination of parallelism and differential philosophical formation that sets up the problems of recognition and misrecognition between Gillian Rose and Jacques Derrida. Derrida's philosophical formation is indissolubly linked with the problems of defending and transforming philosophy as formulated by Husserl and Heidegger, and – after the structuralist revolution wrought by Saussure – Lévi-Strauss and Lacan. Working through this trajectory, what is definitively lost is that belief in the eventual representability of the real that Hegel still believed to be possible, that sense of confidence, if not in ordinary language, then in speculative concepts. Rose continues to believe in a connection between philosophy and social and political theory in which the latter would correct the failings of the former. The philosophers who she sets herself against have simply lost the belief that this way of doing things still makes sense. The question then is whether nihilism is a fearsome opportunity or a symptom. The problem with the symptomatic reading is surely that it reduces philosophy to a contest between powerful symptomatologies.

In a world of angled mirrors, strange shapes are born. Gillian Rose sets herself against Derrida, and everything he stands for. Yet there is a deep perversity in the image she has constructed, as if what he is saying must not be heard. On her map, there is a gulf between her and

Derrida. My bet would be that the distance is not as far as she thinks: Jacquesgillian :: Gillianjacques. Extremes meet?

Conclusion

We have alluded to, without developing, Levinas' inability to read Heidegger, and Habermas' hopelessly misinformed reading of Derrida's 'White Mythology'. We have plotted some of Derrida's early constructions of Heidegger, and their limits, and we have speculated about the structure of misrecognition in his precipitate reading of Heidegger in *Of Spirit*. We have marvelled at Adorno's inability to recognize some of the parallels between his own war on the hegemony of the concept, and Heidegger's move towards the question of Being. Finally, we have scratched our head at Rose's blindness to Derrida's concurrence with her fundamental critique of a certain tendency to abstract otherness in Levinas. Is Freud right? Do we simply need to kill our fathers to find our own place in the sun? And can we only do this if we are blind to what we are doing? Is this ultimately the same thing as the anxiety of influence? What would it be to recognize the necessity of influence? Can we wage war on this anxiety, rather than its projected source? Can we not gratefully attend to our indebtedness? When Heidegger writes about listening (to language) and about thinking as thanking, is he not entering into the conversation at just this point? Is not Derrida's introduction of double reading, his recognition of the necessary failure of authorial mastery, moving along the same lines? Perhaps the deep lesson of misrecognition is that it is perhaps a form of recognition – grasping that the other, to whom one is implacably theoretically opposed, has formulated something disturbingly close to one's own position. One is then faced with a major crisis about the significance of that theoretical background, and all the allegiances it is tied into. The refusal to acknowledge the parallelism spares one all this trouble.

Part III

Unlimited Responsibility

8

Much Obliged

I would like to do a number of things in this chapter: trace the account of *responsibility* that Derrida develops in *The Gift of Death* back to Nietzsche's account of breeding animals with the right to make promises, back to Husserl's sense of an ability to give intuitive redemption to one's claims, and back to Derrida's own previous treatments in 'Force of Law', *The Other Heading*, 'Eating Well', and elsewhere; follow through his account of the gift (and death, sacrifice and the secret) from *Aporias*, *Given Time*, 'Passions', etc.; trace this text to his previous discussions of Heidegger, to Nietzsche's *The Genealogy of Morals*, and Freud's *The Uncanny*; trace through Derrida's discussions of God and religious discourse back to the last chapter of *Of Spirit*, to '*Comment ne pas parler*', and beyond; satisfactorily link Derrida's discourse of the other to that of Lacan and Levinas.

I would like to do these things, and some of these threads are taken up in other chapters, but for the moment the grand synthesis this project represents will have to remain an unfulfilled ambition. What I will do instead is to focus on one or two of Derrida's explicit, powerful and connected claims about responsibility and about God in *The Gift of Death*, to see how we might understand and assess them.[1]

First, in his claim about the shape of the conflict between singular and general responsibility, Derrida argues that

> I can respond only to the one (or to the One), that is, to the other, by sacrificing that one to the other. I am responsible to any one (that is to say, to any other) only by failing in my responsibility to all the others, to the ethical or political generality. And I can never justify this sacrifice, I must always hold my peace about it.[2]

And again:

> There is no language, no reason, no generality or mediation to justify
> this ultimate responsibility which leads me to absolute sacrifice, abso-
> lute sacrifice that is not the sacrifice of irresponsibility on the altar of
> responsibility, but the sacrifice of the most imperative duty (that which
> binds me to the other as a singularity in general) in favor of another
> absolutely imperative duty binding me to every other.[3]

Second, there is Derrida's explicit suggestion about the formal status
of God-talk.

> It is perhaps necessary, if we are to follow the traditional Judeo–
> Christian–Islamic injunction, but also at the risk of turning it against
> the tradition, to think of God and of the name of God without such
> idolatrous stereotyping or representation.[4]
>
> Then we might say: God is the name of the possibility I have of
> keeping a secret that is visible from the interior but not from the
> exterior. Once I can have a secret relationship with myself and not
> tell everything, once there is secrecy and secret witnessing within me
> then what I call God exists . . . God is in me, he is the absolute 'me' and
> 'self', he is that structure of invisible intensity that is called, in Kierke-
> gaard's sense, subjectivity.[5]

It is intriguing to be witness to Derrida's encounter with Kierkegaard. *Prima facie* one might have thought that deconstruction would
take Kierkegaard's oppositions – interior / exterior, objective / subjective – and demonstrate their deep metaphysical indebtedness. Instead
Derrida is clearly intrigued by Kierkegaard's erection of an alternative
economy of thought, one which takes delight in an exaggerated
inversion of traditional privileges (such as: Truth is subjectivity).
Derrida sees Kierkegaard as something of an ally in his own campaign
against good conscience. That he should focus on Kierkegaard's *Fear
and Trembling* can be no surprise. I would like to rehearse Derrida's
argument and raise some questions about it.

Derrida explains Kierkegaard's reasoning as to the paradox involved in Abraham's willingness to sacrifice Isaac in language not
too distant from Kierkegaard's own. It is not enough that Abraham
act genuinely *out of duty* rather than merely in conformity to duty.
Beyond that, his Absolute Duty requires 'a sort of gift or sacrifice', 'a
gift of death'. Both Kierkegaard and Derrida labour mightily to make
us recognize that this Absolute Duty makes a demand on us which
cannot be harmonized (mediated) with the ethical in its ordinary
sense.

Abraham must assume absolute responsibility for sacrificing his son by sacrificing ethics, but in order for there to be a sacrifice the ethical must retain all its value; the love for his son must remain intact, and the order of human duty must continue to insist on its rights.[6]

Derrida is right to emphasize the way in which Kierkegaard stresses that this sacrifice, the grasp of this paradox, takes place neither in public space (language), nor in time. Mediation – that is, a process leading to some resolution – is impossible. The sacrifice occurs at or in an instant which itself cannot be recuperated as a present, as a part of time.

So in the experience of the paradox, Abraham is both himself and not entirely himself. Kierkegaard's subjectivity is not a pure interiority, or if it is interiority, it is one constituted by a relation to an other, and the conflict that Abraham experiences is not between (say) two ordinary principles of duty, which would make him a tragic hero who could, again, work on some sort of reconciliation. It is here that Derrida brings in a reference to 'the absolute singularity of the other, whose name here is God'.[7]

Kierkegaard's account of the Abraham story may seem to depict an extraordinary and extreme occasion, but Derrida suggests that it is also 'the most common thing [something that] the most cursory examination of the concept of responsibility cannot fail to affirm'[8] – as if this could be discharged in truckloads, as if it were not bound up, precisely with paradox.

What puzzles me, however, is how Derrida continues at this point:

> What binds me thus in my singularity to the absolute singularity of the other, immediately propels me into the space or risk of absolute sacrifice.... As soon as I enter into a relation with the other, with the gaze, look, request, love, command or call to the other, I know that I can respond only by sacrificing ethics, that is, by sacrificing what obliges me also to respond, in the same way, in the same instant to all the others.[9]

If I say this claim is *absurd* I might be misunderstood as endorsing Kierkegaard's (or Derrida's) own judgement here, but with this formulation of the paradox, and with the further formulations that Derrida subsequently gives, I have serious unease. Allow me to quote Derrida's own confession:

> By preferring my own work, simply by giving it my time and attention, by preferring my own activity as a citizen or as a professorial and professional philosopher, writing and speaking here in a public

language...I am perhaps fulfilling my duty...But I am sacrificing and betraying at every moment all my other obligations: my obligations to the other others whom I know or don't know...[each and every other deserves, requires response]...in a singular manner.[10]

Later on he writes

I can never justify...the fact that I prefer and sacrifice any one (any other) to the other. I will always be secretive, held to secrecy in respect of this...How would you ever justify the fact that you sacrifice all the cats in the world to the cat that you feed at home every morning for years?[11]

I wonder if I am alone in feeling disturbed by these thoughts – not because I have tried to repress them and now they are returning to haunt me, but disturbed by what one could almost call the hubris involved in them. I am also disturbed by the difficulty of pinning down the role or place of the Other, and consequently the difficulty of linking it back to the Abraham story. Derrida is the philosopher of whom I am perhaps most fond, but agreeing with him here is not the most appropriate form of respect.

First problem: 'I can never justify the fact that I prefer or sacrifice any one (any other) to the other.' Can this be true? Suppose I have promised something to one person, and not to another, in such a way that he relies on my support in ways that others do not. Does that not give me special obligations? Or, suppose one person (or animal) in need is in front of me, and the other is not? What worries me about Derrida's move is that it seems to deny my situatedness, it seems to return us to occupying a universal space in which we could be anywhere. And it is not obvious how to read 'my obligation to the other others, whom I know or don't know, the billions of my fellows (...and animals)'. I could make my worry clearer by asking what are my obligations here? Is it to treat every cat as I treat my own – no better, no worse? No – I *could* treat my own cat better, and could still not 'justify' not applying this ideal standard generally. My concern is that Derrida is de-actualizing obligation. He is giving no privilege to those obligations, precisely that we have not willed, but that we find ourselves in, to those obligations we have voluntarily acquired, to those expectations we have allowed others to have of us. And the thought that there are no fixed boundaries here does not mean that there are none. Hospitality would self-destruct if it were 'infinite'. My point here is that Derrida is engaged in a kind of hyperbolic expansion of obligation which it would be quite as appropriate to consider as an identification with God rather than a response to God in or as the singular other, the other as other. It is worth mentioning various forms of slippage that encourage this move. Let me just describe some of these:

1   *Quantification*: the move from any to all. It is a fallacy to suppose that just because I cannot justify not sharing my loaf with one person rather than another, that I cannot justify not sharing my loaf equally with an army of hungry people. It may not be possible to justify loving this person rather than that, but it is possible to justify not loving everyone.
2   *Justification*. Unless we are holding onto some source of absolute justification, which I thought had long since been abandoned, it is just not true that 'I can never justify this sacrifice'...that 'I will always be secretive'. My justification for teaching my children about poison ivy is that they are my children and I care especially for them. And that's about all. This is not to demonstrate a complacent 'good conscience'. It is not and cannot be an absolute justification, for there can be no such thing. Indeed there is a stronger claim that may be even more plausible – that to describe me as sacrificing all other cats when I feed my own is to mistakenly read my inability to justify this activity as some sort of deficiency. It may just be that justification is not at issue here.
3   *Space and time*. It is possible, of course, to imagine that one dwells no-where and no-when in particular, and this would tend to induce a detachment from special obligations. But to live everywhere is to live nowhere. And to live somewhere at some time is to find oneself with specific obligations.
4   *Good conscience*. The sense that the gaze of all the suffering of the world is upon me would certainly shake me from any good conscience, but it is surely a huge exaggeration of one's own importance.
5   *Silence, and the secret*. Of course, when we are confronted by the vision, often attributed to Hegel, of total openness, total visibility or publicity, it is true that silence, the secret, functions as an interruption, as a form of resistance. But (and again without complacency) the absence of absolute justification does not banish language, it rather makes it more fragile, more open to misunderstanding, etc. Here we should probably remind ourselves of the risk, the uncertainty in language.
6   *Reading Derrida*...'I am sacrificing and betraying at every moment all my other obligations.' I hear the voice of guilt here. And the impossibility of satisfying this anxiety could indeed be

expressed in a paradox. It is not necessary to set up this bondage to an insatiable monster to recognize the importance of doing what one can, which of course is never *enough*, about wider grief and suffering, campaigning for peace, etc. And yet all this would invert the relationship between the ethical and one's infinite obligations – it would return us to a (non-complacent) affirmation of our special obligations, a recognition of our public (ethical) duties, and dispel any complacency about our being able to draw a clear line between them.

Where does that leave us with respect to Kierkegaard? I continue to find a universal interpretation of *Fear and Trembling* unsatisfactory, especially any clear assignation of the ethical, the singular other, etc. Abraham's relation to Isaac is both ethical (universal) and utterly singular, quite apart from his relationship to God. And it is thoroughly bound up (as a relation with his son) to his own self-relatedness. On another occasion it would be possible to pursue a number of short-circuits in Derrida's account – particularly the reference to Abraham as a murderer, or to his sacrifice of Isaac. It seems to be crucial that these things did not in the end happen. When death functions to destabilize, deepen, transform identity, as it does in this case (and in the importantly parallel cases of Hegel's account of the life and death struggle, and Heidegger's account of being towards death), death always appears as a risk, as something offered up, but never completed. The master and slave survive the struggle, Abraham and Isaac walk away from Mt. Moriah, Being-towards-death operates only while I am alive. And in the case of Abraham and Isaac, it seems to be that gift and death function rather differently from the way Derrida suggests. This story is essentially (or at least) a dramatization of the gift of life that Isaac was for Abraham, a gift *acknowledged* by his willingness to return it. Isaac was the unexpected, the unjustified, the impossible *gift* in the first place, and the willingness to sacrifice him was Abraham's grasp of the way the significance of his life, indeed his identity, lay outside himself.

For the most part let me emphasize that at one level Derrida is right about responsibility – right, that is, to insist that it must exceed any prescribable algorithm. But there is so much to be said here. We can talk about the importance of irresponsibility (meaning a super-responsibility beyond the ethical), but while this may be an antidote to a certain kind of 'good conscience' there is a paradox lurking for us here – that it does sound like *a recipe for avoiding a bad 'good conscience'* which would be perilously close to finding a good one – and the further danger remains of a kind of moralization of life, a danger perhaps signalled defiantly in Nietzsche's affirmation of evil.

I would like to turn now to Derrida's remarks about God: 'once I can have a secret relationship with myself and not tell every-thing ... then what I call God exists'; 'he is that structure of invisible interiority that is called in Kierkegaard's sense, subjectivity'.[12]

Here Derrida is echoing and apparently endorsing Jan Patocka's formulation of a God that sustains, or is co-extensive with, a Chris-tianity that has overcome both the orgiastic moment and Platonism, and announces the *mysterium tremendum*, a new sense of responsi-bility, which resides henceforth not in an essence ... accessible to the human gaze, that of the Good and the One [Plato], but in the relation to a supreme, absolute and inaccessible being that holds us in check not by exterior but interior force.[13]

Derrida clearly wants to endorse the structure of this thought, and even to *recognize* God, even if in a way that few theologians would swallow. It opens up a space for a sense of responsibility not wedded to, or protected by, what we could call a narrowly humanistic sense of the subject. Derrida has written that 'responsibility is excessive or it is not a responsibility. A limited, measured, calculable, rationally dis-tributed responsibility is already the becoming *right* of morality.' In his treatment of Kierkegaard, he seems to be trying to show that within Kierkegaard's 'deconstruction' of Christianity there are re-sources for thinking this excess of responsibility, and hence that Christianity (as Patōcka is suggesting) may be seen as contributing to this *stronger* sense of responsibility.

But allow me, for a moment, if I may, to take a step back. Derrida seems to be *defining* God in terms of a structure of (invisible) inter-iority. It looks, at first glance, as though these remarks are continuous with a genre of demystification in which we could include Feuerbach, Nietzsche, Freud and many others.[14] From his earliest writings, Der-rida had diagnosed as a fiction the production of a 'transcendental signified', an entity or value projected outside of language and immune from its workings, and providing some grounding for it – the famous fixed point from which Archimedes could move the world. And this position seemed continuous with Nietzsche's claim that we had not got rid of God if we still believed in grammar – i.e. still believed in there being some sort of ideal underpinning to language. Nietzsche, too, offers us in his *The Genealogy of Morals* a history of responsibility, one which ends with the creation of an animal with the right to make promises. Allow me, if I may, to quote a most celebrated passage, the reading of which Freud kept secret, or repressed or 'fortunately delayed' until he had invented the wheel again:

All instincts that do not discharge themselves outwards *turn inward* –
this is what I call the internalization of man – thus it was that man first
developed what was later called his 'soul'. The entire inner world,
originally as thin as if it were stretched between two membranes,
expanded and extended itself, acquired depth, breadth and height, in
the same measure as outward discharge was inhibited.... Man, from
this point, became pregnant with a future [and is included in the great
dice game of chance].[15]

Nietzsche clearly recognizes that what begins as a form of violence
exercised by an animal on itself ends giving birth to a new kind of
creativity. Bad conscience is an illness *as pregnancy is an illness*. It
eventually leads through asceticism to the ability to recognize the will
to truth itself as a problem. And Derrida, too, seems to want to find in
this interiority the basis for a new resource, a new ground for a
responsibility beyond rules.

When we read what Derrida says about God, we imagine that the
typical response will be to see him as explaining away God, as does
Feuerbach, or Freud, or Nietzsche. And yet, strictly speaking, all
statements of such a form as '*x* is what we mean by God', 'God is
y', can also be understood as grounding and legitimating religious
discourse, even if in a transformed way. I am reminded here of
Derrida's construction of an imaginary dialogue between Heidegger
and certain (advanced) Christian theologians at the end of *Of Spirit*.
When these theologians listen to Heidegger talk of promise, of a new
dawn, beyond a beginning and end of history, etc., they will endorse
his remarks: 'You say the most radical things that can be said when
one is a Christian today.'[16] And when Heidegger talks about
following the path of a 'repetition which crosses the path of the
entirely other in a vertiginous and abyssal way' he is told that this is
exactly what theology has been trying to say. Derrida leaves this
conversation unresolved, as if to say that one cannot in the end decide
between these various options – and I wonder if that is not his
message here too.

We might suppose that the ambivalent or undecidable position in
which Derrida leaves us with respect to God is to be contrasted with
that of Kierkegaard, the overtly religious thinker. When Derrida
defines God in terms of a 'structure of invisible interiority [that
Kierkegaard calls] subjectivity', he seems to be taking what we
might call the psychological reduction of God to an extreme that
Kierkegaard could not himself accept. It is, however, I believe
revealing that Kierkegaard himself is quite capable of putting things
in a very similar way. At the beginning of *The Sickness unto Death*

Kierkegaard argues that the phenomenon of despair demonstrates the impossibility of the idea that the self is *sui generis*, self-constituted. Or rather, what demonstrates it is the fact that not all despair is simply suicidal. We each can and do 'despairingly will to be ourselves' – that is, carry on albeit in despair. His argument is that this can only happen if the self is not just self-related, but if that self-relatedness is itself sustained by a further Power. And the eradication of despair arises when 'by relating itself to its own self and by willing to be itself, the self is grounded transparently in the Power which posited it'.[17] To the extent that this argument is successful, what it does is to argue for a certain mediated structure of self-relatedness to which he gives the name 'Power'. This turns out to be God, but it could be said that the strength of the argument does not rest on that identification – that what Kierkegaard is arguing for is precisely a certain (complex) structure of subjectivity, one in which the power of the other is central.

I understand Derrida to be saying something like this: we cannot think God (and consequently worship, prayer, etc.) outside of the economies and topologies of the subject. God as project, God as introjection, God as hidden, as secret – these point to the most intimate connection between God and the whole topology of the other's relation to the self. If, we ask here about the reality of God – God's independent, external existence, God's existence in space and time – we meet the same kind of difficulties that beset Kant's Aesthetic: What can 'inner' or 'outer' mean if space is (already) a form of intuition? When Kant says famously of the temporalizing schematism of the understanding that it 'is an art concealed in the depths of the human soul whose real modes of activity nature is hardly ever likely to allow us to discover, and to have open to our gaze'[18] – words that pretty *exactly* repeat Derrida's Kierkegaardian location of God – and when we reflect on the strict *impossibility* of such formulations as 'depths', 'real mode of activity', 'nature' etc., we may begin to see how God may never be able to be disentangled from these topological (and, as we see in *The Gift of Death*, photological) schemas.

The question I am left with is how to think this whole topology of alterity. Surely the appearance of paradox, of allegorical expressions, of (clearly) imaginary spaces, etc., are attempts to *represent* relations whose complexity exceeds the standard logics of representation? Perhaps when we talk about an inexhaustible, infinite or absolute responsibility, we confuse the shape of a certain openness to the call of the other, with an impossibility of limiting, or specifying the content of that openness. This reworks my concern about the slide from *any* to *all* – the obligation to share our meal with anyone is not an obligation to share it with everyone. So our obligation is not, I suggest, infinite; it is instead indeterminable. And while thinking of the other as a certain permanent space within the Self *suggests* a positively infinite obligation, this is the consequence of the crudeness of our topological thinking.

In conclusion I would like to echo some of the thoughts of the French thinker who in my view runs Levinas a close second as the figure who haunts Derrida in his work – namely Sartre. Derrida has been relatively silent about Sartre, but one wonders sometimes whether Sartre does not play a secret role in Derrida's self understanding. (Think of Sartre's critique of Husserl's account of the ego, his French reworking of Heidegger, his deep suspicion of good conscience, his hyperbolic affirmation of responsibility, his literary ambition and his political involvements.)

In 1964 (the same year as Derrida published 'Violence and Metaphysics', on Levinas) Sartre wrote a paper 'The Singular Universal'[19] for a Unesco conference – *Kierkegaard Living* – in which he presents Kierkegaard (who, it is worth noting in passing, understood his own life as a sacrifice) as *living on* precisely as Christ might live on in revealing 'that each man is all mankind as the singular universal', showing, against Hegel, 'temporalisation as the transhistorical dimension of history. Each of is Søren as adventure.'[20] He continues, 'Thus Kierkegaard's depth, his manner of remaining other within me, without ceasing to be mine, is today's Other, my real contemplation'; and 'In each of us he gives and refuses himself, as he did during his life, [as is for me] a witness that *becoming an atheist* is a long and difficult undertaking.'[21]

What is both charming and subtle in Sartre's position here, one which may perhaps be Derrida's unavowed secret, is that the place of God, for this atheist, the interiorized Other with whom there is unending conversation, is not a restored Father, but rather Kierkegaard 'himself', and indeed that pantheon of extraordinary humans, many now ghosts, who have triumphantly affirmed, puzzled over and denounced God, and to whose writing we undoubtedly have an undischargable responsibility.

9

Comment ne pas manger: Deconstruction and Humanism

I

As we have seen, Derrida's cat, and his obligations to cats throughout the world, is one of the sites at which the idea of an infinite obligation arises in his work. Coming to terms with the non-human animal, or indeed, knowing when to leave one's terms aside, is perhaps the reef on which the originality of both Heidegger's and Levinas' thinking founders. Derrida's repeated charge against Heidegger is that when it comes to his treatment of the animal, the revolution in thought comes to a halt, and the deep currents of humanism reassert themselves. In this chapter[1] I will be arguing that something similar befalls Derrida himself, in his long discussion with Jean-Luc Nancy: 'Eating Well'.[2]

I would first like to explain why this repeated failure matters. If one thinks of philosophy as an elucidating exploration of the ways in which we already think, then we might not be surprised to find a moral and metaphysical line being drawn between Man and the Animal. A Rortyean neopragmatism would support this: we are men, how could we want to do any more than write and think as men? Indeed, if we consider, as we must, the importance of history, culture, tradition, and language, perhaps we should declare all our interests and involvements. Our philosophical output could all then be subtitled, for example: What it is like to be a WASP [white, Anglo-Saxon, Protestant]. And Rorty encourages just such modesty. If it were not for the fact that this project is dialectically unstable, we would be looking the end of philosophy in the face. The dialectical instability arises from the fact that pragmatist self-declarations are already modes of reflection that, as such, contaminate and exceed their proclaimed limitations. To be able to define one's identity and the limited validity of one's claims is already to move in a space in which those limitations are being breached. There are other instabilities too. There is no one map of the ways in which we plot the animal/human relationship. The consequences of sentimentality towards animals, of our fear or disgust of our symbolic deployment, of our culinary habits, are such as to give us a laminated set of superimposed maps of that relationship. Further instabilities arise when we begin to think through the implications of both the words Man and Animal. Each suggests an unproblematic universalization. So, Man includes Woman, and occludes racial, historical and other differences; and Animal covers everything from cows to caterpillars, apes to anchovies, and more. The instability arises not just because of species diversity, but because its obvious supposed unimportance makes one realize that these terms are, to put it bluntly, metaphysical categories, with all sorts of police work to do, and not simply useful conceptual tools, biological generalizations, etc. If they are metaphysical categories, then they are subject to the deepest forms of scrutiny that philosophy can devise.

Philosophy cannot just be an elucidation of the functioning of our concepts of categories; even the very word 'our' is already problematic. It is problematic whether or not we are explicit about how we intend it. If we are, we make philosophy into *Weltanschauungstheorie* [an account of a world view], in which its critical edge vanishes. If we are blind to the question of 'we' or 'our', we run the risk of projecting a parochialism.

I am claiming that philosophy has to maintain a critical function if it is to avoid a fate worse than death – that of having actually died but seeming to live on in an emasculated form. So, the first reason why this failure to think the animal or animality matters is that it is symptomatic of a wider failure in the philosophical project, or at least any conception of that project for which a serious re-examination of the whole man/animal nexus would be close to a top priority. And, to be quite clear here, the suspicion is that it is within this dyad (among others, such as man/woman, man/God) that the difficulties of thinking, rethinking and defining man are distributed.

The Animal question also matters for practical reason. If the fate of non-human animals (and here I include both individuals and species) is dependent directly and indirectly on the actions and technologies of humans, and if these actions and technologies continue at least in part because they seem justified, and if humanism of some sort is always the framework for such justifications, then practical consequences could flow from a persistent scrutiny of such humanism. Allow me, if I may, a few brief reflections on this bit of scaffolding. First, of course, the argument is only as strong as its premises, and it might be argued that I have more faith than I should both in reason and in its practical relevance. How far do our animal practices survive because they seem justified? Would anything change if we could no longer justify them? The current coexistence of various forms of horrific interhuman violence round the world, with a massive moral and political consensus that condemns it, is not a hopeful precedent. And the manipulability of international law to justify counter-terror gives us no clear promise that right will prosper. Worst of all, there is more than a faint worry that the very concern with justification might not survive the deconstruction of humanism. Our treatment of the animal kingdom, in other words, might eventually be recognized to be the acid test of our true humanity only at the point at which that value has lost all credibility.

Compare the following argument: humans are said to be fundamentally different from animals. But if we are so different, why do we act so *bestially* towards animals? It could be said that we are not acting bestially: morality has always had a practical dimension, reflecting human and other more specific interests. Reason is and should only be a slave to morality. Does this not mean sacrificing critical reflection at the altar of meat-eating? I will return to this issue.

Derrida's most powerful readings of philosophers have been devoted to certain of those – I have in mind especially Husserl, Heidegger and Levinas – who have attempted a revolution in philosophy, who have diagnosed a certain systematic difficulty, inadequacy or failure in the tradition, and tried productively to overcome it. The shape of Derrida's readings of these thinkers is such as to bring out recursive difficulties in the radicality of their new beginnings. The point of these readings, however, has often been misunderstood. People have talked about Derrida's deconstruction of Husserl, his critique of Heidegger, etc. What is very clear, however, is that what is called deconstruction did not fall fully formed from the sky onto Derrida's desk, but has been developed through these various readings. Derrida is deeply committed to a version of the very philosophical radicality that Husserl, Heidegger and Levinas attempted, but one that builds in a certain recursive openness as an antidote to the natural tendencies towards closure of any method. And here I would explicitly link Derridean deconstruction to phenomenology's inaugurating opposition to naturalism and psychologism, and I would link it to Heidegger's allergy to vitalism, life-philosophy, and philosophical anthropology, and to Levinas's rejection of ontology, and the principle of totality. Deconstruction is, *inter alia*, a most powerful attempt to preserve philosophy against plausible complacencies. What it preserves philosophy *for* is a certain capacity to respond, and particularly to respond to what has not been adequately schematized, formulated, etc., perhaps to the inadequacy of any schematization or formulation. In this way, philosophy's critical function makes way for something more receptive and responsive.

It is in this context that the question of humanism arises as a question. It has a curious history within twentieth-century European philosophy. In his *Existentialism and Humanism*,[3] Sartre chose to interpret existentialism as a form of humanism when the alternative was nihilism, even if he was careful to distinguish it from such essentializing humanisms as Christianity and communism. He later repudiated this essay. Heidegger, on the other hand, in his *Letter on Humanism*[4] sees the humanistic tradition as preserving a mistaken primacy of subjectivity against his own more primordial analysis of man's relation to Being. But it is clear from his lectures in the early thirties (as Derrida[5] and Krell[6] have shown) that Heidegger continued to struggle with the question of how properly to characterize man or Dasein in relation to animality without the traditional appeal to reason, or subjectivity or language. Derrida argues that Heidegger's thinking is in the end circumscribed within 'a certain anthropocentric or even humanist teleology'.[7] The lizard lies on the rock, but does not know it as a rock. The lizard has a world, but it is poor in world (*Weltarm*); it has a world in a privative or deprived sense. Heidegger has shifted the question of the animal away from the question of whether or not the animal possesses some special feature, to the question of the animal's fundamental relation to the world. But as soon as the word poor (*arm*) appears, we have a comparison, in which man's relation to the world sets the standard. And when Rilke talks about the fundamental openness of the animal to the world – a kind of innocent vulnerable 'being-out-there-amongst' – Heidegger will insist that there is still a missing 'as such'. Of Levinas, I will only say that the tale of missed opportunity, of aborted radicality, repeats itself. The thinker of otherness, of the most radical alterity, of the unassimilability of the other, can accommodate the animal only by analogy with the human, and indeed constructs the distinctiveness of the human – the unreasonable animal – by contrast with the struggle for survival of the animal, the aim of whose being 'is being itself'.[8] For a thinker for whom phenomenology is the jumping-off point rather than a continuing method, it is revealing that he recognizes the value of 'a specific phenomenological analysis' of our experience of the animal.[9] Reflecting the way in which the animal serves so often as a foil against which we think the human, one is tempted to say here, as elsewhere, and with apologies to Voltaire, that if animals had not existed it would have been necessary to invent them.

I have described deconstruction as the most powerful attempt to preserve philosophy against plausible complacencies. Derrida's diagnosis of Heidegger's thinking as anthropocentric, even humanist, is not, I think, offered in the spirit of any deconstructive triumphalism. Rather it suggests that whatever we may have thought of Heidegger's radicality with regard to the tradition, he has not succeeded in escaping from the very anthropocentrism that substituting Dasein for man in *Being and Time* was to have signalled. There is no suggestion that this would be easy, or that Heidegger's failure is not instructive. But where does it leave us?

It is perhaps worth considering a seemingly pessimistic verdict at this point – namely, that anthropocentrism in some sense is *logically* unavoidable. If Heidegger were the latest in a line of thinkers who had attempted to square the circle and failed, the proper response would not be to try harder, or find some more subtle, more radical approach, but to lay to rest the whole sad episode. But the sense in which it is logically unavoidable is precisely, and for that very reason, an empty sense. The logically unavoidable sense is this: that any account we come up with of 'our' relation to 'animals' will be from 'our' point of view. The challenge, however, remains to construct a point of view that is not *just* 'ours', one that allows us to practise a subtle and multilayered differentiation among animals as well as between various animals and various humans, one which is not subordinated to any hidden teleology.

Against the idea that some sort of anthropocentrism is unavoidable, we do seem to be able to imagine ways of setting aside certain aspects of our being human. Yet, it might be observed, the kind of abstinence from anthropocentric projection described here is something to which no non-human animal could even begin to aspire. Surely the aspiration to it, let alone success in achieving such a rare and complex attitude, would, paradoxically, provide the best possible proof for the superiority of the human species. This is a fallacy. No one is disputing that there are many things that many humans can do that no other animal can do, and that there are many attitudes and capacities of humans that non-human animals do not share. What is being disputed is the move from these and other facts to the judgement of animals as only partial realizations of the human ideal, as subhuman, rather than as importantly different.

If I am right, then, about these pessimistic verdicts, we do not need to conclude that Heidegger's failure to avoid humanism is trivial. If I am right about deconstruction, it is just such a doctrine as humanism that qualifies for the status of a plausible complacency. Plausible, clearly; and complacency in the philosophical sense of being a structurally invisible commitment that as such resists critical interrogation.

What does Derrida have to say about the animal? To answer this question I will turn to the extended discussion between Derrida and Nancy ('Eating Well'). I will argue that Derrida fails deconstruction at a critical moment, and that the question of a humanist teleology hangs, if not over deconstruction, over Derrida's failure of nerve.[10]

2

Derrida: 'I am a vegetarian in my soul.'
(Cerisy Conference, 1993)

I would like to begin this section by quoting Derrida's opening to *The Other Heading*.

> A colloquium always tries to forget the risk it runs: the risk of being just another one of those events where, in good company, one strings together a few talks or speeches on some general subject.[11] If this meeting had any chance of escaping repetition, it would be only insofar as some imminence, at once a chance and a danger, exerted pressure on us.[12]

Allow me, then, to invoke some of the silent or virtual or possible future conditions that exert 'pressure' on us today:

1 From the point of view of natural science, the animal / man boundary is already being breached through genetic engineering.[13] Could not the practical consequences be as great as splitting the atom?
2 Biological diversity is being threatened faster than the concept is becoming current, with the destruction of habitats (especially rainforest).
3 Our concerns with each of these are themselves bound up with a curious technoscientific displacement, in which we humans come to see our fate, indeed our very being, increasingly bound up with our biological existence.
4 We humans live, still live, despite significant dietary shifts, in a carnivorous society, one fed largely by the biofactory flesh of non-

humans. This is not a secret, but it is usually treated as a background truth.

Philosophy is not practical in the way that engineering and medicine is, but it does and can respond to what presses. Is it enough for us to say that the pressure, the imminence, is just truth, or philosophy itself? What would it mean for us to have escaped repetition? We perhaps never think except in response to such imminences, pressures or, as we might say, calls or appeals.

Much of Derrida's recent work – in *The Other Heading*,[14] in 'Force of Law',[15] in the 'Afterword: Toward an Ethics of Discussion' in *Limited Inc*[16] and in 'Eating Well'[17] – has been devoted to thinking through what we might call the ethical dimension of deconstruction in terms of justice or, more frequently, responsibility; where responsibility is thought in terms of a response or openness to what does not admit of straightforward decision.[18] If deconstruction is, or will be, or will or may have been, responsibility (or justice), the urgency of *this* moment may be located in particular topics, issues, etc. But it is also to be found in our continuing response to the call of philosophy itself, reactivating perhaps a certain tradition of philosophy as responsibility. Not everyone will share my sense that the fate of philosophy and our own capacity for philosophizing is bound up with that of deconstruction. However, the ethical and political dimension Derrida has explicitly given to deconstruction answers at least those critics who have thought it alien to such concerns.

In order to assess Derrida's discussion of the problem of the animal in 'Eating Well', I need to show how the concept of responsibility is developed into such a central term.

I have already remarked on the formative influence on Derrida of his reading of Husserl; and Husserl's linkage of philosophical method, its historical and cultural significance, with the idea of responsibility, is well known. Responsibility for Husserl meant living and thinking within the possibilities of reactivation of our original intuitive grasp of phenomena, even if his idea of a community of scholars living in 'the unity of a common responsibility', contributing to 'a radically new humanity made capable of an absolute responsibility to itself on the basis of absolute theoretical insights', is now honoured only in the breach.

Heidegger's meditations on the task of thinking at the end of philosophy, on the plight of the West, on the call, the appeal, are moving in the same element. Heidegger's destruction of the tradition, of ontology, is in the service of what is first a programme of renewal. Later, less of a programme.

Derrida writes

> Now we must ourselves be responsible for this disclosure of the modern
> tradition. We bear the responsibility for this heritage, right along with
> the capitalizing meaning that we have of it. We did not choose this
> responsibility, it imposes itself upon us, and in an even more imperative
> way, in that it is, as other, and from the other, the language of our
> language.[19]

The filiation is clear. Derrida is *taking responsibility for responsibility*
as Husserl had originally laid it out, rethinking reactivation in terms
of language rather than intuition, rethinking language in terms of the
trace, chance, the proper name, signature, rather than in Heidegger's
more poetized ontological way, and insisting on the original displacement wrought by the other. But he conceives of the other, beyond
Levinas, not as limited to the other man, but as the dimension of
initial and permanent ruination of all presence. Being responsible for
responsibility, reactivation, it is in such expressions that the importance for deconstruction of the phenomenological tradition in its
broadest sense appears.

The relation between responsibility and language is an enduring
theme for this tradition at many levels. It is a central issue, for
example, in judging Heidegger's now infamous 'Rectoral Address'.
Our first dismay is at what he is saying; our second at his saying it. But
perhaps the lingering worry is about his willingness to use a language
invented to facilitate reinterpreting the texts of the tradition for
overtly political purposes. *The Other Heading* raises this same question about Derrida. When he writes 'it is necessary to make ourselves
the guardians of an idea of Europe...',[20] it is not difficult to feel a
certain astonishment; but what Derrida has done is to enter the realm
of public discourse by converting the old principle of writing under
erasure into an insistence on bringing to the surface the aporetic
structure of central philosophical concepts. Instead of new words,
or old words with displaced meanings, Derrida works to develop
the contradictory implications of concepts central to the tradition.
Responsibility is one of these concepts and, like 'justice', it is privil-
eged in being able to guide our very reception of it. When Derrida
writes 'Now, we must ourselves be responsible for this discourse of
the modern tradition',[21] he is of course putting a weight on a word
that is part of the modern tradition. When he writes 'we bear the
responsibility for this heritage',[22] his words are inseparable from the
tradition itself. Responsibility is obligation, burden, duty, etc. No
words are forbidden, if ever they were. Indeed, if anything, Derrida

is increasingly willing to draw the most traditional words within his embrace – because it is the disturbing embrace of ex-appropriation, of dislocation. For each word he chooses, deconstruction will be its undoing, and its restoration as a word with which to think. The word 'responsibility' is a case in point; there could be no more potent entrance into ethical and political discourse.

Although many people will associate responsibility with moralism or with some neo-Kantian account of the subject, neither of these could be further from what Derrida means. Accordingly, I will try to get clearer about what is at stake in what he means by 'responsibility' by reconstructing what it is hard not to call Derrida's philosophical 'programme' as laid out in 'Eating Well'.

The full-title of Nancy's interview was '"Eating Well", or the Calculation of the Subject – an interview with Jacques Derrida'.[23] We could talk here about the interview format, and its limitations and opportunities, but I see nothing here to caution against taking these formulations wholly seriously.

First the context. The 1970s and 1980s in particular hosted numerous pronouncements of 'the death of the subject'. The general idea was that the concept of the human subject, as agent, as seat of consciousness or experience, or as origin, had lost its capacity to underwrite philosophical inquiry. Saussure, Levi-Strauss, Foucault, Lacan were obvious influences here. *Who Comes After the Subject?*, the book in which the Derrida/Nancy interview appears, followed a conference devoted to discussion of how to fill the supposed gap in the conceptual map. In beginning to answer the question 'Who comes after the subject?' Derrida takes the opportunity – naturally – to raise the level of discussion from that of the absence or presence of the subject, the life or death of the 'subject', both to the broader philosophical tradition dealing with consciousness and subjectivity (from Descartes onwards) and to the more recent trajectory of the phenomenological tradition which, within Husserl's work, already came to recognize an essential passivity of the subject in the studies of passive genesis. And interestingly, especially for those who despair of references to *the* Western metaphysical tradition, Derrida makes it clear that to speak of 'the' Subject at least, is a fiction, a fable – it always has been a scene of real differentiation. Moreover – and in ways that recall the ambivalent imaginary conversation with Christian theologians within which Derrida suspended Heidegger at the end of his book *Of Spirit* – he sets up, without resolving, a tension between those who would try to reconstruct a subject 'as the finite experience of non-identity to self', and those who would 'still have reservations about the term'. What is striking, however, for all this, is the way

Derrida sets up our relationship to the Heideggerian legacy, and all its dangers. It is in the recognition of these dangers that Derrida answers those critics who would charge deconstruction with political and ethical irresponsibility. I am reminded again of Husserl, comparing those who are afraid of solipsism with children afraid of what is lurking in a dark corner. We should not turn away, he argues, but shine the light into the corner.[24]

Derrida's view of the Heideggerian legacy on the subject has the following crucial double dimension. He writes:

> I believe in the force and the necessity (and therefore in a certain irreversibility) of the act by which Heidegger *substitutes* a certain concept of Dasein for a concept of subject still too marked by the traits of the being as *Vorhanden*, and *hence by an interpretation of time*, and insufficiently questioned in its ontological structure. [Italics in original][25]

Heidegger's thinking, in other words, is a necessary step in a process which it does not complete – which in brief we could call the deconstruction of the subject. Not only is the process incomplete, but its completion is internally threatened because 'the point of departure for the existential analytic remains a tributary of precisely what it puts in question'.

Despite Heidegger's avoidance of the words 'subject', 'consciousness' and so on, what Derrida calls the 'logic' of Heidegger's thought still betrays a commitment to 'the axiom of the subject'. I quote again:

> The chosen point of departure . . . is the entity that *we* are, we the *questioning* entities, we who, in that we are open to the question of Being and of the being of the entity we are, have this relation to self that is lacking in everything that is not *Dasein*. [Italics in original][26]

In other words, Derrida is insisting on the persistence and domination in Heidegger of the value of the proper, of self-relatedness, of identity, of presence, in the very way in which Heidegger sets out on his journey. This is not, of course, news. (See chapter 6 above.) What makes it important is that Derrida both restates despite everything the necessity of Heidegger's moves, and affirms the seriousness of their consequences for ethics and politics. So Derrida's response to Heidegger's politics is that Heidegger did not go far enough and his challenge to us is to rework – dare one say reactivate – Heidegger's own origin. This is how Derrida puts the question, and I should add that it seems to me to quite successfully lay out Derrida's philosophical programme:

First, where we stand with Heidegger:

> [T]he time and space of this displacement opened up a gap, marked a gap, they left fragile, or recalled the essential ontological fragility of the ethical, juridical, and political foundations of democracy and of every discourse that one can oppose to national socialism.[27]

Second,

> Can one take into account the necessity of the existential analytic and what it shatters in the subject and turn towards an ethics, a politics (are these words still appropriate?), in any case towards an other type of responsibility that safeguards against what a moment ago I very quickly called the 'worst'?[28]

It is here that Derrida makes an extraordinary claim. The claim is that through his reading of Heidegger in *Of Spirit*, and with some assistance from others (especially Françoise Dastur), he had located a point within Heidegger which breached the original primacy given to the question: Heidegger's reference to a *Zusage*, an original promise or pledge of language, a moment in Heidegger parallel to Husserl's discovery of passive genesis.

The importance of the claim is that this *Zusage* (Derrida will also speak of an original affirmation, or a 'Yes') displaces the priority or privilege accorded by philosophy, and indeed by most of Heidegger's own work, to the question, and hence to questioning. If we can link the privilege of the question (interrogation) to that of the subject (who sets the questions, insists on answers) then anything that displaces that privilege will perhaps open up a new (post-deconstructive) determination of the responsibility of the 'subject'.

In beginning to answer the question 'Who comes after the subject?', Derrida as usual, and in the context, quite appropriately problematizes the question itself. The very word 'who' already suggests something human, does it not? In trying to pin him down, Nancy provokes one of the longest responses.

I would like to draw attention to his references to calculation and excess, for it is here that the concept of responsibility enters. Traditional dissatisfaction with Derrida's line of argument has often run along these lines: What is at stake in thinking of the subject is indeed its relation to ethical and political questions. In particular it has commonly been suggested that as the central category of both the ethical and the political is action, and as action requires agency, and as all agency requires a subject that can get it together, Derrida's contribution here is negative, nihilistic. Deconstruction is the death

of the subject, the death of politics, and the utter irresponsibility of
thought.

Derrida's response is classical in its form – that the subject is not just
a given agency whose potency might be impugned by sceptical reflection, but a deeply complex concept inseparable from networks of
concepts, from 'a multiplicity of traditional discourses', from 'the
whole conceptual machinery'. Now we could conclude that Derrida
is saying that as we cannot decide what our responsibilities are until
we have sorted out all these conceptual confusions, we must act
cautiously with what Jean-Luc Nancy later calls a 'provisional morality'. But this is not Derrida's position at all. Rather he converts the
condition in which we find ourselves from a negative to a positive one.
It is not that we cannot yet sort out or calculate our responsibilities;
rather, to believe that we could do this would be to fail to grasp a
responsibility that exceeds all calculation. Derrida identifies the spirit
of calculation (classically represented by such Utilitarians as Bentham
– whose motto was said to have been 'Let us calculate' – but also
anyone who could prescribe a hierarchy of duties would also have a
calculating machine) with that of the subject itself: 'the subject is also a
principle of calculability'. We see later the shapes that the incalculable
will take, but it is worth pausing at this particularly sharp formulation:

> I believe that there is no responsibility, no ethico-political decision that
> must not pass through the trials of the incalculable or the undecidable.
> Otherwise everything would be reducible to calculation, program,
> causality, and at best 'hypothetical imperative'.[29]

I will return shortly to the serious question this raises. Derrida's
response to the charge of political impotence was to argue for a two-
stage responsibility – both of relentless questioning – following out
the structure of predicates traditionally associated with the concept of
subject, and their linkage to self-presence, but also a beyond of
questioning, a vigil. We have, of course, been here before. But the
turn that it makes in his work here is most important. Let me focus on
just one sentence:

> Such a vigil leads us to recognize the processes of *difference*, trace,
> iterability, ex-appropriation . . . at work everywhere . . . well beyond
> humanity.[30]

Heidegger used the language of Being, of Dasein, to try to avoid
traditional humanistic formulations. Perhaps unsuccessfully. Husserl's
epoché too was, in principle, capable of an extreme radicalization,

opening up a sphere of transcendental consciousness that was in principle quite as much non-human as human. And in the reference to this 'well beyond humanity', Derrida signals that he too will be trying to overcome the silent humanism to which Heidegger and Husserl in all their radicality succumbed. Derrida is saying that if we already know or determine the call of the other as human, then we have failed to understand its radicality. It is not another device in the humanistic programme. It is not, in that or any other sense, programmable, co-optable.

To violently abbreviate Derrida's story, we could say that, in his view, Heidegger rules out from the beginning the possibility that 'the call heard by Dasein [might] come originally to or from the animal... [that]... the voice of the friend be that of an animal',[31] and, as he says, Heidegger follows Aristotle in denying that we could have a responsibility towards the living in general. Even Levinas, in this respect, for all his apparent radicality seems to be following all too carefully the contours of the human, as I have suggested.

At this point it is not unusual for people to say (or to think and then refuse to say) '... but this is not surprising; we are human! Is it so odd that our thought reflects this?' It is worth spelling out the difficulties with this response: 'we are human'. For all its obviousness, it is an extraordinary remark. I will make two observations:

1 The very issue of what it is to be human is precisely what is at issue deep down in all of philosophy. To assert it in this way is to refuse philosophy, to refuse philosophical reflection, and much more.
2 It has a certain formality to it, which means it can be rewritten 'we are male', 'we are white', 'we are European', on the one hand, with whatever self-justifying consequences are meant to follow. But equally, 'we are living beings', 'we are animals'. In other words, the performative force of the claim is radically undercut by the equally plausible substitutions it allows. Perhaps when it is repeated, we should add 'all-too-human'.

3

Perhaps, however, we are missing something.

It is Derrida's thesis that a particular discourse, or a range of discourses, can be identified here. We are beings locked into a carno-phallogocentric structure of subjectivity, governed by sacrificial discourse. And if this does not determine what it is to be human, it does describe the structure of Western humanistic subjectivity.

What Derrida is doing here is at the very least drawing the question of the animal within what I have called the programme of the 'deconstruction of the subject', and in effect saying that we cannot pursue the responsibilities it enjoins without this incorporation. It is instructive, of course, and yet perhaps as necessary as it is a limitation, that Derrida uses the words 'animal' or 'the animal' – as if this was not already a form of deadening shorthand. Human / animal (or man / animal) is of course one of a set of oppositions which anaesthetizes and hierarchizes at the very same time as it allows us to continue to order our lives. And when man / god was still a good, working opposition, it too could be drawn into the game. What man is to god, animal is to man (and indeed woman has been said to be to man – let us say, in each case dependent beings). But I must break off. My point is just this: there are no animals 'as such', but rather an extraordinary variety of living beings that in the animal alphabet would begin with ants, apes, arachnids, antelopes, aardvarks, anchovies, alligators, americans, australians...

Our responsibility exceeds the limits of calculation; and, if Derrida is right, it is excessive or nothing. Such a list as this is a form of witness. But I am deviating from the frame within which Derrida's discussion is set. Allow me, if I may, to return to it. Derrida defines the sacrificial structure of

> [T]he whole canonized or hegemonic discourse of Western metaphysics or religion, in which the most original form that this discourse might assume today [as discourses that leave] a place open, in the very structure of these discourses (which are also 'cultures') for a non-criminal putting-to-death. Such [he continues] are the executions of ingestion, incorporation, or introjection of the corpse.[32]

But this sacrificial operation takes place both symbolically and actually (and in the case of our treatment of many animals, both). I will not rehearse the way in which he shows how Heidegger and Levinas replicate this structure; his reference to the complicity of 'Heidegger's obstinate critique of vitalism' is particularly illuminating. Suffice it to say that Derrida offers us here a massive project in which the deconstruction of the subject (i.e. the human subject) would be linked to eating flesh, virility, taking possession of nature, the privilege of the head, and the head of state – the general scheme of dominance condensed in that ugly neologism carnophallogocentrism.

> Th[is] subject does not want just to master and possess nature actively. In our cultures, he accepts sacrifice and eats flesh.[33]

Aware that I risk a half-digested regurgitation, I would add that Derrida also alludes to a psychoanalytical graft of a whole discourse on interiorization which would account not only for the formation of such subjects, but also symbolically for the religious and philosophical dreams of interiorization (sublimation, appropriation, etc.). To pursue all this here would be to bite off more than we could chew.

There will be some, I'm sure, who have concluded that my response to Derrida is very far from being an openness to an excessive responsibility and much closer to that of the worst kind of carnivorous ingestion. But, of course, Derrida is not arguing for vegetarianism at all. For the way he sets up the issue is such as to incorporate, interiorize, the actual eating of animals inside the symbolic eating of anything by anyone. The title of the paper, 'Bien manger', is very difficult to translate: *Il faut bien manger* means straightforwardly 'we have to eat', and perhaps less obviously 'we have to eat well'. The *bien*, in other words, operates first as an emphatic, and only more obscurely as an adverb. So, many of the translations here are as ambiguous as Derrida's attitudes to other animals are ambivalent.

We could summarize how this interview ends in the following way: A pure openness to the other is impossible – *and certainly* in this culture. We can no more step out of carnophallogocentrism to some peaceable kingdom than we can step out of metaphysics. Put another way, violence of a sort, 'eating others', is not an option, but a general condition of life, and it would be a dangerous fanaticism (or quietism) to suppose otherwise. The issue is not *whether we eat, but how.*[34]

And if we try to fill out what eating well would consist in, what then? Derrida seems to be replacing Heidegger's *mitsein* (a deep Being-with) and Levinas' conception of the subject as hostage, by the idea that 'one never eats entirely on one's own' – a 'rule offering infinite hospitality'.

Derrida shows how these considerations open onto a vast range of questions about bioethics, the state's attempts to regulate medical advances, etc. I will not pursue these here, but I would pause for a moment with the claim that 'one never eats alone', for it is unclear who the others are here. Words like 'hospitality' sound human, wars (of religion) sound human too. And one does wonder whether Derrida is not reverting to the very humanism he has tried to outflank.

In other respects, too, Derrida's argument is deeply disappointing and needs careful attention. First he assimilates – there is no other word for it – real and symbolic sacrifice, so that real sacrifice (killing and eating flesh) becomes an instance of symbolic sacrifice. With this change of focus, the question of eating (well) can be generalized in such a way as to leave open the question of real or symbolic sacrifice.

And to the extent that, in this culture, sacrifice in the broad (symbolic) sense seems unavoidable, there would seem to be little motivation for practical transformations of one's engagement in sacrificial behaviour. Derrida does have one overriding concern, which sometimes seems equivalent to all he says about responsibility, and it is a concern that would align him with all the great diagnosers of human self-deception – and that is the concern to avoid 'good conscience', at almost all costs. To suppose that one could know one's responsibility (and act on it) would be 'good conscience' – however heavy the burden you took on. Good conscience would allow that my responsibility be calculable, and hence limited, but everything Derrida says about responsibility points in the opposite direction. Responsibility is primarily a willingness and capacity to respond, hence an indeterminable openness – and it is here that Derrida parts company with vegetarianism. Non-cannibalistic cultures are still symbolically cannibalistic. 'Vegetarians, too, partake of animals, even of men. They practise a different mode of denegation.'[35]

A carnivorous diet, it is true, is only the most visible and violent front of our undeclared war on the creatures with whom we share the planet. Although Derrida may seem to be bringing deconstruction down to earth when he says, for example, that 'deconstruction is justice',[36] this formula actually reinforces the separation between deconstruction and any particular concrete practice. Deconstruction is a practice of vigilance and cannot, as such, become some sort of alternative ethical seal of approval. Why then am I tempted to declare, in the face of Derrida's sidestep on this issue, that 'vegetarianism is deconstruction'? 'Vegetarianism', like any progressive position, can become a finite symbolic substitute for an unlimited and undelimitable responsibility – the renegotiation of our Being-towards-other animals. But it can also spearhead a powerful, practical, multidimensional transformation of our broader political engagement. Derrida's ambivalence towards vegetarianism seems to rest on the restricted, cautious assessment of its significance – one that would allow vegetarians to buy good conscience on the cheap. But Derrida does not thereby avoid entanglement in the paradoxes of 'good conscience'. For the avoidance of that widening path of resistance to violence that is vegetarianism could end up preserving – against the temptations of progressive practical engagement – the kind of good conscience that too closely resembles a 'beautiful soul'.

The question of the other animal is an exemplary case of responsibility in Derrida's sense – even if for that very reason it may seem too good. It is an exemplary case because once we have seen through our self-serving anthropocentric thinking about other animals, we are and should be left wholly disarmed, ill-equipped to calculate our proper response. And exemplary because the other animal is the Other par excellence, the being who or which exceeds my concepts, my grasp, etc.

Derrida is reported to have said at the Cerisy Conference in the summer of 1993 that 'I am a vegetarian in my soul'.[37] The proper place for vegetarianism is perhaps not in the soul but in a complex reworking of the investments of the oral sphincter and all its personal and political ramifications. Carnophallogocentrism is not a dispensation of Being towards which resistance is futile, it is a mutually reinforcing network of powers, schemata of domination and investments that has to reproduce itself to stay in existence. Vegetarianism is not just about substituting beans for beef, it is – at least potentially – a site of proliferating resistance to that reproduction. If we allow the imminences and pressures (and ghosts and cries and suffering) to which I have been yielding to have their say, we might well end up insisting that 'deconstruction is vegetarianism'.

There is a place for argument, proof, demonstration in philosophy. I have insisted on its critical function, and claimed that deconstruction's relation to humanism has such a critical aspect to it. But I also suggested that what this critical function opens onto is more or less motivated *possibilities of response*. As far as our relations to other animals are concerned, nothing is prescribed. Or if there is a prescription – thou shalt not kill – one is not obliged to listen. Or if one is obliged to listen to this prescription, this proscription, one does not have to respond. And if one does have to respond, nothing determines how one responds.

Yet there is something that moves in Derrida's account of schemas of domination, something that it is hard not to be moved by. In 'Eating Well', Derrida writes as though he is on the brink of a kind of historico-psycho-anthropology that would displace Heidegger's existential analytic, that would reveal human subjectivity as something like surplus repression, and would give philosophy – deconstruction – the infinite task of reworking these archaic structures. But would not deconstruction be in danger of ending up as a kind of back door naturalism? For all its echoes of what Vattimo calls weak thought, the account I have given of deconstruction, as a certain kind of critical vigilance opening possibilities of response, is worth preserving. My sense, however, is that the poverty of Derrida's response to vegetarianism suggests that the resources of deconstruction are not being fully deployed here.

One last word. Before Heidegger, the history of philosophy zoo would have sheltered bees, asses, monkeys, bats and fish. After

Heidegger, snails become famous. But especially lizards. And it is especially for Heideggerians that I would like to quote part of a poem by the American poet Theodore Roethke.

> *The Lizard*[38]
> He too has eaten well –
> I can see that by the distended pulsating middle;
> And his world and mine are the same,
> The Mediterranean sun shining on us, equally,
>
> [...]
>
> To whom, does this terrace belong? –
> Not to me, but this lizard,
> Older than I, or the cockroach.

10

The Performative Imperative: Reflections on Heidegger's *Contributions to Philosophy (From Eventuation)*

Framing performativity

The task (or opportunity) of thinking after Heidegger might seem to have inherited the suggestion that we set aside philosophy in favour of something less encased in institutional trappings – a way of proceeding that would have found a way of keeping open the very space that institutional repetition inevitably closes down. And yet the very innocence of the word 'thinking', which conjures up Rodin's solitary figure curled in inner contemplation, or the seer seated under the tree in silence, does not begin to capture the shape of what is being called thinking here. If thinking is to take place, it will do so in, through and as a kind of writing, and it will embody a complex set of critical imperatives reflecting hard-won achievements on many fronts. One of the central threads of such thinking will be some sort of negotiated response to the question of performativity.[1] But we need only scratch the surface of this idea to discover that it is the site of monumental struggles on many fronts. It has been tempting to understand Heidegger as having prematurely resolved these issues in favour of some simple principle of self-present authenticity. There is no doubt that, from time to time, Heidegger writes longingly of a 'simple saying', but the thrust of his actual practice is far more compelling philosophically – it is the dramatic staging of the question of performativity in many

simultaneous dimensions. What we will now try to do is to demonstrate just how compelling are the considerations which led Heidegger, and which must continue to lead us, in this direction. Our central
focus will be the grand experiment of 1936–7, Heidegger's *Contributions to Philosophy (From Eventuation)*.[2]

The idea that certain considerations are compelling, and that the
recognition that they are compelling will lead us in a certain direction,
is of course doubly problematic. It is very tempting to suppose that
there are limits to this project. We might be able, for example, to
reconstruct how Heidegger came to think his path was compelling, or
how it might have seemed compelling to someone experiencing the
economic and political turmoil of the 1930s, or how someone who
had swallowed one big implausible assumption might find it compelling, or how someone with religious leanings who had rejected theology, or someone haunted by Hölderlin but with an allegiance to
philosophy, might proceed. But every time we circumscribe significance in advance in this way, we risk cheating ourselves. We do not
know who we are or where we are going sufficiently clearly to be able
to mark the distance between then and now. Those who are loudest in
dismissing or restricting the value of the work of someone from
another era often have the least reflective account of their own.
Many 'friends' of Heidegger have been deeply disturbed by his political record, especially in the 1930s, but we should all be just as
disturbed by those whose sense of the present, this present, is so
normalized that they could not even be tempted by the dreams of
transformation to which Heidegger temporarily signed up. It would
be another dream to be able to lay out all the assumptions that
Heidegger makes, and the conclusions he draws from them, and
show that they were necessary, or unavoidable. Instead I will try to
show that many of the most critical are highly plausible, and this in a
field where plausibility is often the best we can hope for. I bring to my
reading of Heidegger here a version of the choice he sets before us in
What is Called Thinking?, as we discussed in chapter 4 above, that we
can choose to go *counter to* a thinker or to go *to their encounter*. As
we have suggested earlier, going counter to a thinker too soon aborts
the possibility of a reflection not just on the frame of reference he is
working within, but also on one's own. If philosophy were to be itself
a 'science', that is, a problem-solving activity, or again a training
ground in disputation, the unearthing of fundamental frames and
assumptions would be counter-productive. It may be a shorter distance than we realize from being the odd man (or woman) out in a
group, who cannot help to decide what movie we will all go and see,
because he (or she) doesn't want to go to a movie at all, to being

invited to drink hemlock. I will attempt my version of going to
Heidegger's encounter by presenting many of his claims here in
ways that are hard to resist. The upshot will then be to allow us to
be confronted by a Heidegger to whom we have no choice but to
respond philosophically and not just with the apparatus of scholarship.

Before going any further, we must clarify what we mean and do not
mean by the performative. For the word has a recent history that we
need to be critically aware of. In particular, we recall the distinction
between descriptive and performative first elaborated by Austin, and
the subsequent use of the term 'performativity' by Lyotard, which has
been glossed as 'the power of...language games to get themselves
accepted on a short-term provisional basis'.[3] Austin's sense of the
performative now seems dated in that he was drawing attention to a
dimension of language obscured by too much attention being paid to
its descriptive function within a certain tradition. Austin reminded us
that sometimes the words we utter are themselves deeds, as when we
say 'I will' at the appropriate time in a wedding ceremony. It is not so
much that words are instrumental in an external sense, as that they
constitute part of the real. Lyotard's usage, however, seems to stray
into the instrumental when performativity is offered as a standard by
which to judge the power of a discourse to insert itself into our lives.
Here it seems at least as though an instrumental standard is being
deployed in such a way as to challenge metaphysical complacency,
without itself being put into question.

But neither of these senses of the performative quite captures what I
am attributing to Heidegger. To approach that sense we need to
broaden our range of reference. Hegel could be said to have set the
scene when he said that philosophy must cease being the love of
wisdom and become wisdom itself. The implication is that philosophy
has for too long been satisfied with marking out its distance from
truth, by describing it, pointing to it, representing it. Hegel argued
that these very relations marked a distance that needed to be
overcome if knowledge was to be attained. Knowledge was of the
whole, and each such mode of distantiation was a mark of incompleteness, and partiality. Philosophy had itself in some way to bear the
whole, and Hegel's *Phenomenology of Spirit* was something that
needed to be worked through. Reading this book would be what we
might call a participatory engagement. In this respect, it is ironic that
Kierkegaard would precisely criticize Hegel for building a castle and
living in a hut next door. But his response was in effect using Hegel's
own standard against himself, saying that the very form of the system
was the wrong kind of wholeness. It could not in principle include the

individual passion, mortal singularity, when that was the very thing that had to be sacrificed to enter the system. Kierkegaard insists that truth be subjective partly to rile Hegelians, but partly to make the point that we need a full relation to our incompleteness, not a partial relation to a misconstrued completeness. Kierkegaard is in effect saying that Hegel's model of the whole as the system is a monument to the philosophy of representation, while Hegel was insisting that there was no royal road to truth, but that it could only be obtained through the labour of the negative, through undergoing 'the experience of consciousness'. So Kierkegaard could be said to be schematizing Hegel in such a way as to enable him to crystallize the specific path of fulfilment that was engaging him. Where Kierkegaard and Hegel really do seem to differ is in Kierkegaard's sense that the relation to the whole is not to be found in participation with others in community, but in a relation that can only be lived and not represented, as a personal relation to the spiritual ground of my being. Interestingly, both Hegel and Kierkegaard emphasize the role of risk. For Hegel it is the risk of death, in the life and death struggle for recognition. For Kierkegaard, it is the risk of insanity and/or social ignominy, as we set aside the tenets of everyday morality in the leap of faith. For Kierkegaard, the risk of death appears indirectly in the more dire form as the risk of having to survive being the murderer of one's own son (in *Fear and Trembling*).

Performativity arises in Kierkegaard in what he calls the double reflection needed for truth to occur, in which there is both a (conceptual) relation to the object – my words reflect a judgement about the world – and an existential relation to myself, which will appear in the form of pathos, irony, or some other marker of inward significance. It is completed in what he calls the emancipatory intent of such utterances, which open the Other, the listener, to the possibility of self-relation – one which in turn is itself open to the Other, which is 'complete' in acknowledging its 'incompleteness'. This matrix of relations we could call the matrix of performativity. These same concerns – that it's only by risking one's fundamental groundedness that certain possibilities of transformation arise at all ('Live dangerously', 'What does not kill me makes me stronger') and that philosophy is an active agency, not just descriptive of the world ('How to philosophize with a hammer') – course through all of Nietzsche's writings too. And his account of asceticism in *The Genealogy of Morals* could be said to be an explanation of the source of that detachment that would condemn philosophy to the mock triumphs of ever more complete system construction. Uncertainty as how best to characterize Nietzsche's commitment to performativity centres on the same issues that were raised by Lyotard's account. To the extent that language, on Nietzsche's view, is constitutive of at least much of our engagement with the real, we cannot just think of the way we write or read instrumentally. At the very least it is second-order instrumentality. But Nietzsche insists that we need to write in such a way as not only gives voice to this constitutive relation between language and the world, but also marks and keeps open the contingency of that relation, as when he writes, 'My style is a dance – an overleaping mockery of symmetries.' Nietzsche holds both a structuralist view of everyday language, and a rhetorician's view of what it is possible to do with words given a certain command of the language. Nietzsche's writings are not, in this all, all performative. *The Geneaology of Morals* is much more descriptive than *Thus Spoke Zarathustra*. And yet Nietzsche's 'description' here is in fact a highly tendentious construction of the embodied history of mind, such that description is arguably being deployed rhetorically!

That there are precursors to Heidegger's *Contributions* is not surprising. It would not be hard to enlist Kant's references to being able for the first time to set aside the mock battles of previous philosophy now that he has clarified the proper relation of language to the world. And Marx's insistence about philosophy's limits ('Philosophy has only interpreted the world . . .') marks the same frustration with a certain distantiation. We could, of course, conclude that we had identified a key philosophical trope, and gently congratulate ourselves on drawing these various connections. Yet just to treat this sense of philosophy (as tied up with a distance that it can only overcome by a certain transformative movement) as a formal pattern would generate immediately an aporetic moment of the most telling sort. For the formal treatment of this distance would seem at least to reinscribe it within that very distance, and hence be an instance of what is being decried. The philosopher's version of what De Man calls the resistance to theory is not resistance to theory so much as resistance to the distinction between theory and practice.[4] Performativity, we might say, is a clear case of such resistance; and Heidegger, we might say, is in this respect part of a worthy tradition. I do not know whether it is merely an apocryphal story that he wrote *Being and Time* with a copy of Lukács' *History and Class Consciousness* open on his desk. He would have to have had a big desk for all the other books that, from the evidence of the product, seem to have been open on his desk – like Aristotle's *Ethics*, and Hegel's *Phenomenology of Spirit*. There are clearly strong parallels between Lukács' sense of the proletariat being *in the truth* at the point of revolution, and Heidegger's own account of authenticity and his sense of truth as disclosedness. And a sense that Kierkegaard was right to have wanted to reverse the direction of Hegel's grand sweep to encompass the fate of the individual. The critical move in each of these cases would be to show that the turn away from serene detachment does not end with instrumental action, nor with merely subjective expression. Rather philosophy discovers that the shape and modes of engagement of its own practice is the hidden locus of what needs to change.

Performativity does not so much designate one specific dimension of philosophical practice, as a displaced understanding of what is at stake in that realm. In particular, for example, it will not be sufficient to suppose that what is needed is just greater attention to the shape of my agency, or to the terms I deploy, or to the effects of my words. Performativity will be seen to spill over from being a characterization of thinking, to a way of understanding phenomena themselves. And language, and time, and being. In order to close in more effectively on the specific performativity of Heidegger's *Contributions*, let us try to broach those issues as they appear already in *Being and Time*.

Being and Time begins with a question about the meaning of Being; or rather with a double question – for the second question is why the meaning of Being is not, for most of us, a pressing question. It begins with the issue of perplexity and its scope. It begins with the invocation of the need for a reawakening, even to issues that seem to us 'as clear as day'. It begins with a quotation from Plato (from the *Sophist*) and a reference to ancient philosophizing. It begins, let us say, at the beginning – at the question of the beginning, and at the beginning of questioning.[5] And given the problems Derrida ran into in *Of Spirit* (see above, chapter 6), it is important to realize that the space of the question from which Heidegger begins is not straightforwardly one in which a subject asks questions. Rather it is one in which we feel, or don't feel, perplexity, in which what should be questionable is covered over. It is one in which the subject is already problematized with respect to being asleep or awake. *Contributions* will begin with a more desperate version of the same predicament. Philosophy can no longer appear in public because 'all fundamental words have been used up'. Heidegger is announcing a double crisis – a crisis in the human spirit, and a crisis in philosophy. At the heart of the diagnosis is a critique of culture, both the culture of this age and, more weakly, the tendencies of any culture. The crisis in the human spirit is implicit. Perplexity is on the wane; certain kinds of questions are no longer being asked; and philosophy is implicated in that its role as an interrogative resource is threatened by its own normalizing transformation. In each case, Heidegger's account of the shape and scope of the problem is what sets the scene for the kind of prescription he will be offering. It would be easy to reduce Heidegger's starting position to a kind of *Weltanschauung*, a particular view of the world occasioned by the economic and political turmoil of the 1930s, coupled with the religious troubles he experienced during his childhood. But in every such reductive explanation, there is an enormous danger – that we exaggerate what is special about the special circumstances. We do not consider, for example, that peacetime and prosperity might actually blind us to deep truths about our condition. A strong bridge over a gorge traversed at night would give us an unbalanced view of the geography of the region. Scheler once suggested as an alternative to a historical reductionism that particular circumstances 'open and close the floodgates of ideas'. More finely put, instead of supposing that extreme conditions lead us to implausible conclusions, we might say that they certainly can do so, but that more importantly they can open us to the deepest significance of what happens around us. By analogy, there can be traumatic responses to traumatic events, which may indeed be inadequate as responses. But traumatic events themselves, if one can avoid that kind of response to them, may be the most revealing. The same would be true not just of traumatic events, but all times and periods in which the lineaments of the state, of our very existence and happiness are being thrown into question. It might be said that such dramatic circumstances obscure the deep and pervasive significance of what we take to be the everyday – birth, marriage, death, despair, hope, etc. It is perhaps precisely at this juncture that the circumstances that Heidegger (and many others) took themselves to be in come to be particularly important. For if we accept the idea that in the everyday we can find all we need to understand the human condition – that we do not need war, catastrophe, invasion, etc. – then the tranquillization of the everyday in such a way as to deprive it of those resources would constitute a threat to the very experience of living.

To be clear, this tranquillization of the everyday does not just mean the removal of disaster from our ordinary experience. It encompasses just as much the loss of a vital and not overly schematized *capacity for experience*. Is that not, surely, what Heidegger, and Adorno, and before them Husserl, and Nietzsche, were saying? There is, however, in each thinker, a constant tension between the idea that the problem is historical and cultural, even if particularly heightened today (with philosophy being increasingly helpless to do anything about it), and the idea that philosophy itself, after an initially genuine contact with phenomena, has itself hardened into an institutional form, and even contributed to the very historical condition that we face. On this more complex model, philosophy is both potentially a source of interruption of sclerotic representationalism, and also a central carrier of the same liability. If we can talk at all about 'the experience of living', philosophy should not be separated out from it. This tradition at least contends that philosophy, before anything else, is part of that experience, that it only becomes a derived and institutionalized activity when it too has fallen away from its own possibilities.

I have walked up the path to Heidegger's door by setting a certain scene. I am claiming that it would be a mistake to think of this scene simply as historical or cultural. I do not mean it would be a factual error, that there was no *Weltschmerz* around. Rather it would be a precarious interpretive presumption. It is at the heart of our understanding of the significance of philosophy that it reflects perennial concerns, even if the balance and perspicuousness of those concerns varies over time. Some will find these comments useful precisely for illuminating what it is about Heidegger's fundamental commitments that they do not share. They may object, taking a remark of Hegel's in a certain way, that it is not philosophy's job to be edifying. They may suppose, in another Hegelian twist, that Heidegger is making the idealist's (and especially German) error of giving philosophy an exaggerated role in the affairs of men. They may suppose that Heidegger's position is an essentially religious one, cloaked in philosophical pathos. They may suppose that Heidegger's thinking is the latest expression of a regressive philosophical desire – for presence, for unmediated community, for a more primitive cosmic consciousness... The answers to these and like objections go a long way to making Heidegger's way of setting out more persuasive, but also clarify why performativity takes on such a central role in his writing, commending it as a concern to us.

Suppose we take the first objection – that philosophy should avoid trying to be edifying. It is not that being edifying is in itself without merit, rather that philosophy loses its track when it bends itself to this end. That does not mean that philosophy cannot be helpful, but that it should not set out to be helpful, and indeed that it can be more helpful when it is not trying too hard to be. We might suppose, for example, that a flexible mathematics, in which sometimes $2 + 2$ would stretch to 5, might be helpful, but we would quickly discover how much better it is to have an arithmetic that does not bend to our desires! Also, a history that wilfully rewrote the past might be useful in some sense, but it would similarly set the scene for deeper interpretive fractures. Is Heidegger trying to make philosophy edifying? Obviously everything hangs on what counts as edification. Heidegger is not trying to moralize us into being better people, or living better lives. If he is trying to do anything like this at all, it would be closer to what Blake called 'cleansing the doors of perception', helping us to work through sedimented layers of deadening framing and schematizing conceptualization, opening up more profound relationships to experiences of loss and finitude. All this is indirectly edifying, but it would be hard to accuse Heidegger of sacrificing the end to the means, settling for a cheap fix. Everything points in the opposite direction – and everything points to Heidegger offering us one of the most powerful ways of thinking through just what edification could possibly mean.

Perhaps, then, Heidegger is guilty of a certain idealistic hyperbole, giving philosophy an efficacy that it does not deserve. Is he not another in a long line of thinkers who believe that the world should be refigured in line with philosophical recommendations and that the real should be ruled by ideas? Did he not say that German idealism had not been refuted, but rather the German people had not lived up to its promise? What is interesting is that it is this very 'idealistic' model – the very distinctions between the idea and the real, between thought and action – that he is repudiating. We can see this clearly at the beginning of his 'Letter on Humanism', in which he insists that thinking is not opposed to action; rather it is a mode of action itself. This gets very close to making the performative point – thinking is not merely capable of having instrumental effects in other dimensions. But more importantly, it is intrinsically efficacious. This is akin to the claim that human interaction is not just affected by language; it is permeated, riddled with it! Thinking and speaking cannot be reduced to instrumentality not because they occupy a sealed world of their own currency, but because they help to shape, constitute and transform the world in which we live, move and have our being. And, perhaps paradoxically, how we understand thinking and speaking, whether we think of it instrumentally or performatively, does indeed have real-world consequences.

What that does not imply is that we can just switch to doing these things differently. What makes *Being and Time* difficult and the *Contributions* such a challenge is Heidegger's insistence that the performative thinking *from* Ereignis is, as Kierkegaard said about subjectivity, a highly complex achievement, one we can only anticipate and prepare for at present. To give a more direct take on this, we have learned from Nietzsche, from Saussure and from Lévi-Strauss that our language, our thinking, our social institutions are organized on the basis of oppositions: truth and false, inside and outside, appearance and reality, man and woman. Philosophy too would be unthinkable without this skeletal structuration. But while it makes the most critical reflection possible, it also sets limits precisely because this structuration is not itself being questioned when it is being deployed. As we have seen, questioning can itself be 'interrogated' in this respect, as Derrida does. We may suppose that it silently reinscribes a detached subject v. passive world model. Particularly salient here is the oppositional pair subject–object, or act–object, which is at the heart of the instrumental view of agency. We can treat the whole move towards performativity as an attempt to free philosophizing from an unreflective subordination to that model. It is important to realize that one of the most seductive circumstances we find ourselves in is that of having in our knapsack a model known to work well under certain conditions, and needing *something* to deal with a new situation. Instrumental reason in general is enormously 'effective', but the deployment of its structures beyond their proper bounds is both a seductive temptation, and a fatal one. Of course, this is the shape of Kant's central discovery – that our reason applied perfectly well to the phenomenal realm, but to apply it further, to the real, would be like painting on water. Heidegger's concern with the performative transformation of philosophy could be read as a transformation of Kant's insight. Instead of discerning different realms, Heidegger focuses on different modes of relationality. If philosophizing cannot properly be pursued as an instrumental relation, but has been drawn into such ways by the understandable demands of expediency – including the demands for public intelligibility – what transformations of our current 'practices' does it require of us?

Here perhaps, the religious objection may arise. All this talk of the limits of instrumentality surely reeks of religiosity. Is it not obvious that when Heidegger speaks of Being, he speaks covertly of God, and does this not become even more obvious when in *Contributions* he responds so positively to Hölderlin's evocation of the gods, and finally declares that 'Only a god can save us'?[6] Nietzsche long ago warned us of the need to ferret out hidden gods by the odour still being given off by our worship of their decaying remains. 'We have not got rid of God if we still believe in grammar.' And would this not all be understandable given Heidegger's Catholic upbringing, and the interest taken in his work by theologians such as Bultmann? Obviously this question deserves another book. But the thrust of this whole objection can be turned around quite quickly and sharply. Nietzsche's reference to grammar ought to give us pause. Heidegger could be said to have inherited *precisely* this further archaeological task from Nietzsche by subverting our attachment to such fundamental 'grammatical' structures as inside / outside, subject / object, self / world, active / passive, and he explicitly diagnoses as an error the deep essentialism that is fundamentally if unconsciously and silently committed to a creationist model of the world. The reference to the gods can be treated as evidence of his religiosity, but the shift from God to gods surely marks a break at least with everything the Judaeo-Christian tradition stands for.

Instead of supposing that Heidegger is engaged in covert theology, I suggest the following: that Heidegger is recovering for philosophy a dimension of thinking that could be said to have been preserved in theological discourse. This dimension could be named in various ways – perhaps for the moment we could call it 'what escapes and sustains reason'. My model here is this: theology develops and preserves religious awareness, subjecting it to formal and discursive elaboration that sets up an uneasy tension with that very awareness. The modes of awareness that we call religious have to do with those forms of apprehension and relationality that a certain self-understanding of philosophy is unable to deal with. Theology then preserves, at some cost, phenomena that philosophy, once it frees itself from its self-imposed limitations, can then address. Imagine the scene: philosophy leaves a bunch of stuff out in the yard that it does not know where to put in the house. Theology comes along at night and collects these surplus items. The house then burns down, and a subsequent recon-struction of philosophy discovers the cache of its surplus goods in a nearby church.... The key to that transformation of philosophy is its grasp of the significance of certain relations – to absence, to the impossible, to the unrepresentable, the *rapport sans rapport*, etc. – and philosophy's readiness to deal with these relations even though they precisely do not permit systematization or closure. So my re-sponse to the suggestion that Heidegger is a covert theologian, that Being really means God, etc., is that such identifications and assimi-lations do not begin to address what is at stake in Heidegger's relation to the religious or to theology. It is almost unbelievable that someone could claim that Being really means God, and think they had clarified things.[7] What if people had always meant Being when they said 'God'? Would that be the same thing? Heidegger is not so much a covert theologian as someone who attempts to recover for thinking the significance of a set of relations to the unrepresentable to which theology has at times taken a proprietary relation. What is distinctive about Heidegger is that he recognizes that to take these relations seriously means going against, twisting free, of the usual grammar of predicative assertion. Language, and one's 'deployment' of lan-guage as a philosopher, is not exempt from the transformation that this recovery requires. It is precisely because he is not a theolo-gian, not even a negative theologian – and precisely because the thematization either of the unrepresentable, or of the impossibility of its representation betrays its significance – that the performative becomes, for Heidegger, an imperative.

Finally, to complete the process of motivating performativity by responding to common misunderstandings of Heidegger, there is the charge or suspicion that Heidegger is in the final analysis a philosopher of presence, or identity – what I described as a regressive philosophical desire. This worry appears in various forms – philosophical and political – and spans the spectrum from Derrida to Habermas. I discussed this general worry in connection with Derrida's critical readings of Heidegger in chapter 6. Here I sketch the shape of the proper response to this objection in such a way that the performative way forward is called for.

There is no doubt that there are moments in Heidegger's thinking at which a certain drive to presence manifests itself. For example, in *Contributions* he speaks of the search for 'a simple saying'; in *Being and Time* he speaks of returning to 'those primordial experiences from which our concepts have for the most part been drawn'; and when he speaks of community, it is often in terms of a tendency to resolution of destiny through struggle. It might be said that when Heidegger explicitly discusses identity (e.g. in *Identity and Difference*), it is precisely to undo the representational purity of an achieved or pure identity, in favour of 'gathering'; but then again, it could be said that this privileges centripetal movement over the centrifugal, the movement towards unification over dispersion. I propose a different reading. We can find just as many references in Heidegger to the abyssal, to death, to absence, to a future that cannot be represented but only, tentatively, be prepared for; and *Contributions* in particular is flooded with structures in which presentation and the unpresentable are fatefully and irretrievably intertwined. Any thinker who takes seriously, as Heidegger did, the question of how to acknowledge both what we could call metastable identities, the differential conditions on which they rest, and our own determination in relation to possibilities whose actual presence is as yet unthinkable is faced with a whole set of fundamental strategic questions. We may think, for example, that every concept with any trace of a thread connecting it to 'presence' should be banished from our lexicon, but, as we saw in chapter 2, 'The Return of Experience', the most extreme proponents of such a position, Derrida and Blanchot, end up welcoming back, albeit carefully, even the word 'experience'. And Derrida will explain the inevitability of strategic considerations in his response to Jean-Luc Nancy's question about the continued currency of the word 'Subject'. It is not just that there are no easy answers, but rather that the easy answers are nothing like as easy as they look. And where the easy answer involves a purification – cutting out this or that word or lexical cluster – we must always wonder whether there will not be a price to be paid for this violence somewhere else in our thinking, whether the repressed will not return in an unexpected place. There is an analogy, perhaps, with the belief in surgical procedures in medicine. It may be that the immediate outcome is successful, but that the surgery fails to address the root of the problem in a person's lifestyle (or genes). There may be a short-term gain, philosophically, if we stop using the lexicon of humanism, but unless the fundamental essentialism is addressed, the problem will return in reified understandings of the substitutes for the terms we have banished. What may be needed is a way of thinking and writing which systemically discourages essentialism. On the other hand, it may be that danger, and its corollary, vigilance, are ineliminable from these attempts at transformation. When we consider, for example, the relation between philosophy and poetry, or philosophy and the political, or (as we have seen) philosophy and theology, it may be said that there is something in poetry, or in the political or in theology that need no longer be excluded from philosophy, but that may indeed offer resources for furthering our thinking. We may agree with this idea, and yet such a move is in each case fraught with danger. Art may insist on the image, theology on the infinite, and the political on action and implementation. In attempting to negotiate conversations at each of these boundaries, Heidegger took real risks. But I think it was in his diagnosis that philosophy finds itself in a situation in which the risk of failure is the price of success. In *Contributions*, for example, philosophy is assigned the task of preserving Hölderlin's call from the gods. If this is a resource for the transformation of philosophy that we cannot do without, does that mean that Heidegger is then subordinating philosophy to poetry? Not at all. But the danger that it will be taken like this, or that he will at times walk on the wrong side of the track, is one he cannot avoid. I suggest that Heidegger is not so much wedded to 'presence' as to the staging of the struggle between our desire for presence, and its impossibility. This cannot be adequately said; it has to be shown. And again, performativity beckons.

Phenomenology has an inner relation to performativity in two different ways. Husserl's insistence on phenomenology as 'responsibility to phenomena' raises the question as to how this responsibility is to be carried through in language. That secondary responsibility may begin as a certain attentiveness to phenomena that present themselves to me. But in Heidegger's development of phenomenology in *Being and Time*, attention turns away from what presents itself to me, to the mode of presentation, and towards our mode of engagement with the world. Husserl had long thought of phenomenology as the form that philosophy would have to take to meet its hitherto undischarged historical and cultural responsibilities. But it would not be hard to think that the goal of maintaining and restoring the groundedness of language, the sciences, philosophy itself in the complexity of 'things themselves' would require more than presuppositionless description. If justice must be *seen* to be done, the way we write and think must bear witness to the connectedness we avow. Phenomenology as responsibility leads to performativity. The second connection between phenomenology and the performative is instructive for the way this dimension gets elaborated in *Contributions*. Phenomenology, whether in Husserl or in Heidegger, begins with an understanding of phenomena not as 'appearances' which would hide or disguise a noumenal substratum, but rather as showing themselves, as self-showing. The yellow of the lemon is no mere 'appearance', but a way in which the lemon lemons, a way in which the lemon is a lemon. This sense, that the way things shine forth is essential to what they are, does not enjoin a particular manner of thinking or writing. It does, however, lay the ground for the recognition that philosophy, thinking, writing, speaking are subject to the same consideration as phenomena in general. In other words, if we suppose that in writing *about* something, the 'aboutness' guarantees a certain neutrality, we are wrong. 'Aboutness' is a commitment to a certain detachment, which is a particular mode of engagement with its own advantages and liabilities. Of course the same would be true of what we could call mystical performativity, in which there would, *per impossibile*, be no space at all between act and significance.

The performative imperative

[W]e must attempt the thinking-saying of philosophy... This saying does not describe or explain, does not proclaim or teach. This saying does not stand over against what is said. Rather the saying itself is the 'to be said' as the essential swaying of be-ing. This saying gathers being's essential sway unto a first sounding, while itself [this saying] sounds only out of this essential sway.[8]

So far, in this concluding chapter, often drawing on work in previous chapters, I have attempted three things. First, to make plausible the idea that philosophy might have a significant role to play either in resisting contemporary historical trends, or in the perennial task of combating the inherent human tendency to sleepwalking (habituality and routinization). Secondly, to argue that philosophy will not be well placed to deliver this assistance without its own internal renewal and transformation. Thirdly, to claim that this renewal cannot be completed without entering the space of performativity. We are now in a better position to explore what is implied by the subtitle of Heidegger's *Beitrage: Vom Ereignis* – we have translated *Ereignis* as 'eventuation' – and what kind of *contributions* he thinks he is making.[9] While what we have said so far provides something of a motivating frame for what is to come, the audacity of what he attempts is indeed breathtaking.

Aspects of performativity

It is sorely tempting to try to come to the assistance of the reader, and indeed oneself, by making some helpful distinctions between different types of performativity. One could start, for example, by distinguishing methodological, existential, historical and linguistic performativity, and much of what Heidegger says would slide without too much force into one of these categories. The methodological dimension would concern itself with the way in which the performative addresses questions about how Heidegger thinks we should go about doing philosophy. The existential would deal with its relevance to questions of the self's relation to itself, to others and to the world. The historical would take up Heidegger's understanding of what he is doing as 'being-historical thinking'. And linguistic performativity would focus on the writer and thinker's relation to language. It would not be wholly an error to proceed like this, and it would be an error to suppose that one could proceed without having to make any trade-offs at all. The objection that one is beginning by subordinating performativity to representation in the shape of analytical categories is not a fatal objection. Just as there is no 'pure saying', so there is no pure presentation of performativity. If I were to take the analytical route, however, these categories seem peculiarly insensitive to what is being attempted. That philosophy might freely adopt certain 'methods' is itself in question, the word 'existential' has been problematic in Heidegger ever since revisionary doubts about *Being and Time*, the historical is as difficult a category as it is important in Heidegger, and 'linguistic' suggests a genuinely unhelpful possibility of taking up a viewpoint on language which Heidegger is at pains to disavow. Perhaps we could say that in hesitating over this schematizing approach I am myself enacting the kind of hesitation that Heidegger will elaborate.

Are there then no usefully distinct dimensions of performativity? Here is a semi-serviceable less compromising way of dividing up the field of performativity:

(a) Eventuation (anticipation, transition, inceptual thinking)
(b) Withholding (hesitation, reticence, double-bind)
(c) Response-ability (reading the other, preserving the call of the gods, listening to the poet)
(d) Transformations of Self (displacement of mastery, negative capability, openness)

The connections suggested by these clusters will appear and reappear throughout this chapter. But with the issue of avoiding repetition there is announced one of the major thrusts motivating the performative imperative. In section 20 of *Beyond Good and Evil*, Nietzsche gave a classic expression of this problem: 'Under an invisible spell, [the most diverse philosophers] always revolve once more in the same orbit.' Nietzsche spoke of 'unconscious grammatical functions' – our belief in the separateness of subject and object, and although Heidegger will cease to subscribe to Nietzsche's own basis for disavowing representationalism (the will-to-power), Heidegger's grasp of the difficulty of avoiding unconscious repetition is every bit as strong as Nietzsche's. For Heidegger, this problem set in with the very way in which philosophical conceptualization began. But the adumbration of an Other Beginning has to face the additional obstacle of *Machenschaft*, or the contemporary reign of machination. Machination could be described as the concrete logic of calculative rationality. It is no mere optional basis for meaning or decision-making. It is not a logic simply in a formal sense; rather it serves to eliminate what does not conform to its principles. Nor is it confined to some specific area – say commercial transactions. *Machenschaft* is an invasive logic that knows no limits. Heidegger sees it threatening not only the power of thought to have any distinct impact on the world, but as affecting the inner possibilities of thinking itself. *Machenschaft* is not just a force out there to be reckoned with, but, in the shape of representational thinking and calculation, it reaches into the heart of philosophy itself. Later, Heidegger will make the connection even tighter when he describes *Gestell*, the framing characteristic of technology, as the completion of philosophy. The argument is this: if philosophy comes to identify itself with conceptual activity, and if that activity ceases to understand itself as having a necessary grounding (or ab-grounding) in phenomena that make possible such conceptualization, and if conceptualization comes to be guided by the world's receptiveness to this or that mode of conceptualization, then this abridged philosophy, this philosophy that has ceased to raise the question of being, will become part of the problem, rather than part of the solution. The framed world will mirror philosophy's own forgetfulness. This diagnosis of different styles of thinking, with 'calculative' relegated to the less philosophical, is not original with Heidegger. We can find it at various places in Hegel's writing. But whereas for Hegel the solution was arriving at a kind of self-consciousness that would overcome these deficiencies, for Heidegger this very movement of self-consciousness is unreflectively repeating the privilege of the knowing subject. This is an example of how it is possible to think of repetition as a recursive danger, looming up even after one's best efforts at avoidance. This suggests something that Derrida and De Man will take very seriously – that even performativity may suffer the same fate. It will be my claim that Heidegger recognizes this problem at times and takes steps to avoid it.

The particular problem is one we mentioned above, that negation can precisely set the scene for recuperation. If what is being negated has the recursive capacity to curl back and incorporate that which opposes it, then negation may be feeding the fire, rather than quenching it. Atheists who deny God's existence, for example, are sometimes thought to be outflanked by agnostics who say they do not know. But agnostics who accept the discourse and just cannot decide are themselves outflanked by those who smell something fishy about the very question. It might then be thought that *those* people cannot enter the conversation, cannot say anything at all. But what if there were a way of going sideways (i.e. questioning the terms, changing the question); could we then not twist free of the original set-up? Such a response would allow more than resistance to *Machenschaft*, it would open up the possibility of a non-recuperable negation. Heidegger's commitment to enactment and performativity is the key to that twisting free.

Such a transformative resistance is at the heart of phenomenology; but perhaps not just any phenomenology.[10] What Heidegger developed (and Blanchot, Levinas and Derrida took further) was the idea that our fundamental philosophemes could be, and needed to be, reinscribed in a dimensionality in which their own mastery is shown to be conditioned. We could call this dimensionality a 'space' but anything that smacks of a 'framework' immediately reintroduces the representational level we are attempting to set aside. Heidegger will call it an interplay of time–space. Truth, for example, becomes more than a relation of correspondence between a proposition and a state of affairs, and becomes an event of disclosure, one which generates occlusion at the same time. Truth and untruth are not so much opposed as necessary to each other. And if we take seriously that modern philosophy (since Descartes, since Kant) has been predominantly the philosophy of representation, one underpinned by the model of a subject representing its object (the world) to itself in the shape of an idea, then the transformative resistance wrought by phenomenology would have the effect of making this structure of representation itself 'appear'. That this is no simple matter becomes clear when we remember that Heidegger's earlier *Being and Time* could be said to have attempted just such a phenomenological displacement of representation.

Although it may seem too simplistic an opposition, it is helpful to understand what Heidegger is attempting in *Contributions* in its rhetorical contrast with *Being and Time*. By a rhetorical contrast, I mean a contrast in the mode of presentation, the performative stance of these two works. The simple story of opposition would see in *Being and Time* the unwanted vestiges of the project of metaphysical representation. It would interpret *Contributions* as engaging in a post-representational performativity. The original posing of the question of Being in *Being and Time* sets the scene for a thinking of Being that would keep its distance from any and all conceptualizations and yet the whole apparatus of the existential analytic, the apparent foundational status of the ontological, all smack of traditional metaphysical schematization. Heidegger seems to have set up a detour in which he then gets lost. Heidegger seems to settle for telling us *how it is*, existentially and ontologically. His language is not very profoundly affected by what he is trying to get at. Representation seems in control. In fact, however, as some have begun to show, there are moments in *Being and Time* at which there is what we might call an enactment, an appeal to something beyond representation in, for example, the call of conscience, in the role played by anticipatory resoluteness, and by being-towards-death.[11] In each case the text opens itself to what escapes representation. And yet the impression remains – *Being and Time* is a systematic treatise where form folds itself around its object.

Contributions, on the contrary, seems to be a work that has banished representation. Its German subtitle, *From Ereignis*, is what he calls its 'essential heading' (*wesentliche Überschrift*), which says what the public title cannot. There is no doubt that what we are witness to in this book is an uncompromising attempt to mark the moment of thinking as the moment at which a break with representation occurs, at which we cease to speak about, and begin to speak, we cease to write about, and begin to write. There is undoubtedly a partial convergence with such movements as are captured by such titles as

'Writing – an Intransitive Verb' [Barthes], and 'The End of the Book and the Beginning of Writing' [Derrida].

It is a commonplace that we need to move on somehow from the philosophy of representation. But what is meant by representation here? First, the epistemological project of constructing a model of, or systematic account of, what we know about the world. Secondly, ontologically, the articulation of the relationship between subject and object. What we mean by the philosophy of representation is not, actually, a philosophical account of 'representation', but rather an understanding of philosophy driven by the question of representation – one which subordinates questions about human comportment, questions about life and death, questions about the ground of our being, and about the non-cognitive dimensions of language. The philosophy of representation is already a representation of philosophy to itself as centred on and anchored in representation. Overcoming the philosophy of representation does not mean ignoring what falls under the heading of representation. It involves a decentring of philosophy's sense of its fundamental orientation; but in order that this does not simply fall back into representation, a certain twist needs to occur. Reiner Schürmann's account of Heidegger's double-bind is helpful here.[12] Phenomenology would be the demonstration of how phenomena are bound not just by one law (such as representation), but by a second (e.g. relation to the other, to what cannot wholly be made to appear). Twisting free of the one-dimensional perspective of subordination to a single law requires allowing the second to begin to appear. When Heidegger writes 'Poetry, as the act of establishing being, is subject to a two fold control',[13] he is charging the poet (Hölderlin) with the burden of this double-bind – naming the gods, and interpreting the voice of the people. Hölderlin's gods free us from the Promethean illusion that man is the measure of all things.

Philosophical resources

The scene is now set to ask in more detail what philosophical resources Heidegger provides for this performative twisting free, but before that we should consider a fundamental difficulty with this whole account of the philosophy of representation. To put the difficulty in its baldest form: this very characterization seems itself to be a totalizing characterization, a summing up, a schematic account – in short, a *representation* of the very sort that Heidegger is trying to turn away from. If *Machenschaft* is something like what Heidegger elsewhere calls a 'sending of Being', i.e. a fundamental attunement of Being, or way in which Being is determined, do not these very characterizations in effect represent Being in a certain way? Does not the very idea that Being is thought in terms of 'representation', represent how being is thought in a certain way? There is a genuine problem here, one that mandates a certain caution in our thinking, but there are two important responses to be made of a defensive nature. First, there is no suggestion that the structure of 'a knowing subject facing a world' is being deployed here. That was already set aside in *Being and Time*. Secondly, there is a deep difficulty in attributing totalization to Heidegger's own position given that what he is describing is a totalizing logic. The claim that Heidegger himself is into a kind of representational totalization would in effect preclude anyone from diagnosing totalization actually operating in the world. Current critics of globalization could be told, for example, that they repeat the problem in their systematic critique of it. The answer here is surely that it is quite possible for one who diagnoses a totalizing logic to be mistaken, but there is nothing essentially totalizing about the claim itself, any more than one has to be extremely hungry and omnivorous to suggest that there is a big pike in the lake eating up all the other fish. The important corollary is that when we speak of the philosophy of 'representation', we are not speaking of the bare acceptance of the concept of representation, we are talking about reliance on and promotion of the logic of representation, in which the conditions of representability are nonetheless all that matter, even if (as with Kant) they are not identified with the real. Returning to the matter at hand – Heidegger may have succumbed instrumentally to a certain reliance on metaphysical structuration in *Being and Time*, but for a reader with the eyes to see and the ears to hear, it is clear that this is serving as a foil for quite other moves. While his *Contributions to Philosophy* can in no way be reduced to a writing from the standpoint of, or thinking from within... *Ereignis*, the more representational moves that litter this text – for there is a lot of thinking *about*, as well as thinking – are less evidence of a totalizing logic than of unavoidable tactical necessity. As we have said, Heidegger is diagnosing what we have called a 'logic', itself a not-unproblematic term. We could come to think him mistaken. We could come to think that he had mistaken a tendency or a widespread temptation for something more systematic, but we cannot conclude that he himself must be guilty of totalization, just because he points to a systematizing phenomenon. Both the oncologist and the ontologist suppose that the pervasive phenomena they encounter are real. No doubt the big question is what kinds of non-recuperable interventions are possible. The claim that no opposition or resistance of any sort is possible may well deserve to be interpreted as a hysterical mimesis of the imagined original.

Heidegger's own mimesis begins perhaps with the fugal structure of the book. As a book it has to have something approaching a linear form, but as if saluting the pervasive character of the problem, as well as the derivativeness of traditional temporal order, Heidegger plots the transition from the first beginning to the other beginning, a transition which honours the uniqueness of the first beginning as it turns away from it, by the simultaneous opening up of a six-stranded skein of themes and enactable moments which he names echo, playing-forth, leap, grounding, the ones to come, and the last god.[14] If there is some residual sequentiality towards the end, what is more significant is that these six threads collectively provide a way of breaking the hold of the first beginning. It is not that Heidegger holds a coherence theory of truth rather than a correspondence theory, but he has something like a coherence theory of transformation – that a number of switches need to be thrown at the same time. Heidegger is plotting a revolution that works through a new seeing 'as'. In the English translation, our grasp of the *Wesen* of *Sein*, is translated as the sway of truth, suggesting both the sense of truth as a regime, as Nietzsche and Foucault might put it, and also a movement internal to truth itself, akin to the sense of a double-bind in which one law (say of identity) views with another, more recessive. In the sense of truth as regime, truth holds sway. In the second sense, thinking truth requires a bifocal vision, a grasp of the movement within truth's occurrence. To let Heidegger speak for himself:

> In the knowing awareness of thinking in the crossing, the first begin-ning remains decisively the *first* – and yet is overcome as beginning. For this thinking, reverence for the first beginning, which most clearly and initially discloses the uniqueness of this beginning, must coincide with the relentlessness of turning away from this beginning to an other questioning and saying.[15]

The grasp of the first beginning as first opens up the possibility of an other beginning. The particular elements we have recorded outline what he calls 'the still unmastered groundplan of the historicity of the crossing itself'.[16] Heidegger eschews any sense of a historical devel-opment. Rather what this sixfold set of elements does is this: 'It breaks ahead into the free-play of time-space which the history of the crossing first opens up as its realm...'[17] Again we can see this matricial mimesis; provoking a breakthrough to another 'dimension' through a thinking that itself supplies what we might call a semantic

anticipation of such dimensionality. And with this language of crossing and breakthrough Heidegger at least makes it possible both to
grasp the first beginning (Greek philosophy) in its singularity, and to
imagine (not Heidegger's word, but that surely is what is happening
here), an other beginning. Seeing 'as' here requires an interruption. In
Being and Time, such interruptions appeared in the shape of the
broken hammer (which revealed its instrumentality), the experience
of *Angst* (which shatters everydayness), and the anticipation of death
(which could be said to make life 'sway', and sets it off against my
possible 'impossibility'). Here Heidegger will speak of distress as if it
played the same role, but also of the distress at the lack of distress,
which must surely be less of an interruption. But the central player in
the drama of interruption is Hölderlin and his gods. For Hölderlin,
the poet's evocation of the gods is a fragile event that philosophers
need to preserve for the resources it offers us to imagine thinking
differently. The gods call to the poet, the poet calls to philosophy.
What is significant about Heidegger's strategy here is that Hölderlin is
not supplying a sure-fire ready-made interruption. Rather for it to
operate this way, it has to be preserved (explained, honoured,
repeated) – as he says we must do for art in general.[18] The implication
of his *Contributions* is that the crisis of *Machenschaft* is of such an
order that only the resources of Hölderlin's poetry will be able to help.
A strong claim, but one that informs the drama of the whole book:
lodged in the writing of an overlooked nineteenth-century poet is the
key to our transformation, if only we could hear it.

Heidegger brings together what he has to say about the movement
from the first to the other beginning under the heading of inceptual
thinking (*das anfängliche Denken*).

> Inceptual thinking is the original enactment of the onefold of echo,
> playing-forth, leap and grounding. Enactment here means that these
> . . . are taken over and sustained in each case only in human terms, so
> that they themselves are always essentially an other and belong to the
> occurrence of Da-sein.[19]

A brief account will help us to see the strategic and performative
complexities involved in navigating the path from one to the other. It
is clear that for Heidegger certain considerations about time and
being *compel* the peculiar shape he gives to this path. Some simple
thoughts about repetition will guide us here.[20] The idea of starting
again is not just a philosophical cliché, even though it dates back to
Plato's doctrine of recollection. It is neither just philosophical nor is it
just a cliché. It is a piece of sound practical wisdom that if we get lost

we may need to retrace our steps. Or that if a project becomes stale, it may need relaunching. In philosophy the irony is that the call for a new beginning – that Heidegger will have heard loud and clear from his teacher Husserl – is the oldest call in the book, but it is never just a cliché, because it is almost impossible to begin again philosophically without thematizing the very idea of beginning. Heidegger, as Kierkegaard did before him, does this through reflection on repetition. Naively we suppose that returning to the beginning would allow the beginning to be repeated, but this runs up against the problem of historical singularity. Events could only be repeated ('come to pass for a second time') if history were just a stage on which events with a certain ideality happen. This model would make history into a temporal container, whereas beginnings, inaugural events, take up the historical specificity of their time, including the possibilities they project and open up. Heidegger puts this point forcibly when he says 'Only what is unique is retrievable and repeatable' (section 20). His point is this: it is only when we grasp the uniqueness, singularity, and unrepeatability of a beginning that it is possible to begin again. Inceptual thinking is this retrieval of the projective eventuality of the first beginning. This happens at the same time as we realize that we cannot simply repeat its content, but must rather attune ourselves to the possibilities opened up by this grasp of the inceptuality of the first beginning!!

> Because every beginning is unsurpassable, in being encountered it must be placed again and again into the uniqueness of its inceptuality and thus into its unsurpassable fore-grasping. When this encountering is inceptual, then it is originary – but this necessarily as *other* beginning.[21]

Heidegger is offering us an account of the kind of historical attunement needed to be able to begin again, one we can only arrive at by reworking, reinhabiting, philosophy's inaugural appearance. In this work, in coming to grasp what once happened, something happens that did not happen the first time. Inceptual thinking both has inception as its focus (content), and inception is what it brings about. It is in this way that the performative – as re-eventing, re-inauguration – flows from this encounter with beginning. Heidegger will use other expressions too – ones that recall *Being and Time*, where this repetition is thought in terms of *Destruktion*. In particular, this account of beginning, of eventuation, will be thought in terms of a certain relation to being, or be-ing. And in these references to encountering the beginning, we hear anticipations of what Heidegger will describe later on (in *What is Called Thinking?*) as going to the other's encounter when we read. We encounter the other when we go to their encounter. We grasp what it is to begin, we begin to engage in inceptual thinking, when we understand that encounter in 'being-historical' terms. The point is that if the grasp of a singular occurrence is to be completed, it will itself be singularized. And in this way, enactment happens.

If this serves to explain how the enacting or performative dimension arises, it is worth briefly repeating the motivation for it. Heidegger believes it is the only way out. We need an other beginning:

> Because only the greatest occurrence, the innermost enowning, can still save us from being lost in the bustle of mere events and machinations. What must take place is enopening being for us . . .[22]

What philosophical resources are available for escape? I have mentioned already what could be called the logical problem – that negation and opposition consolidate the frame of reference within which they turn. It is this, I believe, that fuels Heidegger's distaste for dialectic, which retains its progressivist optimism as it overcomes limited forms of expression. The labour of the negative seems to rest on the assumption that overcoming opposition will bring us truth. Heidegger, on the other hand, is committed to the animation of the unrepresentable, not its incorporation into a whole. Later sections of *Contributions* (such as section 129) make clear the continuity of these claims with his treatment of Hegel (see chapter 5 above), and his remarks about negation and the Nothing in 'What is Metaphysics?' (see chapter 1 above). Put simply, Heidegger sees dialectics as reducing the operation of the negative to a logical function. Whereas, on his view, the fundamental place of the negative lies in refusal, hesitation, withdrawal – in other words as animating the 'sway' of Being, the double-bind of Being, or its irreducible relation to an unrepresentable otherness. Similarly the whole opposition between affirmation and negation is misconstrued. '[S]hould we [then] be surprised if the "nothing" is misconstrued as what is simply nihilating?' (section 129). Here two claims are being woven together. Heidegger is arguing for the co-constitutive power of the negative, as a dimension of being that 'logic' and 'metaphysics' typically cover over. He is also responding to the cultural fear and suspicion of the negative expressed in the common critique of nihilism. Giving the negative its place is essential for Heidegger to launch his general sigetics, his defence of the many modalities of silence. Silence here does not just mean saying nothing, but rather includes all those modes of reserved speech, or reticence, hesitation, indirectness that enact the unpresentable by pointing to the fact that something is being held back. As Kierkegaard reminds us, such indirectness has real emancipatory power. It frees us, or potentially frees us, from the regime of calculation. Calculation presupposes and demands that everything be available, accessible, open to exchange in a public space. It silences Being, as Heidegger would say, in favour of beings. Reticence, refusal, hesitation are all forms of resistance to such calculation. As a regime, calculation excludes questioning, and demands an unambiguous one-dimensional reality. In the face of this, Heidegger writes: 'What remains for thinking is only the simplest saying of the simplest image in purest reticence. The future first thinker must be capable of this' (section 32). The poet, and then the philosopher (or thinker), must be capable of enduring the flight of the gods, that is, holding open a space of absence, rather than allowing it to be filled up again with worldly goods. As he will make clear in his later essays on language, the point at which words fail us is precisely a moment at which *Ereignis* (eventuation) arises. The secret is not to see in a gap or an absence or a failure something that needs to be filled up, but rather an opportunity for pausing and perhaps protecting what has passed. To take this opportunity is to respond in a certain way and not just to avoid the negative. Here Heidegger is advocating what Keats called negative capability.

A new time?

We can see Heidegger here reworking in a certain way Nietzsche's critique of *ressentiment*, and indeed these remarks about the protective enactment of the negative connect smoothly to the various temporal motifs in this book. Nietzsche traces back *ressentiment* to our seeking revenge against time and its 'it was'. Nietzsche ties *ressentiment* to those reactive responses that recycle the shape of the problem they encounter. The eternal return displaces our ordinary linear progressivist sense of time with another time folded back on the present. Heidegger says he is not repudiating everyday time, and perhaps the same could be said of Nietzsche. Yet they both attempt to free our sense of time from the calculative logic that its measurability sets up. We have already seen something of this in discussing the sense he gives to the idea of an other beginning, but what I am calling the performative imperative is reinforced by considerations of time, as we will see. To put it simply, instrumental action is quite at ease with linear time. Actions have later consequences. Some thoughts will perhaps make a difference down the line, but for Heidegger the line is what is at stake. To the extent that linearity means discursive continuity floating over separate and distinct events, Heidegger needs to rethink time both to allow for radical transformation, and to be able to articulate the time of performance or enactment, in which something is done in or by doing something else, but not as a temporally distinct outcome.

The connection between a transformation of our relation to Being and a rethinking of temporality was the ultimate point of *Being and Time*, even though that ended inconclusively.[23] Moreover, although it would be easy to slide into an existential–anthropological reduction of its significance, a move that anticipates the temporal dimension of enactment in *Contributions* can be found in his account of being-towards-death, which involves such concepts as the moment of decision, and anticipatory resoluteness. Singly and together what is being proposed is a transformation of our way of being that responds to (takes account of, incorporates) the fact that we are mortal beings. First he understands mortality as a limit to our possibility of Being. Secondly, he understands grasping a new relation to that im-possibility as itself a possibility for us. Thirdly, he spells out what needs to be brought into play for that possibility to be realized. We *could* describe this as a cognitive re-organization, but it also bears on every way in which we 'live, move and have our being'. It affects what we care about, our priorities, our sense of the shape of a life, who we take ourselves to be, what we understand being human to be all about, etc. Being-towards-death is both living *as* a mortal, and also living with a certain depth of interrogation as to what it might be to be mortal. This double 'as' structure marks the moment of enactment or performativity. Being-towards-death is neither an attitude nor an action, but a mortally informed way of being. Although I may suppose that my death is in the future, part of what being-towards-death involves is the recognition that my decision as to the significance of death, and my reorientation towards my own mortality, has nothing to do with the future. Being-towards-death makes my mortality real now insofar as I have to address myself in my possibility of Being. Of course, all of this could be said to take time to figure out. And it would be simplistic to suppose that one could throw a switch after breakfast and that a new time would begin after breakfast. There is every reason to think that the process of transformation itself has phases, that it can be anticipated before it can be accomplished, it can be prepared for, it can be toyed with, adumbrated, etc., and that in and through these very intimations, the transformation is actually under way. With these considerations in mind the strange temporality of the transformation being proposed in the *Contributions* can be more clearly understood.

We have seen how the fugal structure of the book, the joining or jointure of the sixfold into a onefold, begins to wean us from linear thinking.[24] And even within the chapter headings, themes from elsewhere are continually popping up. We have seen, too, how thinking the other beginning means repudiating the idea of the New. The other beginning is a singularizing repetition of the first. It is hard to avoid the impression that we have an advantage, coming later, even if our circumstances may be more dire, just because we have the first beginning to work on! So although Heidegger will repudiate the idea of development, it may in fact be the logic of development that is at issue, not the claim that there are no advantages to coming after. Some of Heidegger's thinking here belongs to the world of the always-already, by which many of the most radical thinkers of time this century remind us, in a curious reprise of Plato, that what we take to be up ahead has already happened. This thought was not dormant between Plato and Heidegger. At the beginning of his book *Hegel's Phenomenology of Spirit* Heidegger tells us that the end is in the beginning, even though, it has to be said, this is more reminiscent of an Aristotelian teleology that he would not subscribe to.

There are perhaps two ways in which time is strangely folded in Heidegger. There is the neo-Platonic sense captured in such remarks as 'Whoever seeks has already found . . . Seeking is already holding-oneself-in-the-truth' (section 38). This recalls the Meno in which Socrates questions a slave-boy to demonstrate the knowledge he already possesses without knowing it. And yet Heidegger is not speaking of items of knowledge but rather of an orientation. If the truth were not so much propositional in form as a certain grasp of the spacing or dimensionality of truth, then to the extent that seeking the truth already partakes of that spacing, the very capacity to pursue the truth means that one is already, at least in part, on the way.[25] This would be a case of the sometimes already, not the always already. What this suggests, very much in keeping with what Heidegger is up to in this book, is that once we step aside from teleological development, and from means/ends calculative rationality, there is still considerable room for a deepening grasp of what the proposed reorientation consists in. Indeed, *Contributions* is not just the record of Heidegger's efforts to explain himself. It is itself the working through of what embarking on that reorientation, entering into the 'crossing' over, might mean. Let me take a curious example, which seems to go against what we have just said. In section 42, Heidegger sets aside, one after the other, various understandings of what he is up to, and how to think through the movement from *Being and Time* to thinking *Ereignis*.

> Here there is no gradual 'development'. Even less [does] what is earlier already include ... what comes later. [It] also averts the historical approach, which gives up what is earlier as 'false' ...[26]

Instead, Heidegger describes this 'way' as 'stumbling and getting up again ... Because in the thinking of be-ing [where] everything steers toward what is unique, stumblings are, as it were, the rule!' By stumbling (*Stürzen*), Heidegger effectively conveys the thought that there really is no progress, but rather a series of attempts at thinking which, although they inevitably fail, convey something in their very failure. *Qui perd gagne*, as Sartre would say. This pathos is confirmed by his remark that

> the way itself becomes more and more essential, not as 'personal development', but as the exertion of man – understood totally nonbiographically – to bring be-ing itself within a being to its truth.[27]

What is curious about this example – and his accompanying suggestion that proceeding by way of answering objections would not work because we have not even formulated a coherent position yet – is that there is surely a certain 'development' in coming to realize that we can only here proceed by stumbling. We do get clearer about what is not possible. As I see it, stumbling performs our general vulnerability to failure in such an enterprise, and the specific impossibility of succeeding by what are currently public standards. If stumbling constitutes an interruption to smooth progressivism, at the other end of the spectrum Heidegger will attempt to interrupt linear time, and even the distinction between time and space, by thinking time-space.

However, Heidegger's presentation of time-space interrupts our ordinary sense of time (and space) only in a very particular way that it would be easy to misunderstand. Time-space is not another representation of any sort. It does not replace time or space with a new and improved model. It is not a Minkowskian four-dimensional space–time. The interruption comes not in the replacement of one model of time with another; 'we are not dealing at all with altering representation ... but rather with dis-placing human being into Da-sein' (section 239). One way of understanding this would be to say that what we call space and time have their 'origin' in time-space, and that while for Kant, for example, space and time are forms of intuition located in a subject, for Heidegger, space–time is intimately connected to the essential sway of truth, which itself makes possible anything we might call a subject. Time-space, it has to be said, defies description almost more than any of the other 'concepts' introduced in this book.

Heidegger introduces into this expression various of the modes of separation, withdrawal, constitutive strife, resonance, and grounding that are developed throughout the book. Words do not exactly fail him, but clearly the attempt to think time-space is clearer as a battle against various representations of time and space than any positive characterization. However irritating the translators' persistent determination to capture the verbalizing tendencies in Heidegger's lexical innovations (with formulations like en-ownment, en-thinking, essential swaying), they are genuinely responding to Heidegger's own sense that when it comes to the other beginning, the verb is mightier than the noun.[28] (Could *Contributions* be retitled *Reverberations?*) And to be more concrete, there is surely a dimension of time-space that is an event of writing, by which I mean that it appears as the progressive accumulation of semantic connections to his characterizations of truth, grounding, representation, etc. This may sound an oddly formalistic way of putting it, but there is, I believe, an intimate connection between Heidegger's stumbling writing and the displacement he is trying to achieve. Displacing 'human being into Da-sein', the remark we cited above, seems to be at least in part acquiring certain habits of connectivity, as well as those we discussed above as negative capability. Heidegger's writing, with all his stumblings, exemplify these connections, and reinforce these dispositions. Kant said of the schematism that Nature was unlikely ever to reveal its secret to us. Heidegger's time-space seems to be the attempt to set up lines of communication, however broken, with that secret.

The dispositional ingredients of negative capability can be given names – refusal, hesitation, withdrawal, resistance. Each of these terms is capable of a certain displacement, applying at different moments at man and to Being itself. 'Displacing man into Da-sein' means grasping the ontological significance of these dispositions. *Contributions* shows us how that works. The temporal significance of these dispositions is that they each mark an interruption in smooth instrumental agency and its orderly temporal flow. Heidegger will also make great use of many terms that capture the discontinuous nature of the venture of thinking on which he is engaged. We have seen that the 'way' is one on which he stumbles. He speaks of us as engaged in transition, in which stumbling would be appropriate. He writes of the leap involved in the movement to thinking. 'The leap gives rise to preparedness for belongingness to eventuation.... The most actual and the broadest leap is that of thinking' (section 120). Again what is interesting here is that Heidegger is using this Kierkegaardian expression to capture not a breakthrough in which one positively arrives at some great goal, but rather a leap that opens up 'a preparedness'! Again, the movement from distress to distress at the lack of distress is a leap which, when it 'breaks out, strikes against the staying away of the arrival and flight of the gods' (section 120). This leap, in other words, again does not produce a definite outcome, but rather counteracts a withdrawal. The kinds of breakthrough effected by the leap are themselves provisional and dispositional. But Heidegger's point is that this is where what matters happens.

Nietzsche claimed to have written for an audience that might be 300 years in coming, anticipating those with ears behind ears, a different kind of human, or an *Übermensch*. It is as if the future offered a site into which an imaginary community could be projected. Heidegger's references to the ones to come seem seamlessly grafted onto Nietzsche's thinking. He calls them 'Strangers of like mind who are equally decided for the gifting and refusing that has been allotted to them...the stillest witness to the stillest stillness...' (section 248), the companions for whom Zarathustra had to substitute animals. These strangers of like mind would begin where Hölderlin begins in the Between, between gods and men (or as Nietzsche put it – the tightrope walker's rope is stretched between man and superman). In establishing the essence of poetry, Heidegger says, 'Hölderlin...first determines a new time. It is the time of the gods that have fled *and* of the god that is coming.'[29] What Heidegger means by a new time is sometimes presented as a new era projected into the future at some point: 'it anticipates a historical time'.[30] But this would be another representation, with all the dangers of misunderstanding that that raises. More carefully, what he means by a 'time' – 'the time is needy' – is closer to a radical negative capability, a time of witness to lost gods, a time of hope, anticipation of a new god. A god is a horizon of possibility impossible to imagine, and distressingly easy to lose hope in.

Enacting self-transformation

If Hölderlin understands the poet as cast out, standing between man and god, and the philosopher's task as that of preserving the poet's insight, what possibilities of self-transformation does this open up? It is fashionable to avoid the language of selfhood altogether. And yet, as we suggested above with respect to experience, it is precisely the problematic space of selfhood that opens up the possibility of transformation. It also offers an opening onto the thinking of a whole tradition of selfhood displacers, from Kierkegaard and Nietzsche, who are so present in this book, to Derrida and Levinas, in whose writing Heidegger is so present. For Heidegger, Hölderlin presents the poet as situated *between* men and gods. But he also redeploys the structure of the Between to characterize the position of Da-sein: 'Dasein is the "between" between be-ing and a being' (section 218). But unlike the position in *Being and Time*, by the time of *Contributions* Dasein is not just a post-metaphysical name for man, it is an achievement (much as *subjectivity* becomes an achievement rather than a given, for Kierkegaard). And Heidegger has transposed the position Hölderlin attributes to the poet to the broader transformational possibility he is attempting to enact.

If selfhood in what we could call its illusory form is cut off from its own abyssal groundedness, its relation to its other, the classic problem is how it can come to an awareness of this condition. If, as we have seen, for Heidegger, to seek is already to have found, then not to seek is surely already to be lost. How can one find the light switch in the dark? The answer in *Being and Time* was the call of conscience, in which the authentic self calls to the everyday self, and interrupts. In *Contributions* the same role is played by Hölderlin's naming of the gods. The effect of such an interruption on selfhood is to take us out of ourselves, to turn the enclosure of selfhood inside out. For Kierkegaard, it is despair that opens up the possibility of being 'transparently grounded in the Power that constituted me'; for Nietzsche, it is the relation to the *Übermensch* that releases me from my state of being human – all-too-human; for Levinas, it is the face-to-face relation which brings about a dehiscence of self; and, for Derrida, selfhood is always riven and textually distributed. For Heidegger, the whole question of man's selfhood seems both metaphysically entrenched and yet poised for a kind of reversal. As Heidegger puts it:

> Because selfhood – the site for the moment of the call and the belongingness – must first be set up for decision, the one who is in the crossing cannot know what comes unto him.[31]

What does this reversal look like?

> Man's selfhood ... is a domain of events wherein man will be owned unto himself only when he himself reaches into the open time-space in which an owning can take place.[32]

A little later Heidegger puts another twist on this movement when he speaks of 'transformation of man himself' as a reversal (section 41). How does this happen? 'The transformation of man here means becoming other in what is ownmost to him' (ibid.). Otto Pöggeler and Günter Figal put the point like this: for Heidegger we must learn to be at home in the uncanny, in the remote.[33] This does not mean expanding selfhood to include otherness. It means opening selfhood to an indeterminable relation to otherness. Heidegger offers an example of this reversal in the course of talking strategically about how to deal with the fact that the ordinary philosophical language with which we begin bears with it precisely the limitations we need to shed.

> This difficulty cannot be eliminated at all.... This conditions an approach that within certain limits must extend to ordinary understanding and must go a certain stretch of the way with it, in order then at the right moment to exact a turning in thinking, but only under the power of the same word. For example, 'decision' can and should at first be meant as a human 'act' – not of course in any moral sense but still in terms of enactment – until it suddenly means the essential sway of being. This does not mean that be-ing is interpreted 'anthropologically', but the reverse: that man is put back into the essential sway of be-ing and cut off from the fetters of 'anthropology'.[34]

The implication of such moves, of course, is that becoming at home in the uncanny does not mean forced residence in an unpleasant place. It means, rather, the shedding of a sense of self that is a mere artefact of representationalism. There is, however, a second dimension of reversal of self, one that operates performatively throughout this text, and that is the dimension of will. In ways that seem pretty clearly to be a working through of his political folly, this text repeatedly and in many different ways enacts a displacement of the will. Perhaps the most obvious way in which this happens can be thought by reference to his discussion of decision. In sections 43–49, Heidegger explains what he does and does not mean by decision. We tend to think of decision as 'an activity of man, of an enactment, of a process. But here neither the human character in an activity nor the process dimension is essential.'[35] Later (section 46) he will say that decision is not a matter or choice. Paradoxically, the kind of decision he is talking about is the one that would determine whether we thought of decision in terms of human volition, or in terms of the disposition of being. Decision for Heidegger is not a matter of will, but rather marks the critical possibility of a thinking from eventuation, thinking from the standpoint of being – or not. The will is associated with the subject's illusion of mastery – although it has been well said that the other beginning is not one in which the will would be entirely eliminated but rather one in which the will would no longer have a metaphysical primacy.[36] Nor is the setting aside of the will without its implications for the theme of performativity. It would be easy to understand enactment and performance in wilful terms. There is no doubt that Heidegger does exercise a great deal of control over this text; but interestingly we could say that the control he exercises lies largely in pursuing the effects of refusing a certain model of instrumental agency. This text is, as it were, a stage for the development of transformational possibilities – not possibilities of willing, but of letting something else happen, of displacing the very subject of the will. It is interesting in this context to compare Derrida's 'The *Retrait* of Metaphor', which precisely performs the loss of control, albeit with a certain mastery.[37] If all the displacements of man into Da-sein were not enough to make the point, we should simply reiterate that the central basis for the displacement of the will is the recognition that it is in being or truth itself that mastery is to be found. But to the extent that we can engage in inceptual thinking, we get close to a masterful knowing (section 27). And yet when he writes, 'What is grasped here – and what is only and always to be grasped – is be-ing in the joining of those jointures. The masterful knowing of this thinking can never be said in a proposition', he seems to allow mastery to be reinstated as a property of a middle voice. Perhaps he would argue that the recognition of the privilege of the middle voice is precisely the point at which it is proper that something like will can return, because it is no longer *my* will. Those with theological suspicions would be worried by the echo of 'Not my Will, Lord, but thy Will be done', and the obvious possibilities of covert or displaced will. The obvious general point is that there is a certain tension – perhaps healthy – between the staging of the setting aside of the will, of renunciation, and the care and control that seems to be required for that staging. Perhaps Heidegger would say that what we are calling care and control is a certain measured release rather than a resurrected will. It is worth noting that while Heidegger will explicitly endorse enactment, he is not at all in favour of the language of staging. 'If from time to time the theatrical comes to power, how is it then with the ownmost?' (section 223). Heidegger here identifies exhibition, play-acting with dissembling, and we can only suppose he is thinking of the Nuremberg rallies when he writes 'the theatrical comes to power'. What may perhaps be hardest for him to think is the intimate connection between all those dispositional negativities – withdrawal, reticence, refusal – and theatre, drama and staging. It might not be his first impulse to pursue that connection, but even the sense of phenomena as self-showings that occasionally need to be wrested from concealment seems compatible with the language of staging, for it suggests that self-showing may need help. And nothing could convince us faster of the appropriateness of this language than the careful arrangements of scenes that Heidegger himself is engaged in here. Obviously, it will be important to be able to separate staging as the creation of illusion, from staging as letting something be seen as it is. And we will also need to separate the strategic considerations involved in staging from questions of mere instrumentality. It may turn out that the concern to create one effect or outcome rather than another is common to any activity whatsoever, not least Heidegger's delicate weaving of *Contributions*. The issue would then be not whether there was any commerce with questions of strategy, but whether calculation was in charge! What Heidegger himself may feel able to avow should not here be the last word. When Heidegger speaks of repeated stumblings, it is indeed important that the stumblings themselves are not intended to have an effect, but are the result of a certain innocent effort. Yet the claim that what he is doing resembles a series of stumblings does surely draw on a certain value – authentic uncalculating persistence – to legitimize the style of the text. Is that so bad? Could such considerations ever be wholly renounced? The whole book is framed around questions of danger and the necessary risk of misunderstanding and failure.

Heidegger will deny that enactment can be a co-enactment. And yet it is clear that the reader is projected as a party to this text in such a way that questions of staging are inevitable. 'No one understands what "I" think here...' (section 2), writes Heidegger. 'No one grasps this, because everyone tries to explain "my" attempt merely historically...' (ibid.). The reader of course is being solicited as an ally!

We need to say here too that there is a certain contest over the shape of an other beginning, and if it is not a contest that Heidegger will articulate, it is one that his successors cannot avoid. The contest is between those for whom the other beginning is a realm of purity, in which calculation, willing, representation, subject – are all eliminated. Or whether what is critical is not their elimination at all, but rather the fact that they no longer set the agenda. The difficulty here is of course that for their displacement to take place at all we have to come to see these terms as naming not occasional tendencies and temptations, or incidental phenomena, but as ways of thinking being. It is not wholly clear how these rulers would set aside their power and re-enter civil society! If, as we have seen, these displacements occur through such dramatic phenomena as leaps and reversals, would we not be faced with an all-or-nothing choice: e.g. representation or eventuation? But the all-or-nothing choice may rather be between a certain totalizing ordering of the real, and a structure of selfhood (and much more) in touch with its own possibilities and open to its various Others. Representation, calculation, etc., could perhaps operate within the latter, but without their hegemonic pretensions.

Coming to an end

Reading Heidegger performatively means trying to understand the various modalities of enactment and performance on which his writing relies. We have followed these through in various ways: the problem of escaping from machination, the 'analytic' of negative capability, the necessity of reticence, the deconstructive folding back of linear time, receptivity to interruption, and the reversals that make possible a new kind of selfhood, one drawn out into its relation to Being. We have mentioned, and could have developed more, the parallels between what we could rashly call existential and ontological performativity, parallels that are joined in the word Da-sein. And we have claimed, and sometimes only implied, that this very text, *Contributions*, is a mixture of a training manual and a journal of self-analysis in the way in which it teaches and develops dispositions of negative capability, and deploys them in the service of preparing for a new beginning, for the passing of the last god, for being-historical thinking. And we have seen that in this space, preparing for something is already to have begun. But if the arguments we have offered, and the considerations we have adduced, about the necessity of performativity are correct, then unless I myself have been writing performatively, I will be caught in a performative contradiction, describing what I have shown we need to *do*. I could raise this question another way: in what sense have I responded to Heidegger's sense of the important difference between going counter to the other and going to the other's encounter? What am I doing with respect to Heidegger?

Working within a very different philosophical space, in a new century, it would be very hard not to produce a certain transformation performance even if one were to merely try to present Heidegger's work. Translation itself already enacts choices, some personal, some of wider historical importance. I have not, however, merely attempted what Derrida would call a 'doubling commentary'. Rather I have tried to bring out, and thereby to make its challenge visible and audible, the reasons why Heidegger thought performativity was unavoidable. Now we could agree that it is unavoidable in a technical sense – that even mere commentary could be said to *do* something (bore the audience, reinforce existing prejudice, explain in a new way). And describing and representing are both kinds of doing. Heidegger's claim is stronger – that a performative thinking, with all the hesitation and subtlety that he opens up, is necessary if man is not to be dissolved in calculation. Such a thinking has to be able to reopen possibilities, respond to the call of the uncanny, risk unintelligibility, and set aside any assurance of success. On the whole I agree with this account. There is plenty of work still to be done by the accountants of thinking, but there are particular challenges posed by the task of continuing to be able to think outside the box. I have attempted, at some risk, to make some of Heidegger's moves harder to refuse, by translating them, at least in part, into an idiom that does not in advance require full membership of the Heidegger club. More specifically I have intervened at various points with a move that has the following shape: that escape from machination (representation, calculation, etc.) is escape from a totalizing logic, not escape from any commerce with these effects whatsoever. The real leap would then be reconfigured as a shift from a space of calculation and representation, in which no form of alterity can appear, to one that vigorously preserves that possibility without banishing calculation entirely. The desire for purity has almost as many problems attached to it as those it leaves behind. Am I attributing that desire to Heidegger? His references to a 'simple saying' do suggest that Heidegger is not immune to the temptations of a certain experience of presence. But if I am right, what is more significant is the whole stage that Heidegger sets out, in which this desire is but one of the characters.

When in 1976 Heidegger said famously that 'Only a god can save us', he was echoing the logic of his interest in Hölderlin's poetry. We need a god because the problem we have is of the same order (the flight of the gods). A god would be a power lying outside the frame we find ourselves in. But while it is true that we should fear our enemy, should we not also be wary of those who would save us? Is not the welcoming of a god the replication of a logic of traumatic loss, which would require an absolute solution to an absolute problem, after being forcibly detached from its reliance on more subtle distinctions? The fascistic appropriation of the desires that follow traumatic loss is well documented. Heidegger's Führer flirtations in 1933–4 can perhaps be understood in these terms. But *Contributions* is wrestling with a much more interesting question: Can the imaginative[38] and symbolic resources of poetry be preserved without being attached to the desire for or the belief in instrumental action? This is a fine risk. It is one Heidegger believes he has to take under emergency conditions. And he is, of course, quite right that in a situation in which what is needed cannot happen without risk, not taking a risk is not an option. Could someone convert everything he is saying into a blueprint for action? Every move he makes in *Contributions* works against that temptation. Does it all then turn into a kind of passivism? Of course not. What my diagnosis does here is to restage the fundamental wager that Heidegger is making, in such a way that it can be connected up to the work of other thinkers.[39] But this is work for another day.

Notes

Introduction: Aspects of the Plot

1 I explain precisely what I mean by corruption here in an essay 'Philosophy: The Anti-Oxidant of Higher Education', which can be accessed at www.vanderbilt.edu/ans/philosophy/Faculty/woodarticle.html
2 This is a reference to section 5 of Heidegger's *Contributions to Philosophy*, discussed in detail in chapter 10.

Chapter 1 Thinking at the Limit

1 S.T. Coleridge, *The Friend* [1818], Ayer Publishing Co., 1971. The passage quoted here is from vol. III, section 2, Essay XI.
2 How can we handle the problem of faith and God? The tradition from Hegel, Kierkegaard, Nietzsche, Heidegger and Merleau-Ponty to, more recently, Ricoeur, Levinas, Nancy, Marion and Derrida gives us much fuel for thought. In my view, we need to start from the following observations:

(a) The *problem* of faith is inseparable from the way we define reason (see Kant, Hegel, Kierkegaard). The recognition that reason has both limits and conditions opens the way to attempts to think those limits and conditions which will at least overlap with religious thought. Both phenomenology and hermeneutics make *faith* in some sense indispensable.

(b) If we come to see ordinary linear time as a levelling-off of a more primordial existential time, then the challenge that arises is how to think the infinite in the finite, how to think of salvation on earth, how to think eternal life *through* rather than *after* death. It is in this way that we might try to think of the life of Christ.

(c) It seems to me at least, an obligation, as a philosopher, to resist religious formulations for as long as possible, quite as much as those of traditional metaphysics. There is no royal road or short-cut to philosophical insight, and religious belief cannot be immune to philosophical reflection. This is how we should understand Heidegger's *Being* – as a way of opening up philosophy to questions it had become accustomed to pass on to theology. It is this detour, this long route, which is taken by Ricoeur.

(d) There is every reason to want to encourage the separate development of philosophy, theology and poetry, precisely so that each will continue to force the other to rethink its own limits and, in doing so, keep itself young and vigorous.

(e) What about the question of negative theology? When Dufrenne, for example, made this charge against Derrida, he resisted it vigorously. It suggests a reactive opposition to theology rather than a displacement of it.

3 'Philosophy as a Rigorous Science', in *Phenomenology and the Crisis of Philosophy*, New York: Harper, 1965, p. 76. (Hereafter *PRS*.)

4 *PRS*, p. 72.

5 *PRS*, pp. 72–3.

6 *PRS*, p. 140.

7 These three difficulties can be attributed to the names of Heidegger, Derrida and Levinas respectively.

8 Reference is being made here to Heidegger's essay entitled 'The End of Philosophy and the Task of Thinking' [1964], published in *On Time and Being*, trans. Joan Stambaugh, New York: Harper & Row, 1972.

9 This talk was presented at the Second City nightclub in Chicago some time in the 1950s.

10 'Truth and Falsity in their Ultra-Moral Sense', in *The Existentialist Tradition*, ed. Nino Languilli, Humanities Press, 1971, p. 75.

11 If not flawed, at least in need of a certain normative qualification. A metaphysical dualist could say that of course we are in some important sense embodied, but that it is just this embodiment that generates all that clouds our thought, that sways our reason, and that turns us away from the contemplation of form. Imagine a mathematician who had qualms about talking of three or five rather than three apples or five oranges. A certain somatic abstraction is the lifeblood of philosophy... Perhaps one of the most valuable gifts of Nietzsche and Freud is to allow us to name the forms and consequences of the various modes in which we set aside the body, something it was hard to do if thinking could only begin on the other side of that operation.

12 From Wittgenstein's 'Lecture on Ethics' [1929], in *Philosophical Review*, Jan. 1965.

Chapter 2 The Return of Experience

1 Martin Heidegger, *Contributions to Philosophy (From Enowning)*, trans. Parvis Emad and Kenneth Maly, Bloomington: Indiana University Press, 1999, p. 19.

2 Such a 'return' of experience nicely illustrates the necessarily strategic aspects of judging whether or not by drawing on this or that word one will be drawn in to a whole frame of reference commonly associated with it.

3 'Letter on Humanism', in *Martin Heidegger: Basic Writings*, ed. David Farrell Krell, London: Routledge & Kegan Paul, 1978.

4 '"Eating Well", or the Calculation of the Subject', Jean-Luc Nancy interview with Jacques Derrida, in Derrida's *Points...Interviews 1974–1994*, Stanford: Stanford University Press, 1995.

5 In *Poetry, Language, Thought*, New York: Harper & Row, 1971, p. 210. (Hereafter *PLT*.)

6 See here the work of John Llewelyn, for example, *The Middle Voice of Ecological Conscience*, London: Macmillan, 1991; and of Charles Scott, for example, *The Question of Ethics*, Bloomington: Indiana University Press, 1990, and *On the Advantages and Disadvantages of Ethics and Politics*, Bloomington: Indiana University Press, 1996.

7 'Eating Well'.

8 *Notebooks 1914–1916*, Oxford: Basil Blackwell, 1961, p. 73.

9 Quoted in Michael Murray (ed.), *Heidegger and Modern Philosophy*, New Haven: Yale, 1978, p. 80.

10 From 'Language', in *PLT*, p. 189.

11 'What is Metaphysics?' trans. R.F.C. Hull and Alan Crick, in Martin Heidegger, *Existence and Being*, ed. Werner Brock, Chicago: Henry Regnery, 1949, p. 336. (Hereafter *WM*.)

12 *WM*, p. 340.

13 Rudolf Carnap. 'The Overcoming of Metaphysics through Logical Analysis of Language' [1931], in *Logical Positivism*, ed. A.J. Ayer, New York: Free Press, 1966.

14 *What is Called Thinking?* [1954], trans. Fred D. Wieck and J. Glenn Gray, New York: Harper, 1968.

15 The possibility that God might be reduced to playing a structural role in a calculable thanking relationship shows us just how complex things can get. This is not of course Heidegger's take on things at all; Heidegger tries to preserve thanking from any possibility of completion, let alone a theological framing. Derrida goes further. See, for example, his various meditations on the aporetic logic of the gift, such as: *Given Time: 1. Counterfeit Money*, trans. Peggy Kamuf, Chicago: University of Chicago, 1992; *Aporias*, trans. Thomas Dutoit, Stanford: Stanford University, 1993; *The Gift of Death*, trans. David Wills, Chicago: University of Chicago, 1995. 'The gift' is both a logic of (albeit impossible) exchange

that we can uncover in places where it is not apparent. In other cases it may be the very structure of its impossibility that needs to be brought out.

16 Expressions of the form 'Deconstruction is this or that' are not completely frivolous although there is something faintly odd about them, given that deconstruction does not subscribe to the essentialism that these 'is' propositions suggest. If we were to dismantle these formulae, we would first find an underlying claim of the form that the question, concept, theme or philosopheme in question is best illuminated by the aporetic workings of deconstruction. The further claim is that deconstruction itself can then be better understood in the light of this other concept. Thus 'Deconstruction is justice' captures both the sense that justice, in a narrower sense, arises at the point at which we grasp the inadequacy of restricting ourselves to rule-governed responses, and the sense that the practice of deconstruction brings to bear considerations of justice on a wider territory. When, below, I claim that 'Vegetarianism is deconstruction' (and then vice versa), I am making the claim that vegetarianism need not be thought restrictedly in terms of the eating of meat, but more broadly as a practice of respect, in which the object of our interest escapes the gaze in which we typically contain it.

17 *Of Grammatology* [1967], trans. Gayatri Spivak, Baltimore: Johns Hopkins, 1976, pp. 60–1. (Hereafter *OG*.)

18 'Sauf le nom', in *On the Name*, ed. Thomas Dutoit, trans. David Wood, John P. Leavy and Ian McLeod, Stanford: Stanford University Press, p. 43.

19 See, for example, ' "Genesis and Structure" and Phenomenology [1959]', in *Writing and Difference*, trans. Alan Bass, Chicago: University of Chicago Press, 1978; and 'Form and Meaning: A Note on the Phenomenology of Language [1967]', in *Speech and Phenomena*, trans. David Allison, Evanston: Northwestern, 1973.

20 See Kierkegaard, *The Sickness unto Death*, trans. Walter Lowrie, New York: Doubleday Anchor, 1954.

21 *OG*, p. 165.

22 *OG*, p. 165.

23 *OG*, p. 166.

24 Introduction to *Phenomenology of Spirit*, trans. A.V. Miller, para. 14.

25 *OG*, p. 62.

26 *OG*, p. 166.

27 See his *Positions* [1972], trans. Alan Bass, Chicago: University of Chicago, 1981.

28 ' "Eating Well", or the Calculation of the Subject', Jean-Luc Nancy interview with Jacques Derrida, in Derrida's *Points ... Interviews 1974–1994*, Stanford: Stanford University Press, 1995.

29 His use of the word 'experience' in *The Experience of Freedom* deserves a separate treatment. See Jean-Luc Nancy, *The Experience of Freedom* [1988], trans. Bridget McDonald, Stanford: Stanford University Press, 1993.

30   *The Writing of the Disaster* [1980], trans. Ann Smock, Lincoln and London: University of Nebraska Press, 1986. (Hereafter *WD*.)

31   *OG*, p. 15.

32   *WD*, p. 24.

33   See my *On the Way: Ethico-Political Interrogations*, New York: Routledge [forthcoming].

34   I deal more fully with Heidegger's reading of Hegel in chapter 5, below.

35   Martin Heidegger, *Hegel's Phenomenology of Spirit*, trans. Parvis Emad and Kenneth Maly, Bloomington: Indiana University Press, 1988; and his *Hegel's Concept of Experience*, New York: Harper & Row, 1970.

36   Martin Heidegger, *Hegel's Concept of Experience*, New York: Harper & Row, 1970. (Hereafter *HCE*.)

37   See, for example, Howard Caygill's entry on 'Experience' in his *A Kant Dictionary*, Oxford: Blackwell, 1995, p. 185.

38   *HCE*, p. 21.

39   *OG*, p. 57.

40   Ibid.

41   *OG*, p. 59.

42   See his *Concluding Unscientific Postscript*, trans. David Swenson and Walter Lowrie, Princeton: Princeton University Press, 1941, pp. 178ff.

43   For a fuller treatment, see my 'Kierkegaard, God and the Economy of Thought', in *The Kierkegaard Reader*, ed. Jane Chamberlain and Jonathan Rée, Oxford: Blackwell, 1997.

44   *WM*, p. 340.

45   The need for this constant re-examination is intimately tied up with the fact that at a certain point we run out of rules for the application of rules, and yet there is still something to be said, albeit of a different order.

46   *The Gift of Death*, trans. David Wills, Chicago: University of Chicago Press, 1995, p. 53.

47   Ibid., p. 54.

48   Ibid.

49   See, for example, Edmund Husserl, *Experience and Judgment*, trans. James S. Churchill and Karl Ameriks, Evanston: Northwestern University Press, 1973.

50   See his essay 'Simulacrum, or The End of the World', in *Writing the Future*, ed. D.C. Wood, London: Routledge, 1990.

51   See especially *WD*.

52   The logic of my argument is not dissimilar to the common objection to Descartes' universal doubt. The fact that we can doubt anything does not mean we can doubt everything.

53   *The Gift of Death*, p. 69.

54   Compare here Derrida's discussion of our various 'double duties' and the impossibility of choosing between them, his account of the need to go through the 'undecidable', each of which emphasizes the need to remember in each decision the struggle in which it is grounded, which is

already an antidote to any hyperbolic quantification of our obligations. The specific issue of the 'open door' at the borders of a nation is addressed in his *Of Hospitality* (with Anne Dufourmantelle), Stanford: Stanford University Press, 2000, in which he plays off a conditional hospitality (for example, immigration based on the labour needs of the host country) against an unconditional (or pure) hospitality which, for all its 'impossibility', must not be lost sight of, or excluded in advance. These arguments would function as brakes on any over-hasty formula that would establish a sensible balance between (say) security and exposure. The claim (which I expand below), in chapters 8 and 9, that hospitality requires that we are always willing to open a closed door does not in fact determine any particular regime or economy of closure.

55 See here my 'Responsibility Reinscribed (and How)', in *Responsibilities of Deconstruction*, PLI: *Warwick Journal of Philosophy*, ed. Jonathon Dronsfield and Nick Midgley, vol. 6, Summer 1997.

Chapter 3 The Voyage of Reason

1 An early version of this chapter was presented to the Festival Internazionale del Nuovo Teatro di Chieri: International Meeting on 'Discovery' and 'Conquest', Italy, July 1992, at the invitation of Gianni Vattimo.

2 See, for example, *Le Séminaire: Livre XX. Encore* (Paris, Editions du Seuil, 1972), p. 108. I owe this reference to William Richardson's 'Lacan and Non-Philosophy', in *Philosophy and Non-Philosophy since Merleau-Ponty*, ed. Hugh J. Silverman, New York: Routledge, 1988, pp. 120–35.

3 'Preface' to *The Gay Science*, 2nd edition [1887].

4 It has to be admitted that the question of mastery is not one that can be ever quite resolved in Heidegger. While he abjures any first-order sense of man as subject having mastery over nature or the world, one of the fruits of a renewed grasp of our fundamental attunement is that it makes possible a distinction within the idea of mastery. 'Because philosophy is such a mindfulness, it leaps ahead into the utmost possible decision and by its [own] opening dominates in advance all sheltering of the truth in and as beings. Therefore, philosophy is *masterful knowing*, even though not an "absolute knowing" in the style of the philosophy of German Idealism' [*Contributions*, p. 31]. The question of whether Heidegger is finding a subtle way to restore mastery, or whether, on the contrary, he is setting the desire for mastery within a structure of essential non-mastery – our openness to being – is one that will be taken up again in the last chapter.

5 In *On the Way to Language*, New York: Harper & Row, 1971; in *Holzwege* ['What are Poets For?']; in *Vortrage und Aufsätze* ['... poetically man dwells']. These latter essays can be found in *Poetry, Language, Thought*, New York, Harper & Row, 1971. (Hereafter *PLT*.)

6 'Language', in *PLT*, pp. 192–3.
7 The year Freud first used the word psycho-analysis; four years before *The Psychoanalysis of Dreams*.
8 From *Through the Looking Glass*, in *The Complete Illustrated Works of Lewis Carroll*, London: Chancellor Press, 1982, p. 184.
9 Ibid.
10 'The *Retrait* of Metaphor' in *Enclitic* 2, no. 2, Fall 1978, pp. 6–33. French original in *Psyché*, Paris: Galilée, 1987.
11 Lordship is a translation of *Herrschaft*. Also mastery!
12 G.W.F. Hegel, *Phenomenology of Spirit* [1807], trans. A.V. Miller, Oxford: Oxford University Press, 1977.
13 Heidegger, Sartre, Levinas and Derrida, for example.
14 Immanuel Kant, *Critique of Pure Reason*, trans. N. Kemp Smith, London: Macmillan, 1964, Bvii.
15 See Galileo, 'Against the Aristotelians', in *Telos*.

Chapter 4 Heidegger and the Challenge of Repetition

1 'His' is retained from the original contexts cited. Please read 'his or hers'.
2 *Critique of Pure Reason*, 'Transcendental Dialectic'.
3 *What is Called Thinking?*, p. 77. (Hereafter WCT.)
4 In *Kant and the Problem of Metaphysics*.
5 Cf. Derrida, in *Of Grammatology*.
6 *WCT*, p. 77.
7 It will at some point have to be asked whether this supposed shallowness does not deny to a certain criticism a performative validation that could belie its apparent 'naïveté'.
8 *Of Grammatology*, p. 158.
9 *Spurs*, p. 101.
10 See Jean-Luc Nancy, *The Inoperable Community*.
11 See 'Why I stay in the provinces'.
12 *Poetry, Language, Thought*, 'Language', p. 190.
13 'Es gibt': a German idiomatic rendition of 'there is'; compare the English questions 'What gives?', 'What's up?' or 'What's happening?'
14 'The End of Philosophy', in *On Time and Being*, p. 63.
15 *Being and Time*, p. 36.
16 *On Time and Being*, p. 14.
17 Op. cit.
18 Op. cit., p. 15.
19 Op. cit., p. 17.
20 By 'performativity' I mean the space of our attempts at embodying in our manner and stance of writing, at various levels, the truth we seem to be seeking, contesting, but never entirely escaping, the conceptuality of 'performance', 'embodiment', 'enactment', etc.

21   See the last page of *On Time and Being*.
22   I am returning here to my discussion of this topic in *The Deconstruction of Time* ('Nietzsche's Transvaluation of Time', pp. 28–9) where I understood the moment [*Augenblick*] in terms of a 'non-appropriative exceeding', a 'willing... higher than any reconciliation', as Nietzsche's attempt to think a repetition that affirms risk and the possibility of loss. The shape of this return here is indebted substantially to Will McNeill's discussion of this topic in chapter 7, 'Vision and the Enigma', of his *The Glance of the Eye*, Albany: SUNY Press, 1999.
23   Nietzsche, vol. 1, p. 297, quoted in McNeill, p. 224.

Chapter 5 Heidegger's Reading of Hegel's *Phenomenology of Spirit*

1   This chapter began its life as a paper delivered to the Hegel Society of Great Britain, Pembroke College, Oxford, 11 September 1990, at their conference *The Presence of Hegel in Contemporary Thought*. I begin by reflecting on the philosophical implications of the very title of the conference.
2   Published in English as *Reason in History*, Indianapolis: Bobbs-Merrill, 1953.
3   I make no claims to completeness in this review.
4   *Being and Time* [1926], trans. Joan Stambaugh, Albany: SUNY Press, 1996.
5   *Hegel's Phenomenology of Spirit*, trans. Parvis Emad and Kenneth Maly, Bloomington: Indiana University Press, 1988. (Hereafter *HPS*.)
6   *Hegel's Concept of Experience* [1950], New York: Harper & Row, 1970.
7   *Identity and Difference* [1957], trans. Joan Stambaugh, New York: Harper & Row, 1969, p. 42.
8   See H.G. Gadamer, *Hegel's Dialectic: Five Hermeneutical Studies* [1971], trans. P. Christopher Smith, New Haven: Yale University Press, 1976.
9   *Two notes on ontological penetration and totalitarian politics*: 1. I leave aside discussion of the obvious phallocentric overtones of this phrase. Although it is 'my' phrase, it is just such overtones that make it so appropriate for thinking through the desire of ontology. 2. Ontological penetration is not unconnected to the idea of there being levels of truth. Heidegger distinguishes propositional truth from truth as disclosure. But then the question of penetration takes on a vital temporal dimension. There is a difference between *being able* to return to the grounds of truth *as such* (or to its unground) and allowing those grounds to pervade or penetrate propositional truth (for example) at its own level. This was an issue with which Heidegger seems to have dealt satisfactorily at vital points. The whole idea of Nazi science rested on the subjection of

propositional truths to racist ideology, parading as deeper grounds, often dressed up in philosophical, sometimes mystical garb. It is to his credit that Heidegger refused this. And in his essay on the *Essence of Truth*, he does not repudiate propositional truth, he simply says it is not fundamental, resting itself on truth as disclosure. Heidegger wants to say there is a further dimension of truth which both founds and unfounds ordinary truth. And if such claims are not themselves propositional, there must also be another kind of truth, in which thinking and something like the speculative use of language cross. The question of linkage between ontological penetration and totalitarianism is enormously complex. At one level it has to do with the corruptibility of a discourse: '[T]he race problem ... is, according to the word of Der Führer, the key problem of world history... *It was essentially an intuitively grounded sureness of judgement, which conditioned the radical position* taken by the Party in these things' [my emphasis]. *Völkischer Beobachter*, 9/8/ 35, quoted in Robert Brady, *The Spirit and Structure of German Fascism*. At another it has to do with those features of the method, structure, and the analytical and penetrating power of a philosophical discourse that are not intrinsically philosophical, that can be deployed elsewhere. This may not always be, or not necessarily be, sinister; but it does raise disturbing questions for the consideration of philosophical responsibility. It may be true that nothing one says as a philosopher cannot be corrupted. It may even be impossible to say anything significant that could not, *quite legitimately*, have unintended unsavoury implications. But that does not absolve us of the duty to reflect on how best to limit and direct the reception of our texts. And if philosophy were straightforwardly a discourse of power or mastery (which we have questioned, see chapter 3 above), or *often mistakenly construed as such*, this would be all the more necessary. Moreover, ontological penetration raises yet another question, which is that of the status of that which has been passed through – not unlike that posed by *Aufhebung* in Hegel. What was so frightening about the rise of the Third Reich was its dismantling of existing mediating institutions, and their replacement by centralized politicized command structures, embracing culture, youth, university teaching and research as well as the economy. Here penetration did not mean understanding the deeper significance of x, or being able to draw on hidden depths, to return to the origins for a dip. It meant radical internal reorganization and the setting up of chains of command and responsibility to implement change. This reorganization did not of course just mean adjusting the arrangement of existing parts. It involved everything from removal from office to deportation and death. What gives this licence is a certain kind of penetration of the existing order that can reduce not only individual existence, but also the particular ethical order, to nothing but moments to be overcome. It is perhaps no accident that Heidegger would repudiate the very idea of 'overcoming' in his later accounts of thinking.

10 I am thinking here of the Nazi's exploitation of Nietzsche's bellicose utterances, and Eichmann's references to Kant's ethics at Nuremberg.

11 'The Onto-theo-logical Constitution of Metaphysics', in *Identity and Difference*.

12 *Kant and the Problem of Metaphysics*, trans. James Churchill, Bloomington: Indiana University Press, 1962, p. 207.

13 *Positions*, p. 77.

14 *HPS*, p. 23.

15 *HPS*, p. 24.

16 This was begun in my 'Political Openings: Heidegger 1933–4', in *Graduate Faculty Philosophy Journal*, vol. 14, no. 2; vol. 15; no. 1, 1991, *Heidegger and the Political*, pp. 465–78.

17 *HPS*, p. 27.

18 *HPS*, p. 31.

19 *HPS*, p. 31.

20 Note here the etymological connections between *Not* and *Notwendigkeit* (necessity) and *genötigt* (compelled).

21 *HPS*, p. 41.

22 *HPS*, p. 51.

23 *HPS*, p. 51.

24 *HPS*, p. 66. It is perhaps no acccident that Derrida writes (in *Of Grammatology*) of making the value of presence 'tremble'.

25 *HPS*, section 7, 'Mediatedness as the essence of what is immediate and the dialectical movement', pp. 66–80.

26 *HPS*, p. 68.

27 *HPS*, p. 71.

28 See Jacques Derrida, *Of Spirit: Heidegger and the Question*, trans. Geoffrey Bennington and Rachel Bowlby, Chicago: University of Chicago Press, 1989; and David Wood (ed.), *Of Derrida, Heidegger and Spirit*, Evanston: Northwestern University Press, 1993.

29 *HPS*, p. 75.

30 *HPS*, p. 138.

31 *HPS*, p. 141.

32 *HPS*, p. 146.

33 *HPS*, p. 146.

34 Georg Lukács, *History and Class Consciousness*, trans. Rodney Livingstone, London: Merlin Press, 1971.

35 If this leans towards Heidegger away from Hegel, it has to be said that the seriousness with which Hegel takes the ethical life and its institutions, and the difficulty of finding such a recognition in Heidegger, would move us in the other direction. But the same considerations (about the difference between the temporality of radiant presence and that of dispositional access and vulnerability) would apply again.

36 *HPS*, p. 32.

Chapter 6 Heidegger after Derrida

1   J. Derrida, *Positions* [1972], trans. A. Bass, Chicago: University of Chicago Press, 1981, p. 53.
2   Ibid., p. 55.
3   Ibid., p. 54.
4   'Geschlecht II', in *Deconstruction and Philosophy: The Texts of Jacques Derrida*, ed. John Sallis, Chicago: University of Chicago Press, 1987.
5   Derrida's philosophical career is marked by constant and developing reference to Heidegger. Here is a longer list – still selective – of texts in which Heidegger is a major reference point. Full details are supplied in the Bibliography. Derrida's texts [JD] come first, followed by Heidegger's [MH] in brackets. JD: 'The ends of Man' (MH: Letter on Humanism), JD: 'Difference' (MH: 'The Anaximander Fragment'), JD: 'Ousia and Gramme' (MH: *Being and Time*), JD: 'The End of the Book and the Beginning of Writing' (MH: *Being and Time*; *The Question of Being*; *Introduction to Metaphysics*; *Essence of Grounds*), JD: 'Restitutions of the Truth in Painting' (MH: 'Origin of the Work of Art'), JD: 'Letter to a Japanese Friend' (MH: *Being and Time* #6; *Metaphysical Foundations of Logic*; *Basic Problems of Phenomenology*), JD: *Spurs: Nietzsche's Styles* (MH: *Being and Time*; *The Question of Being*; *Nietzsche*), JD: 'Geschlecht: sexual difference / ontological difference' (MH: *Metaphysical Foundations of Logic* #10), JD: 'Envois' (MH: 'The Anaximander Fragment'), JD: *Of Spirit: Heidegger and the Question* (MH: *Being and Time*, 'The Self-Assertion of the German University' [Rectoral Address]), JD: 'Positions' (MH: *Being and Time*, et al.), JD: 'On Reading Heidegger' (MH: various texts), JD: 'Geschlecht II: Heidegger's Hand' (MH: *Being and Time*; *What is Called Thinking?*), JD: 'Eating Well' (MH: *Being and Time*), JD: *Aporias* (MH: *Being and Time*; *On the Way to Language*), JD: *Given Time* (MH: *Being and Time*).
6   *Of Grammatology* [1967], trans. G.C. Spivak, Baltimore: Johns Hopkins, 1974, p. 70.
7   Ibid.
8   Ibid., p. 22.
9   See his 'End of Philosophy and the Task of Thinking' [1966] and 'Letter on Humanism' [1947], both in *Martin Heidegger: Basic Writings*, ed. D.F. Krell, New York: Harper & Row, 1978; and his 'Way Back into the Ground of Metaphysics' [1949], in *Existentialism from Dostoevsky to Sartre* (2nd edition), ed. and trans. by W. Kaufmann, New York: New American Library, 1975.
10 *Positions*, p. 54.
11 While I have retained the existing English translation 'Appropriation' here, I have preferred an alternative translation, 'Eventuation', in the case of the sub-title of *Contributions to Philosophy*. See chapter 10 below.

12 *On Time and Being*, trans. J. Stambaugh, New York: Harper & Row, 1972, p. 23.

13 *Metaphysical Foundations of Logic*, trans. Michael Heim, Bloomington: Indiana University Press, 1984.

14 Ibid.

15 *Spurs: Nietzsche's Styles*, trans. Barbara Harlow, Chicago: University of Chicago Press, 1979.

16 *Of Grammatology.*

17 'Ousia and Gramme', in *Margins*, trans. Alan Bass, Chicago: University of Chicago Press, 1982.

18 See note 5.

19 Extracts from *Discussion* following the presentation of an early version of this chapter, in *Research in Phenomenology*, vol. XVII, 1987, p. 114.

Chapter 7 The Actualization of Philosophy: Heidegger and Adorno

1 *Of Spirit: Heidegger and the Question*, trans. Geoffrey Bennington and Rachel Bowlby, Chicago: University of Chicago Press, 1989.

2 Theodor Adorno, 'The Actuality of Philosophy', trans. Benjamin Snow, *Telos* 31 (Spring 1977), pp. 120–2. (Hereafter *AP*.)

3 Here Adorno shares an unlikely bed with Rudolf Carnap, whose infamous remarks about Heidegger in his 'The Elimination of Metaphysics through the Logical Analysis of Language' showed an impatience of reading that set the scene for much subsequent Anglo-American reception of Heidegger.

4 *AP*, p. 122.

5 He wants philosophy to focus rather on 'concrete inner-historical complexes from which [philosophical questions]...are not to be detached'.

6 *Being and Time*, trans. Joan Stambaugh, Albany: SUNY Press, 1996, p. 4.

7 'What is Metaphysics?' [24 July 1929], trans. David F. Krell, in *Martin Heidegger: Basic Writings*, London: Routledge & Kegan Paul, 1978. (Hereafter *WM*.)

8 *WM*, p. 101.

9 See Philippe Lacoue-Labarthe, *Heidegger, Art and Politics*, trans. Chris Turner, Blackwell, 1990, p. 117. Adorno later admitted to and regretted this review 'from the bottom of his heart' (1963). I thank David Krell for this reference.

10 Adorno is acutely aware of the difficulty of his own position – a difficulty Lyotard later came up against (in his *The Postmodern Condition*) – of using abstract and general categories to outline the necessity for a philosophy of interpretation of non-intentional fragments, linked to materialism. Adorno compares the relation between the philosopher and the sociologist to that between an architect, who develops the

blueprint of a house, and a cat-burglar, who climbs the wall from the outside and takes what he can reach. Adorno sees his own interpretive philosophy as somewhere in between.

11 *Of Spirit*, chapters 3 and 4.
12 Heidegger, *Being and Time*, p. 434.
13 Ibid., chapter 4.
14 Op. cit., p. 29.
15 Op. cit., p. 28.
16 Op. cit., pp. 67–8. It is noteworthy already in these lectures how many of Heidegger's examples involve references to the university, and particularly its employees – 'those who are registered as students or employed as teachers' (p. 67). Note also his reference to the caretaker (p. 62) in which one might think the concerns of the 'Rectoral Address' were prefigured.
17 Op. cit., p. 74.
18 Martin Heidegger, *The Basic Problems of Phenomenology*, trans. A. Hofstadter, Bloomington: Indiana University Press, 1988, p. 178.
19 Martin Heidegger, *Hegel's Phenomenology of Spirit*, Bloomington: Indiana University Press, 1989, p. 146.
20 Op. cit., p. 147.
21 Martin Heidegger, 'The Self-Assertion of the German University', trans. Karsten Harries, *Review of Metaphysics*, 38, no. 3, p. 473.
22 *An Introduction to Metaphysics* [1935], trans. Ralph Manheim, Garden City: Anchor, 1961. (Hereafter *IM*.)
23 See *Being and Time*, section 20.
24 *IM*.
25 These remarks were originally presented in the form of a discussion of Gillian Rose's *Judaism and Modernity* at the Centre for Research in Philosophy and Literature, University of Warwick, 27 April 1994. Gillian Rose (1947–1995) was a friend and adversary, who showed me in practice what Nietzsche had long insisted on, how close these apparent opposites can be.
26 My remarks would not be complete without at least mentioning *The Broken Middle*, and indeed Gillian Rose's three other books, *Hegel contra Sociology*, *Dialectic of Nihilism* (sub-titled *Poststructuralism and Law*), and her introduction to Adorno entitled *The Melancholy Science*. But my remarks will not be complete however much I do or say. There will always be a gap between what needs to be said, what the work calls for, and what I am able to say about it. So I will pretend that a necessary failure justifies this particular avoidance of a synoptic review.
27 *Dialectic of Nihilism*, Oxford: Blackwell, 1984, p. 131.
28 Ibid., p. 132.
29 This line of thought can also be found in Peter Dews's *Logics of Disintegration*, riven by the same paradox – an ahistorical insistence on history.
30 *Judaism and Modernity*, Oxford: Blackwell, 1993, p. 78. (Hereafter *JM*.)

31   *JM*, notes on back cover.
32   *JM*, p. 5.
33   'Violence and Metaphysics' in *Writing and Difference* [1967], trans. Alan Bass, Chicago: University of Chicago Press, 1978, p. 152.
34   Ibid., p. 153.
35   See my 'Comment ne pas manger – Deconstruction and Humanism', in *Animal Others: On Ethics, Ontology and Animal Life*, ed. Peter Steeves, Albany: SUNY Press, 1999.
36   Ibid., p. 125.
37   *JM*, p. 6.
38   Jürgen Habermas, *The Philosophical Discourse of Modernity*, trans. Frederick Lawrence, Cambridge: Polity, 1987.
39   Jacques Derrida, 'White mythology: metaphor in the text of philosophy', in *Margins of Philosophy* [1972], trans. Alan Bass, Chicago: University of Chicago Press, 1982.

Chapter 8 Much Obliged

1   *The Gift of Death*, trans. David Wills, Chicago: University of Chicago Press, 1995. (Hereafter *GD*.)
2   *GD*, p. 71.
3   *GD*, p. 71.
4   *GD*, p. 108.
5   *GD*, p. 109.
6   *GD*, p. 66.
7   *GD*, p. 66.
8   *GD*, pp. 67–8.
9   *GD*, p. 68.
10   *GD*, p. 69.
11   *GD*, p. 71.
12   *GD*, p. 109.
13   Quoted in *GD*, p. 131.
14   *Feuerbach*: 'Only in man's wretchedness does God have his birth-place ... God is what man would like to be; he is man's own essence and goal conceived as a real being' (*Principles of the Philosophy of the Future*, Library of Liberal Arts, 1966, p. 48).
     Nietzsche: 'What if God himself should prove to be our most enduring lie?' (*Gay Science*, section 344).
     Freud: 'The god of each [human being] is formed in the likeness of his father ... and ... at bottom God is nothing but an exalted father' (*Totem and Taboo*, Routledge & Kegan Paul, 1950, p. 147).
15   *The Genealogy of Morals*, New York: Vintage, pp. 84–5, section 16.
16   *Of Spirit*, Chicago, 1989, p. 111.

17 *The Sickness unto Death*, Anchor, 1954, p. 147 (bound together with *Fear and Trembling*).

18 Kant, *Critique of Pure Reason*, trans. Norman Kemp Smith, London: Macmillan, 1964, A141/B180–1.

19 Sartre's paper 'The Singular Universal' is to be found in the collection *Kierkegaard*, ed. J.J. Thompson, Doubleday, 1972. (Hereafter *SU*.)

20 *SU*, p. 263. In an interview in *Points* (trans., p. 202), when asked to describe his own project, the first word Derrida uses is 'adventure'.

21 Sartre writes: 'In a letter to H.P. Berford (Sept. 12 1869) Pastor A.F. Schiodte wrote of Kierkegaard "He once said to Levin that it was a bit of luck for him, Levin, that as a Jew he was free of Christ. For if he, Kierkegaard, was free of Christ then he would have lived in a completely different way, would have enjoyed life, and gotten along quite well"' (*SU*, p. 249).

Chapter 9 *Comment ne pas manger*: Deconstruction and Humanism

1 A version of this chapter appeared in *Animal Others: On Ethics, Ontology and Animal Life*, ed. Peter Steeves, Albany: SUNY Press, 1999, pp. 15–35.

2 Jacques Derrida (with Jean-Luc Nancy) ' "Eating Well", or the Calculation of the Subject: an Interview with Jacques Derrida', in Jacques Derrida, *Points… Interviews 1974–1994*, Stanford: Stanford University Press, 1995.

3 Jean-Paul Sartre, *Existentialism and Humanism* [1946], trans. Philip Mairet, London: Methuen, 1957.

4 Martin Heidegger, 'Letter on Humanism' [1947], trans. Frank A. Capuzzi and J. Glenn Gray, in *Martin Heidegger: Basic Writings*, ed. David Farrell Krell, London: Routledge & Kegan Paul, 1978.

5 See, for example, Jacques Derrida, *Of Spirit: Heidegger and the Question* [1987], trans. Geoffrey Bennington and Rachel Bowlby, Chicago: University of Chicago, 1989.

6 See David Farrell Krell, *Daimon Life: Heidegger and Life-Philosophy*, Bloomington: Indiana University Press, 1992.

7 Derrida, *Of Spirit*, p. 55.

8 See, for example, 'The Paradox of Morality: An Interview…', in *The Provocation of Levinas: Rethinking the Other*, ed. Robert Bernasconi and David Wood, London: Routledge, 1988. He writes, 'It is via the face that one understands, for example, a dog. Yet the priority here is not found in the animal, but in the human face' (p. 169).

9 See *The Provocation of Levinas*, p. 172.

10 I will deal on another occasion with the issues raised by 'L'animal que donc je suis (à suivre)' in *L'animal autobiographique*, Paris, Galilée, 1999.

11 Jacques Derrida, *The Other Heading*, trans. Michael Naas, Bloomington: Indiana University Press, 1992, p. 4.

12 Ibid., p. 5.

13 One notable theoretical elaboration of this boundary crossing is to be found in Donna Haraway's various writings, especially *Simians, Cyborgs, and Women*, New York: Routledge, 1991, and *Modest_Witness@Second_Millenium*, New York: Routledge, 1997.

14 Ibid.

15 Jacques Derrida, 'Force of Law: The "Mystical Foundation of Authority"', in *Deconstruction and the Possibility of Justice*, ed. Drucilla Cornell et al., New York: Routledge, 1992.

16 Jacques Derrida, *Limited Inc*, Evanston: Northwestern University Press, 1988.

17 See n. 1.

18 In other more recent texts, *The Politics of Friendship*, *Of Hospitality*, 'History of the Lie: Prolegomena' and *On Cosmopolitanism and Forgiveness* [see Bibliography for details], a recurrent strategy is to show that each of these concepts is answerable to two incompatible logics or economies. The first goes under many names: calculation, the ethical, exchange, reciprocity; the second such logic we could call that of the undecidable, the infinite, the impossible, the 'to come', the pure. That these two economies are irresolvable permanently prevents us identifying the significance of any of these expressions with their place in the first kind of economy. This scheme then operates as a powerfully recursive way of resisting ethical complacency. But Derrida is at pains to insist that this second logic is not simply that of Kant's equally unrealizable regulative idea. Rather, he insists that it is tied to the recognition of the interruption, the call, the appeal, the advent of a wholly unexpected possibility. These formulations seem to represent a move away from the sense that attending to local concerns involves an absolute sacrifice of one's infinite obligations, and a clearer grasp that this broader space of one's responsibility needs to be thought modally, as an openness whose shape is always to be negotiated anew.

19 *The Other Heading*, p. 28. (Hereafter *OH*.)

20 *OH*, p. 29.

21 *OH*, p. 28.

22 *OH*, p. 28.

23 See n. 1.

24 Husserl, *Ideas*.

25 'Eating Well', p. 104.

26 Ibid.

27 Ibid.

28 Ibid.

29 Ibid., p. 108.

30 Ibid., p. 109.

31 Ibid., p. 112.

32   Ibid., p. 112.
33   Ibid., p. 114.
34   Ibid., p. 115.
35   Ibid., pp. 114–15.
36   'Force of Law', p. 15.
37   I have Simon Critchley to thank for passing on this gem.
38   Theodore Roethke, *Collected Poems*, London: Faber & Faber, 1985, p. 218.

Chapter 10 The Performative Imperative: Reflections on Heidegger's *Contributions to Philosophy (From Eventuation)*

1   This chapter develops with specific reference to Heidegger's *Contributions to Philosophy* dealt with in diverse ways in my *Philosophy at the Limit*, London: Unwin Hyman, 1990. See especially ch. 1 'The Faces of Silence', and ch. 8 'Performative Reflexivity'.
2   The existing English translation of *Beitrage zur Philosophie (Vom Ereignis)* [1936–8], Frankfurt: Klostermann, 1989, is entitled *Contributions to Philosophy (From Enowning)*, trans. Parvis Emad and Kenneth Maly, Bloomington: Indiana University Press, 1999. The word 'eventuation' seems to have more of the right resonances going for it.
3   See Christopher Norris, *Paul De Man*, New York: Routledge, 1988.
4   Paul De Man, *The Resistance to Theory*, Minneapolis: University of Minnesota Press, 1986.
5   See John Sallis's exemplary discussion of this moment in 'Where does *Being and Time* begin?', in his *Delimitations*, Bloomington: Indiana University Press, 1986, pp. 98–118.
6   *Der Spiegel* interview from 1976, printed on his death in 1986.
7   It is disappointingly predictable that people who take themselves to be philosophers can make such claims with a straight face. For the accountants of the real, perhaps, everything is what it is and is not another thing. But it is hard to understand how sophisticated minds can conclude that Heidegger was a Nazi, or that Heidegger was a theologian, without further ado, as if these ascriptions and identifications were not of the same naive form that philosophy would treat as suspect in other circumstances. The closest Heidegger gets here is the early claim that he is a theo-*logian*, which seems to mark the very attempt to reappropriate the 'content' of theology for 'thinking' that I have been describing.
8   *Contributions*, section 1.
9   The modesty of the word 'contributions' anticipates the theme of reticence and intimation that play such a role in this book. It echoes in this respect Kierkegaard's *Concluding Unscientific Postscript*, which suggests a modest ambition, and both enacts and thematizes indirect communication, a version of Heidegger's sigetics.

10   See my 'Deconstructive Phenomenology,' in *Journal of the British Society for Phenomenology*, 1998.
11   See, for example, Karen Feldman's 'The Performative Difficulty of *Being and Time*', *Philosophy Today*, vol. 44. no. 4, 2000.
12   See Reiner Schurmann's 'Riveted to a Monstrous Site', in *The Heidegger Case*, ed. Tom Rockmore and Joseph Margolis, Philadelphia: Temple University Press, 1992. I am grateful to Stephan Pollan for alerting me to this paper, and that by Pöggeler. It is important to note that this double-bind is not quite the same as that introduced more famously by Gregory Bateson in his extraordinary book *Steps to an Ecology of Mind*, Chicago: University of Chicago Press, 2000. For Bateson the double-bind typically led not to the tragedy of Agamemnon as to schizophrenia.
13   Quoted from 'Hölderlin and the Essence of Poetry', in *Existence and Being*, trans. Werner Brock, Chicago: Gateway, 1949, p. 287.
14   Der Anklang, Das Zuspiel, Der Sprung, Die Grundung, Die Zukunftigen, Der letzte Gott (from section 1).
15   *Contributions*, section 1, p. 5.
16   Ibid.
17   Ibid.
18   See his 'Origin of the Work of Art', where he speaks of the need for preservers.
19   *Contributions*, section 27.
20   We are drawing here on sections 21ff devoted to Inceptual Thinking. This discussion of Repetition would be further illuminated by comparisons with Kierkegaard's essay of that name.
21   *Contributions*, section 20.
22   *Contributions*, section 23.
23   There is extensive discussion of these themes in my *The Deconstruction of Time*, Evanston: Northwestern University Press, 2001.
24   See section 39: 'Each of the six joinings of the jointure stands for itself, but only in order to make the essential onefold more pressing.'
25   This is why Kierkegaard's repetition of Lessing's fork 'Would you rather possess the truth or the perpetual striving after truth?' is such a good device for emancipation. One quickly sees that the choice is spurious.
26   *Contributions*, section 42.
27   Ibid.
28   I am indebted here to Miguel de Beistegui's course on the Time-Space sections of *Contributions*, at the Collegium Phaenomenologicum, Città di Castello, July 2000. I would like to take this opportunity also to thank all those who participated in this three-week seminar, devoted solely to this book, especially the joint directors, John Sallis and Charles Scott.
29   Quoted from 'Hölderlin and the Essence of Poetry', in *Existence and Being*, trans. Werner Brock, Chicago: Gateway, 1949, p. 289.
30   Ibid., p. 290.
31   *Contributions*, section 19.
32   Ibid.

33 Otto Pöggeler, 'Heideggers Begegnung mit Hölderlin', in *Man and World*, 10: 1 (1977), p. 263; Günter Figal, 'Forgetfulness of God: On the Core of Heidegger's Contributions to Philosophy' – written for Hermann Heidegger's 80th birthday [unpublished manuscript].
34 *Contributions*, section 41.
35 *Contributions*, section 43.
36 Here I must defer to Bret Davis's brilliant work on *Heidegger on Willing and Non-Willing*, forthcoming from Northwestern University Press.
37 'The *Retrait* of Metaphor', in Enclitic 2, no. 2, Fall 1978.
38 It may be thought that Heidegger would resist this reference to imagination. Interestingly, properly qualified, this is not so. '*As thrown projecting-open grounding, Dasein is the highest actuality in the domain of the imagination*, granted that by this term we understand not only a faculty of the soul and not only something transcendent but rather *eventuation* itself, wherein all transfiguration *reverberates*' (section 192).
39 In another paper, 'Reading and Writing After Heidegger: Glimpses of Being in Heidegger's Development', I argue for a radical redirection of Heidegger's search for an other beginning towards a recovery of the layers of incomplete development that constitute our adult Dasein. My suggestion is that our exposure to the question of Being is the direct result of our history of incomplete development, in which we go through various fundamental modes of orientation to the world, without ever completely letting go our childish schemes. The implication of this, of course, is that we need not maintain an absolute separation between our actual human 'development', its subsequent reflective reworking, and the limits and possibilities of philosophical renewal. And there may not be quite such a divide between the last god, and our first human contact.

Bibliography

Adorno, Theodore. 'The Actuality of Philosophy', trans. Benjamin Snow, *Telos*, 31 (Spring 1977), pp. 120–2.

Aristotle. *Metaphysics*, trans. John Warrington, London: J.M. Dent, 1961.

—— *Physics*, trans. Richard Hope, Lincoln: University of Nebraska Press, 1961.

Bateson, Gregory. *Steps to an Ecology of Mind*, Chicago: University of Chicago Press, 2000.

Brady, Robert. *The Spirit and Structure of German Fascism*, London: Victor Gollancz, 1937.

Carnap, Rudolf. 'The Overcoming of Metaphysics through Logical Analysis of Language', in *Logical Positivism*, ed. A.J. Ayer, New York: Free Press, 1966.

De Man, Paul. *The Resistance to Theory*, Minneapolis: University of Minnesota Press: 1986.

Derrida, Jacques. *Aporias*, trans. Thomas Dutoit, Stanford: Stanford University Press, 1993.

—— *On Cosmopolitanism and Forgiveness*, London and New York: Routledge, 2001.

—— '"Eating Well", or the Calculation of the Subject', trans. Peter Connor and Avital Ronell [Jean-Luc Nancy interview with Jacques Derrida], in Derrida's *Points...Interviews 1974–1994*, Stanford: Stanford University Press, 1995.

—— 'Force of Law – "The Mystical Foundation of Authority"', trans. Mary Quaintance, in *Deconstruction and the Possibility of Justice*, ed. Drucilla Cornell et al., New York: Routledge, 1992.

—— 'Geschlecht I', in *A Derrida Reader*, ed. Peggy Kamuf, New York: Columbia University Press, 1991.

—— 'Geschlecht II', in *Deconstruction and Philosophy: The Texts of Jacques Derrida*, ed. John Sallis, Chicago: University of Chicago Press, 1987.

Derrida, Jacques. *The Gift of Death*, trans. David Wills, Chicago: University of Chicago Press, 1995.

——*Given Time: 1. Counterfeit Money*, trans. Peggy Kamuf, Chicago: University of Chicago Press, 1992.

——*Glas*, trans. John P. Leavey and Richard Rand, Lincoln: University of Nebraska Press, 1986.

——*Of Grammatology*, trans. Gayatri Spivak, Baltimore: Johns Hopkins UP, 1976 [includes 'Linguistics and Grammatology', and 'The End of the Book and the Beginning of Writing'].

——'History of the Lie: Prolegomena', trans. Peggy Kamuf, in *Futures: Of Jacques Derrida*, ed. Richard Rand, Stanford: Stanford University Press, 2001.

——*Of Hospitality*, trans. Rachel Bowlby, Stanford: Stanford University Press, 2000.

——*Edmund Husserl's 'Origin of Geometry': An Introduction*, trans. John P. Leavey, Lincoln: University of Nebraska Press, 1989.

——*Limited Inc*, trans. Samuel Weber, Evanston: Northwestern University Press, 1988.

——*Margins of Philosophy*, trans. Alan Bass, Chicago: University of Chicago Press, 1982 [includes 'Ousia and Gramme', 'Différance', 'The Ends of Man'].

——*The Other Heading*, trans. Michael Naas, Bloomington: Indiana University Press, 1992.

——'Passions', trans. David Wood, in *Derrida: A Critical Reader*, ed. David Wood, Oxford: Blackwell, 1992.

——*Politics of Friendship*, trans. George Collins, London: Verso, 1997.

——*Positions*, trans. Alan Bass, Chicago: University of Chicago Press, 1981.

——*The Postcard*, trans. Alan Bass, Chicago: University of Chicago Press, 1987 [includes 'Envois'].

——'On Reading Heidegger', *Research in Phenomenology*, 17 (1987), pp. 171–88.

——'Sauf le nom', in *On the Name*, ed. Thomas Dutoit, trans. David Wood, John P. Leavey and Ian McLeod, Stanford: Stanford University Press, 1995.

——*Speech and Phenomena*, trans. David Allison, Evanston: Northwestern, 1973.

——*Of Spirit: Heidegger and the Question*, trans. Geoffrey Bennington and Rachel Bowlby, Chicago: University of Chicago Press, 1989.

——*Spurs: Nietzsche's Styles*, trans. Barbara Harlow, Chicago: University of Chicago Press, 1979.

——*The Truth in Painting*, trans. Geoff Bennington and Ian McLeod, Chicago: University of Chicago Press, 1987 [includes 'Restitutions of the Truth in Painting'].

——'Violence and Metaphysics', in *Writing and Difference*, trans. Alan Bass, Chicago: University of Chicago Press, 1978.

——'White Mythology: Metaphor in the Text of Philosophy', in *Margins of Philosophy*, trans. Alan Bass, Chicago: University of Chicago Press, 1982.

Dews, Peter. *Logics of Disintegration*, London: Verso, 1987.

Feldman, Karen. 'The Performative Difficulty of Being and Time', *Philosophy Today*, 44, no. 4, 2000.

Feuerbach, Ludwig. *Principles of the Philosophy of the Future*, trans. Manfred H. Vogel, New York: Hackett, 1986.

Figal, Günter. 'Forgetfulness of God: Concerning the Center of Heidegger's *Contributions to Philosophy*', in *Companion to Heidegger's Contributions to Philosophy*, ed. Charles Scott, Susan Schoenbohm, Daniela Vallega-Neu and Alejandro Vallega, Bloomington: Indiana University Press, 2001.

Freud, Sigmund. *The Ego and the Id*, trans. Joan Riviere, New York: Norton, 1990.

——*The Interpretation of Dreams*, trans. Joyce Crick, London: Oxford University Press, 2000.

——*Totem and Taboo*, trans. A.A. Brill, London: Routledge, 1999.

——'The "Uncanny"', in *On Creativity and the Unconscious*, New York: Harper & Row, 1958.

Habermas, Jürgen. *The Philosophical Discourse of Modernity*, trans. Frederick Lawrence, Cambridge: Polity, 1987.

Haraway, Donna. *Modest_Witness@Second_Millenium*, New York: Routledge, 1997.

——*Simians, Cyborgs, and Women*, New York: Routledge, 1991.

Hearne, Vicki. *Adam's Task*, New York: Vintage, 1987.

Hegel, Georg Wilhelm Friedrich. *The Difference between Fichte's and Schelling's System of Philosophy* [known as the *Differenzschrift*], trans. H.S. Harris and Walter Cerf, Albany: SUNY Press, 1977.

——*Phenomenology of Spirit*, trans. A.V. Miller, Oxford: Clarendon, 1977.

——*Science of Logic*, trans. A.V. Miller, George Allen & Unwin, 1969.

Heidegger, Martin. 'The Anaximander Fragment', trans. David Krell and Frank Capuzzi, in *Early Greek Thinking*, New York: Harper & Row, 1976.

——*The Basic Problems of Phenomenology*, trans. A. Hoftstadter, Bloomington: Indiana University Press, 1988.

——*Being and Time*, trans. Joan Stambaugh, Albany, SUNY Press, 1996.

——*Contributions to Philosophy (From Enowning)* [1936–8], trans. Parvis Emad and Kenneth Maly, Bloomington: Indiana, 1999 [German text: *Beitrage zur Philosophie (Vom Ereignis)*, Frankfurt: Klostermann, 1989].

——'The End of Philosophy and the Task of Thinking', in *On Time and Being*, trans. Joan Stambaugh, New York: Harper & Row, 1972.

——'The Essence of Truth', trans. John Sallis, in *Martin Heidegger: Basic Writings*, ed. David Farrell Krell, London: Routledge & Kegan Paul, 1978.

——'Hegel and the Greeks', in *Pathmarks*, trans. William McNeill, Cambridge: Cambridge University Press, 1998.

——*Hegel's Phenomenology of Spirit*, trans. Parvis Emad and Kenneth Maly, Bloomington: Indiana University Press, 1989.

——'Hölderlin and the Essence of Poetry', in *Existence and Being*, trans. Werner Brock, Chicago: Gateway, 1949.

Heidegger, Martin. *An Introduction to Metaphysics*, trans. Ralph Manheim, Garden City: Anchor, 1961.

—— *Kant and the Problem of Metaphysics*, trans. James S. Churchill, Bloomington: Indiana University Press, 1962.

—— 'Letter on Humanism', trans. Frank A. Capuzzi and J. Glenn Gray, in *Martin Heidegger: Basic Writings*, ed. David Farrell Krell, London: Routledge & Kegan Paul, 1978.

—— *The Metaphysical Foundations of Logic*, trans. Michael Heim, Bloomington: Indiana University Press, 1984.

—— 'Origin of the Work of Art', in *Martin Heidegger: Basic Writings*, ed. David Farrell Krell, London: Routledge & Kegan Paul, 1978.

—— *Poetry, Language, Thought*, New York: Harper & Row, 1971.

—— *The Question of Being*, trans. William Klubak and Jean T. Wilde, New Haven: College and University Press, 1958.

—— 'The Self-Assertion of the German University', trans. Karsten Harries, *Review of Metaphysics* [1985] 38, no. 3, pp. 473 [otherwise known as the Rectoral Address].

—— *On Time and Being*, trans. Joan Stambaugh, New York: Harper & Row, 1972.

—— *On the Way to Language*, trans. Peter Hertz, New York: Harper & Row, 1971.

—— *What is Called Thinking?*, trans. Fred D. Wieck and J. Glenn Gray, New York: Harper, 1968.

—— 'What is Metaphysics?' [24 July 1929] trans. by David F. Krell, in *Martin Heidegger: Basic Writings*, London: Routledge & Kegan Paul, 1978 [earlier translation by R.F.C. Hull and Alan Crick in Martin Heidegger, *Existence and Being*, ed. Werner Brock, Chicago: Henry Regnery, 1949].

—— 'Why I stay in the provinces', in *Heidegger, the Man and the Thinker* (ed. Thomas Sheehan), Chicago: Precedent, 1981.

Husserl, Edmund. *Cartesian Meditations*, trans. D. Cairns, The Hague: Nijhoff, 1973.

—— *Experience and Judgment*, trans. James S. Churchill and Karl Ameriks, Evanston: Northwestern University Press, 1973.

—— 'Philosophy as a Rigorous Science', in *Phenomenology and the Crisis of Philosophy*, trans. Quentin Lauer, New York: Harper, 1965.

Kant, Immanuel. *Critique of Judgement*, trans. J.H. Bernard, New York: Hafner, 1972.

—— *Critique of Practical Reason*, Chicago: University of Chicago Press, 1949.

—— *Critique of Pure Reason*, trans. Norman Kemp-Smith, London: Macmillan, 1964.

Kierkegaard, Søren. *Concluding Unscientific Postscript*, vol. 1, trans. Howard Hong and Edna Hong, New Jersey: Princeton, 1992.

—— *Fear and Trembling*, trans. Alastair Hannay, Harmondsworth: Penguin, 1986.

—— *The Sickness unto Death*, trans. Walter Lowrie, New York: Doubleday Anchor, 1954.

Krell, David Farrell. *Daimon Life: Heidegger and Life-Philosophy*, Bloomington: Indiana University Press, 1992.

Lacan, Jacques. *Le Séminaire: Livre XX. Encore*, Paris, Editions du Seuil, 1972.

Lacoue-Labarthe, Philippe. *Heidegger, Art and Politics*, trans. Chris Turner, Blackwell, 1990.

Levinas, Emmanuel. 'The Paradox of Morality: an Interview with Emmanuel Levinas', trans. Andrew Benjamin and Tamra Wright, in *The Provocation of Levinas: Rethinking the Other*, ed. Robert Bernasconi and David Wood, London: Routledge, 1988.

—— 'Simulacrum, or The End of the World', trans. David Allison et al., in *Writing the Future*, ed. D.C. Wood, London: Routledge, 1990.

Llewelyn, John. *The Middle Voice of Ecological Conscience*, London: Macmillan, 1991.

Lyotard, Jean-François. *Dérive à partir de Marx et Freud*, Paris: Union Générales d'Editions 10/18, 1973.

—— *The Postmodern Condition*, trans. Brian Massumi, Minneapolis: University of Minnesota Press, 1985.

McNeill, William. *The Glance of the Eye*, Albany: SUNY Press, 1999.

Marx, Karl and Engels, Friedrich. *The German Ideology*, New York: Prometheus, 1998.

Merleau-Ponty, Maurice. *The Visible and the Invisible*, trans. Alphonso Lingis, Evanston: Northwestern University Press, 1968.

Murray, Michael (ed.). *Heidegger and Modern Philosophy*, New Haven: Yale, 1978.

Nancy, Jean-Luc. *The Inoperable Community*, trans. Peter Connor, Lisa Garbus, Michael Holland and Simona Sawhney, Minneapolis: University of Minnesota Press, 1991.

Nietzsche, Friedrich. *Beyond Good and Evil*, trans. Walter Kaufmann, New York, Vintage: 1966.

—— *The Gay Science*, trans. Walter Kaufmann, New York: Vintage, 1974.

—— *Thus Spoke Zarathustra*, trans. Walter Kaufmann, New York: Penguin, 1978.

—— 'Truth and Falsity in their Ultra-Moral Sense', in *The Existentialist Tradition*, ed. Nino Languilli, Humanities Press, 1971.

Norris, Christopher. *Paul De Man*, New York: Routledge, 1988.

Pöggeler, Otto. 'Heideggers Begegnung mit Hölderlin', in *Man and World*, 10, no. 1 (1977), p. 263.

Richardson, William. 'Lacan and Non-Philosophy', in *Philosophy and Non-Philosophy since Merleau-Ponty*, ed. Hugh J. Silverman, New York: Routledge, 1988.

Roethke, Theodore. *Collected Poems*, London: Faber & Faber, 1985.

Rose, Gillian. *Hegel contra Sociology*, London: Athlone, 1981.

—— *Judaism and Modernity: Philosophical Essays*, Oxford: Blackwell, 1993.

Sartre, Jean-Paul. *Existentialism and Humanism*, trans. Philip Mairet, London: Methuen, 1957.

—— 'The Singular Universal', trans. Peter Goldberger, in *Kierkegaard*, ed. J.J. Thompson, New York: Anchor, 1972.

Schürmann, Reiner. 'Riveted to a Monstrous Site', in *The Heidegger Case*, ed. Tom Rockmore and Joseph Margolis, Philadelphia: Temple University Press, 1992.

Scott, Charles. *The Question of Ethics*, Bloomington: Indiana University Press, 1990.

—— *On the Advantages and Disadvantages of Ethics and Politics*, Bloomington: Indiana University Press, 1996.

Steeves, Peter (ed.). *Animal Others: On Ethics, Ontology and Animal Life*, Albany: SUNY Press, 1999.

Wittgenstein, Ludwig. *Notebooks 1914–1916*, Oxford: Basil Blackwell, 1961.

Wood, David. 'Comment ne pas manger – Deconstruction and Humanism', in *Animal Others: On Ethics, Ontology and Animal Life*, ed. Peter Steeves, SUNY, 1999.

—— *The Deconstruction of Time*, reprinted with a new Preface by the author, Evanston: Northwestern UP, 2001.

—— 'Deconstructive Phenomenology', in *Journal of the British Society for Phenomenology*, 1998.

—— (ed.) *Of Derrida, Heidegger and Spirit*, Evanston: Northwestern University Press, 1993.

—— 'Identity and Violence', in *On the Work of Edward Said: Cultural Differences and the Gravity of History*, ed. Keith Ansell-Pearson, Benita Parry and Judith Squires, London and New York: Lawrence Wishart, 1998.

—— 'Kierkegaard, God and the Economy of Thought', in *The Kierkegaard Reader*, ed. Jane Chamberlain and Jonathan Rée, Oxford: Blackwell, 1997.

—— *Philosophy at the Limit*, London: Unwin Hyman, 1990.

—— 'Responsibility Reinscribed (and How)', in *Responsibilities of Deconstruction*, PLI: *Warwick Journal of Philosophy*, ed. Jonathon Dronsfield and Nick Midgley, vol. 6, Summer 1997.

Index